# Margaret Garner

# *Margaret Garner*

*The Premiere Performances of Toni Morrison's Libretto*

EDITED BY LA VINIA DELOIS JENNINGS

University of Virginia Press  Charlottesville and London

University of Virginia Press
© 2016 by the Rector and Visitors of the University of Virginia
All rights reserved
Printed in the United States of America on acid-free paper

First published 2016

9 8 7 6 5 4 3 2 1

Library of Congress Cataloging-in-Publication Data
Names: Jennings, La Vinia Delois, editor.
Title: Margaret Garner : the premiere performances of Toni Morrison's
    libretto / edited by La Vinia Delois Jennings.
Description: Charlottesville ; London : University of Virginia Press,
    2016. | Includes bibliographical references and index.
Identifiers: LCCN 2015043816 | ISBN 9780813938677 (cloth : alk. paper) |
    ISBN 9780813938684 (e-book)
Subjects: LCSH: Morrison, Toni. Margaret Garner. | Danielpour, Rich-
    ard. | Margaret Garner. | Libretto. | Music and literature.
Classification: LCC ML2110 .R3 2016 | DDC 782.1026/8—dc23
LC record available at http://lccn.loc.gov/2015043816

Cover art: Margaret Garner, A Meditation on Laboulaye's Lady Liberty,
    Donna Sully, 2015, oil on canvas. (© Donna Sully)

# Contents

# Foreword

*Performing* Margaret Garner

\* DENYCE GRAVES \*

I was approached by Richard Danielpour backstage in my dressing room at the Metropolitan Opera after a performance of *Carmen* sometime during the 1997–98 opera season. I don't remember the exact date, but I know it was before the birth of my daughter. Danielpour came into my dressing room, introduced himself, and explained that he was going to write an opera about the story of Margaret Garner based on the *Beloved* text by Toni Morrison. I said, as I often do when speaking with composers about new projects, "Great! It sounds wonderful." He asked if I knew of Garner's flight from slavery and capture, and I responded that I didn't but that I would purchase and read Steven Weisenburger's *Modern Medea,* an account of her life. I certainly knew of Toni Morrison and had read her Pulitzer Prize–winning novel *Beloved* and seen its film adaptation, so I was somewhat loosely acquainted with Garner's 1856 run for freedom. I was, in any case, acquainted with the writings of Toni Morrison. I remember reading her first novel, *The Bluest Eye,* in college at my mother's insistence.

Now here was a phenomenal project being proposed with the author of *Sula, Song of Solomon, Tar Baby, Jazz,* and *Paradise* as well as the two novels I've already mentioned above, as its librettist. If it actually took flight, I'd be interacting with Toni Morrison! I had the utmost respect for her work, and just being in the same room with her would be a great honor. Wow! How proud my mother would be, and what an unforgettable treasure the experience would be in my life. Furthermore, I felt Ms. Morrison possessed a very serious regard when I'd seen her in photos and in interviews, and I was intrigued by the attentive gaze she projected to the world and wanted to know what lay beneath it. I saw her as noble, highly intellectual, and stoic and wanted so very much to learn firsthand what life had shown her. She, like my parents, grew up in an unforgivable time of sociopolitical tensions and challenges, and no doubt those experiences influenced and colored her perspectives. But how had they contributed to her formidable aura? Thus, I imagined listening to her stories as if I were listening to the spellbinding tales of the legendary Scheherazade herself. Toni Morrison struck me as a woman who had a deep understanding of life, and I was attracted to that kind of knowledge and wanted very much to sit with her as I romantically imagined her sharing experiences that inspired her writings.

Normally, I try not to get attached to projects before I know that they're really going to happen, but I was so excited about this prospect that I was willing it into being. After reading Margaret Garner's story, I remember being frozen at the impossible, horrific act that she'd committed spontaneously. "How could any mother do that?" I contemplated. My initial censure of her would later evolve, as did I, as the work on the operatic representation of her life became integrated into my daily life.

After our backstage meeting, Danielpour and I communicated often, as we had exchanged contact information. He also asked for my performing calendar so that he might discuss the project with me as I toured. He began sharing information about the musical developments of the opera as he embarked on the long and arduous task of composing it. He even traveled to Paris, where I was living at the time, to show me a duet that he'd just completed. After he arrived on a lovely fall day at my residence in Boulogne-Billancourt, the city's western suburb, we had coffee and chatted in the courtyard of my Rue Denfert Rochereau home before we sat at the piano and began reading, then singing, through parts of his composition. He wanted to know how it "sat in the voice," if the tessitura was good—was it comfortable and in a register that I could freely express the musical and dramatic nuances, and so forth. I gave thumbs-ups to all of his queries. Thereafter, he sent me composed sections as he completed them. We then exchanged e-mail or talked by telephone. The musical scoring was coming together with Morrison's libretto, and we were thrilled with its development. I remember feeling that *this* project seemed serious; it might actually have a life!

I asked Danielpour about the toilsome process of constructing an opera. I was very interested in knowing how he began. Did he sit alone with the words and wait for melody to arrive? Or did he "hear" it from a dramatic standpoint first? Did he "borrow" from melodies that he'd heard?

Or did he sit at the piano and just begin to put music down on paper, or was it a computer he used? And how did he get what he constructed to move people in a meaningful way? Was it a skill that's learned or a talent that's inherent? I always wanted to stand quietly nearby and watch the process. Most of the composers whose music I'd studied were dead, so here was a direct opportunity to learn and understand more about their craft. My job as a singer is always to deconstruct the constructions of composers, and in the midst of that process I am always on my knees in awe at the breadth and depth of their creative and technical prowess.

During the months of working on *Garner*, Danielpour told me that he'd go to Copland House, in the Lower Hudson Valley, or a composing sanctuary like it. He also shared that Morrison's libretto was so descriptive, so powerful and exact, that the music and rhythm came clearly to his creative mind. He said that it was already there, that he felt the libretto sang right away and that there was little for him to do but follow the natural inflections and rhythms of her words. I'm certain that this isn't wholly true, but I understood what he meant and appreciated the insight into Morrison's ease at writing lyrical verse and his deftness at putting music to words. Danielpour's comment, however, did remind me of reading that Michelangelo had been asked how he created a sculpture. The great Renaissance artist answered that the sculpture existed inside the marble and that he merely chipped away anything that wasn't it.

Several months later, after the score was completed, Danielpour invited me to his New York apartment to hear Laurent Phillipe, the pianist for *Garner*, play through the entire work. We grew increasingly excited as the piece took musical form and lifted off the page. We could visualize it dramatically and knew we had our hands on something important, something moving, beautiful, and powerful. Now we needed a venue to perform it.

It was 1999, and Andrea Bocelli and I were singing *Werther* with Michigan Opera Theatre. Taking a meeting with David DiChiera, the founding General and Artistic Director for MOT, I enthusiastically told him about the opera that Danielpour had written and outlined the plot of Morrison's libretto. I shared that the music—melodic and heartbreakingly beautiful—formed a perfect marriage with the command and intensity of the story itself. I ended by asking if he would consider it in MOT's future. He replied that he had been searching for an opera that would pay homage to the African-American experience and that our timing was perfect. He said yes.

DiChiera's green-lighting of the project gave us the authority to talk with other opera companies and to solicit their participation. I met later that same season with Robert Driver, the General Director of Opera Company of Philadelphia. We had lunch at Café des Artistes near Lincoln Center with one of his company's major financial supporters. Driver, too, signed on to the project, and we were off and running! Cincinnati Opera later joined MOT and Opera Company of Philadelphia. The triumvirate would share the production of *Margaret Garner*, with performances debuting in each of the northern cities. The opera had a life, and Danielpour and I were ecstatic! Now there was the work of orchestrating the score; of securing a conductor, a director, the set and costume designers; casting the singing roles; and arranging all the other essentials necessary for the success of a premier grand opera.

From the beginning Danielpour was certain that he wanted Stefan Lano as the conductor. They apparently had a long-standing working relationship, and he referred to Lano many times as his "brother." By happenstance, Stefan Lano and I had worked together at the Met on Stravinsky's *The Rake's Progress* and that experience had been a happy one for me. He is clear, precise, studied, reliable, and very musical. It was easy to express enthusiasm for this wonderful choice. I adore him as a musician and as a human being, plus he always smells so delicious.

The selection of Donna Langman as the costume mistress was another sweet coincidence. I'd met her early in my career when she made the costumes for a *Carmen* I did with Washington Opera in 1992. I fell in love with her designs for that production and asked if I could purchase them to use in my concerts. She later went on to create more than thirty concert gowns for me and an assortment of casual wear. She designed and personally sewed my wedding dress as well as the formal wear for my entire wedding party. Donna is a beautifully gifted designer and seamstress, and over the years through our working together has become a treasured friend. So from the outset the artistic team being assembled was a dream, at least from my standpoint. The entire production's launch seemed to have been ordained and anointed.

During this time, Danielpour had begun to fine-tune the opera and those persons who had been selected to give it body and breath received the final version. Years of writing, rewriting, planning, meeting, workshopping, and auditioning had culminated in the composition's completion. Seven years after our initial Met meeting, Danielpour and I, along with a group of highly trained and talented artists, arrived in Detroit to complete the creation of *Margaret Garner: A New American Opera.*

Often when I arrive at an opera engagement, particularly now that I've been in the profession for a while, it's a bit of a reunion with colleagues with whom I've worked a number of times over the years. The Detroit engagement would be no different. I'd be working with familiar faces.

Gregg Baker, a baritone whose voice is so resonant and powerful that it makes my bones rattle when I am near him as he sings, had been cast as Robert Garner, the husband of Margaret. I've known him since 1986. While he has performed a plethora of roles, Gregg is perhaps best known for his portrayal of Crown in *Porgy and Bess*. There is no more compelling a Crown than Gregg; no one is more masculine and intimidating as he is in the role. What an artistic privilege it would be to watch him flesh out Robert's character as a husband and father who is not only strong physically and mentally—attributes that come naturally for Gregg—but also sensitive, tender, and squashed down, or "locked down," as Toni Morrison puts it in Margaret's act 1, scene 3, aria, "A Quality Love." And because of the opera's antebellum setting, the portrayal of the role would also require Gregg to complicate the persona of Robert Garner, whose enslavement demanded that he be eagerly compliant and submissive, which would be no easy task for the alpha male that Gregg is.

I was also reunioning with Rod Gilfry, who would be creating the role of the slave master Edward Gaines. A lyric baritone who possesses a beautifully warm, round instrument, Rod and I had sung in many concerts together, but we had never performed in an opera with one another. Our working relationship was always one of generosity and kindness, and he is a heck of a sweet guy. He once went home for a single day during a professional engagement, traveling from coast to coast and back again, in order to hang Christmas lights with his wife. So I eagerly anticipated seeing this sweet guy radically transformed into the cruel, cunning, abusive, and arrogant slave master of a Kentucky plantation.

Since I did not participate in the "Garner" workshops that preceded the Detroit rehearsals, I met the other members of the cast for the first time during the weeks of rehearsals leading up to the world premiere. Despite all of my excitement and preparation prior to arriving in Detroit, there was a *great* part of me that resisted involvement in *this* opera and the telling of *this* story.

While I am proud to be an instrument for Margaret Garner's story and other stories like hers, it is an incendiary story and message that kicks up pain, anger, and resentment for African Americans. The painful saga of American slavery smacks in the face all of the hard-won battles that propelled all Americans forward, and it drags us all backward. It unearths and keeps alive in the minds and hearts of far too many of us a separation of the races, an affirmation of racists' thoughts and practices, and an unvoiced but felt disconnect of "us" and "them." It is a dynamic that continues to want to define us and to make us less. It is a dynamic that refuses to allow us once and for all to shatter the damaging stereotypes that history and familiarity want to return to and dole out. It is a dynamic that is ever pervasive, and I didn't want to be a part of it, even though I worry that these very comments continue its perpetuation.

Racism is so deeply embedded in our terra firma socially and economically and through the media and marketing. It is part of the underlying fabric of this country, and I wanted no role in forwarding it. I didn't want to give its message a voice, a stage, or an audience. Part of my resistance came from the fact that in my profession artists who are nonwhite are consistently raced. Critics and members of the performing arts at large reference opera singers of African descent as the "African-American mezzo-soprano" or the "African-American baritone." I have never once read a review that identified a performer of European descent as "the white soprano" or "the white tenor." Leading with race when the performer is nonwhite is an ignorant and arrogant "habit," and I find it infuriating.

Well, I didn't want to contribute to limited and limiting thinking by accepting a role whose prerequisite was that I be African American. Neither did being African American automatically render me capable of singing the role or conveying an honest portrayal of Margaret Garner or of any enslaved woman of African descent. I prefer to be considered and judged by that which I have actively and conscientiously achieved through diligent instruction, study, dedication, and persistence, and to be chosen for my artistry and ability.

In my career, I purposely had not gone the route of *Porgy and Bess* and other popular "African-American operas" or musicals, like *Treemonisha* or *Showboat*, which repertory companies readily offer. I wanted to make a name for myself with classical, standard repertoire and to be seen and heard on a broader scale from the outset, rather than be solely defined as a singer of "African-American roles," an artistically confining and professionally limiting typecasting that can be very difficult to break free of. And the role of "Margaret" *demanded* an African American.

We were resuscitating a story set before the Civil War, a historical period that many if not most Americans are burned out on revisiting. I know I was. I thought, "Ah, not another 'slave' narrative." I wanted to be part of a vision that stripped away the lie and perception of whites being all powerful and having everything and blacks being powerless and having nothing. I wanted to be part of an empowering message and to impart the lives of an empowered people. I wanted to be a part of a paradigm shift. Why did so many representations of persons of African descent have to continue depicting lines of racial divide? How could we show the range of our talents if we are consistently shown performing "African-American parts" that reach back hundreds of years when persons of African descent were deprived of self-determination and self-actualization?

The narrative of the libretto also called for black and white choruses, which created a racial rent in the cast's interactions during the rehearsal period. The black people hung out with the black people, and the white people hung out with whites. I hated this self-imposed segregation and the unspoken tensions that arose just by doing the work. Yet, ironically, having those tensions surface enabled us to tell the story authentically. I remember when I was a young artist with Houston Grand Opera during its production of *Showboat*, and I went to speak with General Director David Gockley because of the racial divide that developed. I asked to be released from the production. And I was. "Can't we move forward from a new 'set point,'" I thought. "These 'habits' do not match who we are."

Now, with *Margaret Garner*, I tossed and turned for weeks, deliberating over whether to stay with or leave the cast. I had obviously invested time and energy in helping the opera come to life onstage; how could I not go through with its world premiere performance? I feared I would never be taken seriously again in the operatic world if, after petitioning so fervently for this work, I reversed my support and chose not to participate in it. Plus, *the role was written for me!*

I was on trial with myself and my own beliefs, but I knew that the production would take place with or without me. I thought of Margaret Garner; I thought of my grandmother, whom I'd never met; I thought of my mother; I thought of my stepfather, who doesn't know the day of his birth because administrators of a hospital denied his mother admittance; I thought of the fact that so much of African-American history has been lost. I thought of that hurtful time out of which daughters like me were born . . . in spite of these atrocities. I thought of the opportunity and responsibility I had to sing because they could not. This is my time *and* their time—my time to bow before the heavy price they paid for me and others and their time to be heard. I *had* to do this. I *owed* this. The fact that I was singing in the world's greatest opera houses and concert halls is because of the debt that Margaret Garner paid, and that awareness bloomed into full-blown appreciation.

And so I began.

We began the rehearsal process with roundtable discussions about the characters with the opera's director, Kenny Leon. Kenny is noted for his direction of many theatrical works on and off Broadway that particularly illuminate diversity in the human experience. Apart from his many accomplishments, Kenny is a really cool, hip individual who has a keen professional sense and knows what's going on in the world today. So I knew that his approach and vision would be gritty and honest. He's also a very "real" person, without pretense, so there was an immediate familiarity between us as he directed. He's also crazy handsome, which doesn't hurt.

Kenny was making his operatic directing debut and working with him was an unusual and beautiful experience. One thing that was at first jarring about him was his colloquial language. He went instantly to the core of matters, stripping away all exterior facades, and, in doing so with an unaffected manner, immediately created an atmosphere of genuine comfort. We could then interact without inhibitions. It freed us and set the tone for artistic discovery. He allowed each of us to find our distinct way to a character, and he worked with what each of us individually brought to a role's construction. I think that's important in the field of performance because opera is a collaborative effort, and as there are many opinions to take into consideration, as well as egos, directing can sometimes devolve into dictating. So it was liberating to have the creative ideas of the performers folded into the staging.

When building an operatic character, the singer must not only learn the rhythms, notes, and dramatic markings and work them into the voice, but she must also inform herself about the character as much as possible in order to build a broad frame of reference from which to draw and shape a representation. One does this by reading as much material as possible about a character's life, historical moment, and particular circumstances. But notwithstanding all these considerations, at the end of the day the singer has to "play" what's drawn out in the libretto, which will not be as extensive as its source work, if it is an adaptation from a novel or other literary genre. The libretto is a separate work, *but* the more one can draw from all the information she has at her disposal, the better. The more detailed and educated the singer is about the character, the more detailed and layered the portrayal will be.

I read *Modern Medea* in its entirety and reread *Beloved*. I also rescreened Jonathan Demme's film based on the novel and visited Maplewood Farm in Richwood, Kentucky, where the events depicted in the libretto took place. However, in this particular case, my own history afforded me the greatest advantage in terms of background knowledge. Despite its specificity of time and place, Margaret Garner's story is the story of my ancestors I learned about growing up. Parallel remnants of her story I'd witnessed firsthand, as did my mother and my great-grandmother. Garner's story is coded in my DNA.

And Garner's story is also the story of my colleagues: everyone brought her or his truth and real-life experiences to the table, which offered personal relatability to this powerful story. It is America's history, all of ours, the performers and the audiences. Everyone in rehearsal was uncomfortable with it, black and white alike, and the discomfort fueled a powerful verisimilitudinous engine that allowed *Garner* to take off. This shameful time hit us all at our core, and we were about to play out one of its most horrendous moments onstage covered in music to expose a festering wound that we have not allowed to heal.

I felt a great pressure and a great responsibility to "get it right," to do justice to Margaret. I took the role very seriously and tried in my portrayal to make her neither a victim nor a heroine but rather a woman: a woman in love with her husband and children, a woman who understood the incredible fragility of life, a woman who treasured her family and tried to preserve its dignity under a grossly offensive system.

In addition to the carefully nuanced libretto, these moments were carefully drawn musically as well. We had the poignant words of Toni

Morrison and the haunting melodies of Richard Danielpour, so it became a question of spinning out the product of their collaboration as beautifully as I could vocally, of projecting it as honestly as I could dramatically, and of "allowing"—allowing the truth to ring through, allowing myself to be a vessel.

Margaret's soliloquy in the intermezzo of act 2 required this mediation. To sing "Darkness, I salute you" was an exercise in finessing and not overwhelming the raw moment. I had to learn to pace myself, so that I didn't overblow it vocally or dramatically, which was easy to do given the personalness it bore for me. I'd aim at striking a balance between vocal purity and beauty and heartfelt, dramatic emotion. Sometimes the result, depending on my level of commitment, would fall stronger to one side than to the other, and that, too, worked. But then there were times that I successfully balanced the two, which, of course, is why performing artists practice. Singers are always chasing perfection, and their reliance on vocal technique ensures the most consistent delivery.

Performing Margaret Garner, an intensely dramatic role, was very different from portraying Carmen, for example. Carmen is a magnificent, fictional creature whom I love and who has taught me a lot, but Margaret is real in every sense. There is nothing contrived or forced about her; history did not afford her that luxury. There are, however, moments of lightness and sweetness when her story exhales. We all needed them. The lullaby scene is one of them. In a moment of gentleness, we see Margaret and her baby bonding. Later we see the love she has for both her children, even though her slave master has sexually violated her and usurped her husband's rightful paternity. We see the largesse of heart she possesses, but so much of the role is emotionally charged that I had to learn to pace myself and yet to give each moment my all.

I remember the moment of enacting the slashing of the children's throats and the difficulty—vocally and dramatically—of performing it. *And* it was the centerpiece of the entire story. Danielpour had written an *ossia* (option) of a high C on the word *slavery*, as Margaret, in act 2, scene 2, slashes the children's throats, screaming, "Never to be born again into *slavery!*" The staging required my negotiating the logistics of picking up the children, slashing their throats while holding them, and then singing a high C! I could devote myself entirely to the physical staging and execute the throat slashings well, then throw the children's bodies upstage away from the curtain, which was to come down immediately afterward, and ride solely on the high drama and not concern myself with beauty of tone. *Or* I could invest my energy vocally in the beauty of tone—after all it was an opera—and sing to the best of my ability. More often than not I devoted myself to the former, which was very effective dramatically. In this instance, I could serve only one performance god at a time, but I certainly tried to be a devotee to both. Technique, once again, is the only way to ensure that the opera singer gets as close to the idea of perfection as possible. Each moment calls years of training to the surface and challenges the performer. It was never an easy night in the theater, and I was always drained at the end of it.

The role of Margaret also demanded other physically challenging moments, and I have the scars to prove them. The demand on my body began early on with the up and down motions of the *"Crack uh back / Cut uh cane / Pull uh mule / Chop uh cotton"* harvest scene in act 1, scene 2, and then progressed to the rape in scene 3, which was very violent. Rod and I both "went for it," making the latter scene that concludes act 1 as realistic as possible with lots of kicking, screaming, hair pulling, and clothes tearing. In act 2, the slave posse's discovery of the fugitive Garner family in Ohio was also very physical, requiring yet another vigorous tussle between Rod and me. The scene calls for Margaret to toss hot coals at Edward Gaines, and they battle on the ground during her capture. These onstage clashes are directly responsible for my recent knee surgery.

While the killing of the children was certainly costly physically and emotionally, the hanging scene concluding the opera wrung me of any energy I had reserved in a night's performance. One evening at the final dress rehearsal in Cincinnati while the stage technicians were still adjusting the rigging for the final scene's hanging scaffold, the safety wire malfunctioned and the noose caught fast around my neck, suspending me in the air. I flailed about wildly until they cut me down. I was later treated for rope burns around my neck. I felt like Mère Marie de L'Incarnation, the nun who after taking the vow of martyrdom was spared going with her sister nuns to the guillotine in the wake of the French Revolution executions, in Poulenc's *Dialogues of the Carmelites.* Mère Marie de L'Incarnation later develops a mystical line around her neck as a sign of solidarity with the executed sisters. Despite my injuries, I would not have performed the role of Margaret with any less psychical fortitude and physical intensity. The women depicted in the libretto were of extraordinary emotional strength, and Margaret was certainly among the strongest to have acted as she did and to have withstood the daily demands of enslavement. I could have done without the near hanging of course, but the consistently high level of involvement from the cast and creative team was very inspiring, and we raised each other's performance with each rehearsal.

Although she was present at many workshops, Toni Morrison attended few early rehearsals in Detroit. Edits affecting the libretto, like musical cuts or word changes, needed her approval, but for the most part her work had been completed before the cast received the sheet music. Her visibility increased when the rehearsals moved out of the rehearsal room and into the theater. It was her habit to sit in the back of Detroit Opera House's auditorium, where the sound is usually the best.

On occasion, I spoke with Ms. Morrison about crafting the libretto *Margaret Garner: Opera in Two Acts.* I wanted to know what had been the most difficult aspect of writing the libretto. She replied, "To boil it down to one sentence." As a novelist, she's accustomed to going into great detail about matters pertaining to characterization, dialogue, setting, and plot. One of her challenges as a librettist had been to make the literary text as concise as possible.

Later she and I did publicity junkets together. By that time, I'd had my daughter, and I have several photos of Morrison holding her. I also had the joy of watching her coo over my baby. That memory is a real treasure. But our contact was not to the extent of my earlier romantic imaginings. Our working relationship was warm yet unfamiliar, and not wanting to force an intimacy, I resignedly sighed and admired her from afar as I had always done. And she remains to me yet a mystery.

Sadly, Danielpour's behavior became tyrannical as we moved closer to the May 7, 2005, world premiere, which caused great tension among the cast and deteriorated our working relationship with him. His overbearingness cast a suffocating pall over the production. Everyone was gasping for air under his vise grip. In the face of Danielpour's turbulent transformation, Lano took "hold" of the baton and banded the esprit de corps. He encouraged our work and kept us focused on our goals as the pressure mounted. It was nice to feel as if we were actually making a contribution to what was being created and not just following orders. Musically and rhythmically there were several tricky spots in the score, so Lano called numerous musical rehearsals to ensure the entire cast was solid. When a singer is learning and interpreting new music, it makes all the difference in her rapid success if there is a reliable conductor in the pit.

Michigan Opera Theatre's marketing department did an extraordinary job with the publicity campaign and community outreach for the opera. The department had arranged an itinerary of interviews, promotions, and social gatherings. So the word got out, and the buzz was buzzing. As the production came together, its enthusiasm was contagious. There were moments of great heartbreak and moments of exquisite joy. We grew increasingly impatient for the premiere night to arrive. And we were all determined to give our best.

Although I desperately wanted to go, I turned down the wonderful invitation from Oprah Winfrey to attend her "Legends" weekend in California, which she had been planning for more than a year. The three-day event in May unfortunately conflicted with the performance schedule for *Margaret Garner*. I couldn't risk having my return flight canceled, or getting stranded in an airport, or subjecting my voice to climate changes. But, boy, did I want to be there. Rats! Toni Morrison, whom Winfrey had designated as one of her honored Legends, attended the world premiere performances of *Margaret Garner*, but *her* work as librettist was done. *Mine* was still in front of me. Sometimes the greatest offers come while you're engaged elsewhere.

*Margaret Garner*, as the time wound down to the world premiere, was part of my breathing. Everyone in my home knew the music for the entire opera. We discussed the libretto's plot at dinner and got into heated debates over it. For months, it was the leitmotif in every conversation and the sound track of our lives. My family members attended rehearsals often, and they would share their observations. Because the images and the language in the opera are graphic, I did not allow my children to see several scenes, especially the hanging scene. I remembered having a conversation with Rod Gilfry about his singing the title role of *Billy Budd*, and he told me that his daughter when she was younger saw him hanged in the production and confessed to him at the age of twenty-five that she still had nightmares about it. So I vigilantly protected my children from the visually charged scenes because you can't un-see what you've seen.

I felt initially that Margaret Garner's brutal infanticide was unforgivable, but by the opera's premiere I had come to see it, based on her testimony, as she had: as a legitimate, outraged response to a savage institution. The unspeakable acts of cruelty that she, her husband, her children, her family, and her people were subjected to daily would break anyone. It was out of love that she sought to spare her children a lifetime of enslavement horrors. Many African Americans have deep beliefs in God, and I believe that Margaret thought her children better off in the arms of the Divine. In that spontaneous, passionate moment she was, in her way, loving them. Under similar conditions, who knows what each of us might be capable of ? It was a horrific time, and horrific circumstances prevailed under an inhumane and evil institution.

After years in the making and weeks of rehearsals and preparation, we were at opening night and the Detroit theater was packed. I had the usual jitters that never go away, but they subsided once I began to sing. My prayer was to be present. I'd asked the spirit of Margaret many times to come and sing through me. I was so encouraged by the complete commitment on the faces of my colleagues who assisted in keeping me tied to Margaret with their absolute sincerity. Stefan, Gregg, Rod, Angela M. Brown—who sang the role of Margaret's mother-in-law—choruses black and white, orchestra, music, words, spirit, thank you. *Margaret Garner: A New American Opera* was thunderously received. It was a gift to witness its conception and to be a part of its birth. It paralleled the unfolding of my own life's story as my daughter, too, was conceived and born during the opera's gestation. It afforded me firsthand experience of a fierce mother's love and brought new and added dimensions to my awareness of and compassion for Margaret Garner's plight. Her powerful, unforgettable story has impacted the musical world deeply. I am stopped often on the street by people who attended the premiere performances, and I still receive correspondences from fans expressing that the opera moved them profoundly. It truly gives us all a reason to sing aloud in praise of the human spirit and its defiant refusal to be crushed and silenced. We all created something breathtakingly beautiful, and I am very proud of that offering.

I am the African-American mezzo-soprano Denyce Graves.

# Acknowledgments

Many people and institutions, far and near, assisted with making this volume a reality, and to each of them I extend my warmest gratitude. I thank the Schomburg Center for Research in Black Culture; Jennifer B. Lee, Curator for the Performing Arts at Columbia University's Rare Book and Manuscript Library; and Amelia Peck and the Antonio Ratti Textile Center at the Metropolitan Museum of Art. The professionalism extended to researchers at the Metropolitan Museum is unparalleled. I thank its Ratti Textile Center staff for bringing out of storage the mid-eighteenth-century Star of Bethlehem Variation quilt, whose pattern the set designer Marjorie Bradley Kellogg chose for the *Margaret Garner* stage surround, so that I might see firsthand the spectacular artistry of the two enslaved Kentucky women who sewed it into being.

In addition to each of the essayists, I thank Keith Mitchell, Carolyn Denard, and Don Denard for giving their very best to this project. I thank Kenny Leon and Kellogg for granting me interviews. Denyce, you are a joy to write with. And thank you, Frank Simkonis, for your generosity.

The University of Tennessee has consistently supported my research, and I wish to acknowledge its sage development of internal resources to empower professionally its professoriate. I thank the John C. Hodges Better English Fund and SARIF for funding my field research and for providing me with technical support in the form of Julie Tyler.

Finally, I thank Ignatius Gettelfinger for his unique insights into things personal and professional.

# Cast of Characters

*Principal Roles*

Margaret Garner,* a slave in her mid-twenties, Robert's wife
MEZZO-SOPRANO
Robert Garner,* a slave in his early thirties, Margaret's husband
LYRIC BARITONE
Cilla,* a slave about fifty years old, Robert's mother
DRAMATIC SOPRANO
Edward Gaines, the handsome and charismatic master of Maplewood
Plantation, in his late thirties or early forties
LYRIC BARITONE

*Secondary Roles*

Casey, the foreman of Maplewood Plantation
DRAMATIC TENOR
Caroline Gaines, the daughter of Edward Gaines, engaged to
George Hancock
LIGHT LYRIC SOPRANO
George Hancock, engaged to Caroline Gaines
TENOR
Auctioneer, a professional salesman (doubles as Judge I)
LYRIC TENOR
Eight Slave Catchers**
FOUR T; FOUR BAR
(*divisi:* lyric and Verdi baritones)
A Foreman/The Hangman
NON-SINGING ROLE

Three Judges** (Judge I doubles as auctioneer)
> T, BAR, B-BAR

Two Militia Officers
> NON-SINGING ROLES

Margaret's two children,* a five-year-old girl and a two-year-old boy
> NON-SINGING ROLES,

The Townspeople/The Guests (aka, "White Chorus")
> SATB: min. 36 voices

The Slaves* (aka, "Black Chorus")
> SATB: min. 36 voices

*Although much latitude is possible in casting, these roles must be sung by black performers.

**These roles can be sung by members of the White Chorus.

# Synopsis

✳ MARY LOU HUMPHREY ✳

## Act 1, Scene 1: Kentucky; April 1856

The opera begins in total darkness, without any sense of location or time period. A large group of slaves gradually becomes visible, shackled and caged on a trading block. In a call-and-response song, they beg for deliverance from their suffering.

The scene shifts to the lively town square in Richwood Station, Kentucky; it is April 1856. In preparation for an auction, members of slave families are separated from each other, so that they can be sold individually. The local townsfolk bid enthusiastically for these "picknies and mammies and breeders and bucks," even though they consider them nothing more than personal burdens in need of civilizing.

In the crowd of onlookers is a handsome man named Edward Gaines, a native of the region but absent for twenty years, accompanied by his daughter Caroline. He interrupts the auction when an "old estate rich in history" is brought to the block, asserting that this property, Maplewood Plantation, belonged to his deceased brother and therefore cannot be sold. As no one disputes the claim, Gaines acquires Maplewood. However, the self-assured Gaines is dismayed to learn that none of the townsfolk remembers him, but only his well-respected older brother. The younger Gaines informs them that he has survived life's challenges; once happily married, he now is a widower with a child to raise. He grandiosely proclaims that he will fill Maplewood with a multitude of

Mary Lou Humphrey's synopsis prefaces the libretto for *Margaret Garner*. Words by Toni Morrison. Music by Richard Danielpour. Copyright © 2005 by Associated Music Publishers, Inc. (BMI), and G. Schirmer, Inc. (ASCAP). International copyright secured. All rights reserved. Reprinted by permission.

possessions, and announces that he intends to retain all the plantation's "goods and property"—that is, its slaves. The enslaved who were waiting to be auctioned therefore are reunited with their families.

While Gaines signs the ownership papers for Maplewood Plantation, the slaves celebrate with dance and music. The singing of Margaret Garner, an attractive young slave, captivates Gaines; after the crowd disperses, he takes her red scarf, which she had dropped accidentally. He nostalgically recalls his childhood, even though he had been forced to leave town under purportedly disreputable circumstances. He promises himself that this time the townsfolk will not forget him.

### Act 1, Scene 2: Harvest time; about six months later

Singing a wry, somewhat defiant work song, the slaves head back to their quarters after a day of toiling in the fields. Cilla, the mother of Margaret's husband, Robert, joins the couple for supper; their spirits are lighthearted while they prepare the evening meal. Yet when Margaret insists upon seeing her baby immediately after saying grace, Cilla, warmhearted yet worldly-wise, cautions her against such an intense attachment to the child. Margaret persists, however, and sings a lullaby to the baby while Robert and his mother eat dinner. Casey, the treacherous foreman at Maplewood Plantation, unexpectedly appears at the cabin and delivers shocking news: Robert is being sent away that night to another plantation. Margaret is to remain at Maplewood, but now will work in the plantation's main house. When Casey tosses a fancy dress at Margaret, it is clear that Gaines expects sexual favors from her. Robert voices his anger, but Margaret reassures him of her faithfulness, and the two pledge their love.

### Act 1, Scene 3: Maplewood Plantation; in the early summer of 1858

In the parlor at Maplewood Plantation, a reception is being held to celebrate the marriage of Caroline Gaines to George Hancock. The guests include the local townspeople, whom Edward is very eager to impress. However, a discussion at the party about the nature of love quickly develops into a heated disagreement between Edward and George. To break the tension, the newlyweds begin the reception's traditional "first dance." The guests quickly join in the waltz; ironically, only Gaines is without a partner.

When the dance concludes, Gaines graciously toasts the couple. But then Caroline accidentally makes matters worse again by asking Margaret, now the house servant, for her opinions on love. The guests are outraged that a person of "quality" would ask a slave for her opinion. To show their disapproval of Gaines, and the social manners he seemingly allows at Maplewood, the haughty guests leave the party abruptly. Distressed by their rudeness, Gaines lashes out at Caroline, who has ruined what he had hoped would be a proud moment; now, he claims, his neighbors have "more reason to gossip and despise" him. He dismisses her attempts to mollify him, yet watches wistfully as the newlyweds leave for their honeymoon.

After the party, Gaines notices Margaret returning to clear the glasses, and lingers to observe her. Unaware of his presence, she continues to reflect upon the nature of love. Edward emerges from his hiding place and accosts her. She resists his advances and begins to struggle vigorously. But Edward is determined to have his way; he overpowers her and drags her forcibly from the parlor.

End of Act One

*Act 2, Scene l: Maplewood Plantation; Sunday, February 24, 1861, in the early evening*

Anticipating a visit from Robert, who has been meeting her secretly on Sunday nights, Margaret goes to Cilla's cabin. Upon arriving there, she is puzzled to find Cilla packing a carpetbag. She becomes highly agitated when she notices that her children [she now has two] aren't there, and that Cilla is folding their clothing. As Margaret has seen Casey lurking nearby, she fears the worst—that he is coming for the children and plans to sell them. Cilla tries to reassure Margaret that all is well: Robert is attending to the final details for an escape attempt that night.

Margaret, whose life has been sustained by her quest for freedom, begins to cry when Robert arrives and confirms that they are scheduled to leave in just three hours. He attempts to calm her anxieties, and Margaret is overwhelmed by love for her husband, a man of great moral courage and strength of character. Suddenly, Margaret notices that Cilla is not packing any of her own things. In spite of Margaret's pleas to join them, Cilla proclaims that she is too old to begin a new life; her joy is simply to see her son's family safe and living elsewhere. Although sympathetic with Margaret and Robert's dreams for a free life, Cilla has made peace with her own, and sings of her reliance upon God.

Footsteps are heard approaching, and Cilla and Margaret are terrified when Casey storms into the cabin. At the same time, Robert inadvertently walks into the trap when he returns with the children. Casey pulls out a pistol, and Robert impulsively attacks him. A violent struggle ensues, but Robert [wrestling the gun from him] cannot bring himself to shoot Casey. Yet when Casey calls Margaret a "black slut," Robert strangles him to death. Cilla instantly understands that Robert's action has doomed the family, and she and Margaret beg him to run, regardless of any personal danger they might be in. Cilla drags Casey's body away; Robert and Margaret sing of their love and make plans to meet later [on the escape route].

*Act 2, Scene 2: In the Free State of Ohio; March 1861*

Three weeks have passed since Robert and Margaret successfully escaped from Maplewood, and crossed the frozen Ohio River on the Kentucky border to reach Cincinnati, a city in the "Free State" of Ohio. Now both outlaws, they live with their children in an underground shed, in hopes of avoiding recapture by their masters.

Standing outside underneath a huge elm tree, Robert and Margaret discuss speculation about the country's new President. Margaret shudders when she hears of Lincoln's belief that the "Union is sacred" and that "a house divided cannot stand," for she knows that means war is inevitable.

Ever hopeful and sharing Margaret's dream for a better future, Robert asserts that freedom is nearly theirs—after all. They now live in a state whose name means "beautiful"! Here, their children will be able to grow up with dignity, and their own marriage will be respected as sacred. He will protect Margaret always, just as the elm tree always protects them.

Only moments after Robert insists that they return to the shed because of the potential dangers facing them outside, Edward Gaines arrives, accompanied by slave catchers. He pounds on the shed door, promising that no harm will be done; he just wants to claim his property. Intoxicated, Gaines breaks down the shed door. An exchange of gunfire leaves neither man hurt, but the slave catchers tie up Robert. As he is being dragged outside, Gaines grabs Margaret. He laments that his bed is cold; he wants her to heat it up, just as she once did with hot coals. Breaking loose, Margaret recklessly plunges her bare hands into the fire and grabs several pieces of coal; she lunges at Gaines, attempting to burn him. Gaines yells that she can pretend to be as crazy as she likes; he doesn't care even if she mangles herself in the process. Margaret sees Robert outside, standing on a tall box underneath the elm tree. A noose has been placed around his neck, and he is surrounded by fiery torches planted in the ground. His cries of love to her are cut off when one of Gaines's men kicks the box away. Determined that her children not be forced to endure a lifetime filled with slavery's horrors, Margaret violently attacks and murders them: first slitting the throat of her daughter and then stabbing the younger one. Shocked by the bloody carnage, Gaines and his men surround Margaret.


*Act 2, Intermezzo*

In this moment "out of time," total darkness envelops the stage. Gradually, the image of Margaret, alone, becomes visible. With defiant and noble grandeur, she embraces her life's circumstances.


*Act 2, Scene 3: In a Courtroom; in early April 1861*

Margaret Garner sits in the middle of a courtroom, surrounded by militia officers. After capturing the runaway slave in Ohio, Edward Gaines had her transported back to Kentucky, where she now stands trial for the "theft and destruction" of the two dead children, considered his property. Local citizens fill the courtroom gallery, for they have followed the case with great interest and curiosity, and eagerly await Margaret's sentencing by the three presiding judges.

Caroline Gaines tries to rationalize with her father, and contends that Margaret stands wrongly accused: a mother who *kills* her children cannot be said to *steal* them. The proper charge, she insists, is murder—for Margaret killed *human beings*. The judges argue vehemently that Margaret's case is one of "property" and the financial loss suffered by Gaines. Furthermore, Margaret has no legal right or claim to her children; slaves own nothing, least of all their master's other slaves. The onlookers concur rowdily. Laughing cynically at Caroline's perceived naïveté, the judges add that the veracity of their beliefs is confirmed and defended by the Bible.

Caroline senses the hopelessness of the situation, and makes a personal appeal to her father on Margaret's behalf. She pleads that a man of her father's stature could influence the debate on slavery that is tearing apart the country, as well as their family. Margaret is not the only one guilty of a crime, she admonishes; everyone bears some of the blame for the discord. But Gaines merely reiterates that he has committed no crime; society and the law affirm his behavior. When the judges declare that Margaret is to be executed for theft, the onlookers express relief— for it confirms their deeply held conviction that they are superior to Margaret.

Having sat quietly throughout the proceedings, Margaret suddenly rises from her chair, and glares at those in the courtroom. She states emphatically that indeed she is not like them; she is a unique individual over whom no one present has any power. Citing their full legal authority, the judges officially sentence Margaret to be executed by sunrise. They quickly recess to their chambers, and the condemned prisoner is led from the courtroom. Dismayed by the verdict, Caroline again begs her father to urge the court for clemency. Betraying no sign of emotion, although secretly disturbed by the trial, Edward coolly states that Margaret must suffer the consequences of what she has done. Caroline retorts that her father also must accept responsibility for his actions, then walks out.

Left alone in the silent courtroom, Edward Gaines contemplates the course of his life, and wonders why he feels so troubled. His relationship with Caroline, once so close and loving, has deteriorated badly. Feeling under tremendous stress, Gaines realizes that he must choose between the love of his radical daughter and the traditional way of life to which he has always aspired.

*Act 2, Scene 4: In the town square of Richwood Station, Kentucky; the next morning, at dawn*

A group of local citizens—including the town authorities; Caroline and George; and Cilla; as well as some slaves transported from nearby plantations—processes somberly into the town square. Great sorrow fills the air, for they are accompanying Margaret Garner to her execution. All are sobered by the imminence of death. Seemingly, the only person not in the crowded plaza is Edward Gaines.

The hangman brings forth the condemned prisoner, whose hands still are bandaged from the burns she suffered while defending herself against Gaines's unwanted advances. Margaret is led up the scaffold steps. When she reaches the top of the platform, the hangman places a noose around her neck and positions her on the gallows' trap door.

Edward Gaines runs in, excitedly waving a legal document—the judges have granted Margaret clemency. All will be well again, if Margaret admits and repents her crime; she simply will be returned to his custody. Although Caroline is overjoyed and relieved by this turn of events, as well as proud of her father's decision to seek justice, Gaines fails to find any sign of approval or appreciation from his neighbors. The hangman leaves Margaret's side, and walks over to accept the document from Edward for careful review.

Upon hearing the judges' decree, Cilla immediately offers words of gratitude and praise to her God. Margaret, still standing on the gallows, expresses her desire to live peacefully in a just world. Yet when the crowd is momentarily distracted, she seizes the opportunity for "freedom"— by deliberately tripping the trap door's lever and hanging herself. The crowd is stunned by her suicide, yet a sense of awe permeates their sorrow. Caroline notices Margaret's red scarf in her father's front pocket; she removes it, then silently ascends the scaffold and reverently ties it around Margaret's waist.

Edward—as bewildered as anyone by Margaret's deed—realizes that peace will always elude him. For though he made the "right" choice—to fight for Margaret's life—he did it for the wrong reason. His actions were motivated by a desire to win his daughter's respect, and not from any deeply held moral convictions.

The hangman unties the noose around Margaret's neck, and frees her from the gallows. Holding her body tenderly in his arms, he walks slowly through the crowd. All of the onlookers—townspeople and slaves alike—express their need for repentance; Cilla proclaims her desire to join Margaret soon. As the curtain descends slowly, the crowd in the town square prays that Margaret's final journey home be a peaceful one.

# Margaret Garner

# Introduction

*Writing* Margaret Garner

✳ LA VINIA DELOIS JENNINGS ✳

Over lunch at Manhattan's Cafe Fiorello across from the Metropolitan Opera on July 9, 1996, Toni Morrison and composer Richard Danielpour discovered their mutual interest in bringing the story of Margaret Garner to the operatic stage. He disclosed that for ten years he had carried around the idea of scoring an opera about the Kentucky woman who in 1856 had killed her daughter to prevent her return to slavery. Morrison, in turn, revealed that for some time she, too, had wanted to rework as a libretto the story of Garner that she had first imaginatively treated in *Beloved* (1987). Admitting that he had not read her Pulitzer Prize–winning novel,[1] Danielpour invited Morrison to write the libretto for the score that he was now ready to transform from an idea into a reality.

While they had previously collaborated on two song cycles—*Sweet Talk* (1997) and *Spirits in the Well* (1998)—for dramatic soprano Jessye Norman, Morrison agreed to reunite with Danielpour only after he showed his plot sketch to her. Morrison, who is as adept an editor as she is a fiction writer, found the prospect of resolving problematic areas in the sketch exciting. She felt compelled to improve it.

Their third collaboration led to Morrison writing the 2004 English-language libretto *Margaret Garner: Opera in Two Acts* for Danielpour's *Margaret Garner: A New American Opera*. Michigan Opera Theatre world premiered their joint effort on May 7, 2005, in the Detroit Opera House to sold-out performances. The Detroit premiere was the first staging of the opera that had been commissioned by three opera companies at a cost exceeding $5 million. *Margaret Garner*'s debut openings and runs at Cincinnati Opera in Music Hall, starting on July 14, 2005, and the Opera Company of Philadelphia in the Academy of Music, commencing on February 10, 2006, completed its tri-city tour at the commissioning companies' opera houses.

Critics who attended the opera's opening night in Detroit wrote glowing reviews of Morrison's libretto. Lawrence B. Johnson of the *Detroit News* stated that although *Margaret Garner* is the first opera for both Richard Danielpour and Toni Morrison, "the new work is a hand-in-glove masterpiece of words fitted to music."[2] Janelle Gelfand, for the *Cincinnati Enquirer*, commented that "seamlessly joined to [Danielpour's] music were Morrison's powerful, eloquent words, in what may be the most exquisitely crafted libretto of our time,"[3] while David Patrick Stearns at the *Philadelphia Inquirer* noted that the libretto by "Morrison has moments of poetic wisdom."[4]

Morrison's libretto did not cease to please even when its plot departed from Garner's factual timeline or her earlier fictional adaptation of Garner's story. *Cincinnati Post* reviewer Mary Ellyn Hutton lavished high praise on Morrison's libretto despite its historical adjustments:

> Margaret Garner did not disappoint the opening night crowd. . . . It seems destined to take its place among America's most popular contemporary operas. Morrison's libretto is superb, both for its content and its pithy, poetic language. . . . She has made a keenly operatic adaptation of the Margaret Garner story, one which diverges considerably from history, but packs an emotional wallop of its own. . . . No matter. Morrison has given Danielpour a powerful, streamlined vehicle for his music, which is colorful and accessible.[5]

Similarly, *Wall Street Journal* critic Heidi Waleson did not object to the libretto's departing from *Beloved:*

> Michigan Opera Theatre . . . was rewarded with a well-made, affecting American opera. . . . "Margaret Garner" is based on the true story of a slave who ran away from a Kentucky farm in 1856. . . . Ms. Morrison used the story as a source for her bewitching, nightmarish 1987 novel, "Beloved." The opera is nothing like "Beloved." . . . The opera is a more traditional theatrical narrative. . . . In the novel, Ms. Morrison wrote her own arias in prose; in the libretto, her lines are short, spare and poetic, a sturdy yet flexible frame that leaves ample space for Mr. Danielpour's richly lyrical, tonal musical language.[6]

While Margaret Garner's infanticide is unquestionably a story well suited for grand opera—the various operatic versions of the impassioned Medea murdering her young sons bear that out—selecting an enslaved subject from the annals of American history had already proven topically viable for the literary form in the decade leading up to Morrison's lyrical treatment. The libretti for *Slipknot* (2003; T. J. Anderson, composer), by poet Yusef Komunyaaka; for *York: The Voice of Freedom* (2002; Bruce Trinkley, composer), by Jason Charnesky; and for *Amistad: An Opera in Two Acts* (1997; Anthony Davis, composer), by Thulani Davis are cases in point. Komunyaaka's libretto for *Slipknot* treats the true story of a twenty-one-year-old enslaved, Worcester, Massachusetts, man named Arthur who was executed in 1768 for the rape of a white woman who never charged him with assaulting her. Charnesky's *York: The Voice of Freedom* reclaims the name and history of the African-American man that explorer William Clark owned and brought along on the famous transcontinental 1803–1806 expedition with Meriwether Lewis. Thulani Davis's *Amistad: An Opera in Two Acts* recasts the events surrounding the 1839 slave revolt headed by the African Cinque on the slave ship *La Amistad* off the coast of Cuba that led to an international legal battle and a US Supreme Court case in 1841.[7] In contrast to depicting the experiences of the enslaved female as *Margaret Garner* does, these earlier libretti feature male enslaved subjects.

Two libretti, however, featuring enslaved couples bound by love and marriage but not based on historical figures had been written and performed a quarter of a century before Thulani Davis's *Amistad*. Composer and librettist John Duncan's one-act (six-scene) opera *Gideon and Eliza* (1972), which premiered at Xavier University of Louisiana, in New Orleans, depicts a husband and wife with a child divided by enslavement attempting to reunite as a family.[8] Its plot resonates more closely with Morrison's construction of Robert and Margaret Garner's strong love and determination to free their family. Oscar Brown Jr.'s two-act libretto for *Slave Song: An Opera* (1972; Alonzo H. Levister, composer), mingling romance with tragedy, tells the story of Cato and Crecie, a young couple enslaved on the Charleston, South Carolina, plantation of Judge Stacey Talbot, who has recently hired a harsh overseer to manage his human property. Brown and Levister worked on the project for a dozen years before the opera, set in 1830, was performed on March 24 and 25, 1972, in Cramton Auditorium at Howard University, Toni Morrison's undergraduate alma mater.[9] She earned a BA in English from Howard University in 1953 and taught there for seven years before taking an editing job in Syracuse, New York, in 1965. The premiere performances of both operas in March of 1972 on the campuses of historically black universities followed the January 1972 world premiere by Morehouse College and the Atlanta Symphony Orchestra of Scott Joplin's recovered opera *Treemonisha* (1910), set on a post-Reconstruction Texarkana plantation in 1884.

While libretti were once celebrated and published to be read in the absence of music, in the main, the libretto presently receives little attention by music and performance critics and virtually none by literary scholars. The aim of this volume is to rescind the inattentiveness the latter group has shown the libretto as literature. The essays herein record for posterity key events that occurred around and because of Toni Morrison's return to and success with the Margaret Garner infanticide story in the form of the libretto, a lyrical text designed to be paired with music and to be sung. The contributors, scholars specializing in the literary canon of Toni Morrison, the historical Margaret Garner, and the performance of opera, provide a critical foundation for assessing the libretto apart from its musical counterpart and appreciating it aesthetically for its merits as literary art and historical critique. They had the privilege of attending one or more of the commissioning opera companies' performances of *Margaret Garner*, serving as literary or history consultants for the opera's mounting or outreach campaign, and/or organizing community and conference events leading up to and during its tri-city tour. Some of the contributors also attended later stagings of the opera in Charlotte, North Carolina; at Lincoln Center in New York City; and in Chicago. Others studied its radio broadcast.

Mezzo-soprano Denyce Graves's foreword opens the volume, giving an in-depth, personal account of the conception and gestation of *Margaret Garner*, from Richard Danielpour's first visit with her backstage at the Metropolitan Opera during the 1997–98 season, to his request that she sing the title role, to the opera's 2005 world premiere in Detroit. It was for Graves that Danielpour composed the opera; for him she was the perfect operatic embodiment of Margaret Garner.

Eight essays that contain eyewitness accounts of the performance and critical assessments of Morrison's libretto follow Graves's foreword, Mary Lou Humphrey's plot synopsis that prefaces the published libretto, and this introduction. First, Michael Halliwell, an international opera singer affiliated with the Sydney Conservatorium of Music, introduces the reader to the role of the libretto, its closer parallel with the novel rather than with the play, and the design of operatic music and thus Danielpour's compositions to narrate, not accompany, Morrison's lyrical text. Next, after positing that the archives are a textual territory given to suppressions, Steven Weisenburger, whose 1998 seminal study *Modern Medea* reclaims the specific events of Garner's life from historical neglect, argues that Morrison, striving to be faithful to the complete archival record, leaves the paternity of Margaret Garner's children wholly unresolved and thus her libretto "cracks" under her attempt to do justice to both the living and the dead.

Two essays by individuals affiliated with Cincinnati's National Underground Railroad Freedom Center at the time of *Margaret Garner*'s premiere follow Halliwell's and Weisenburger's contributions. Delores M. Walters, a member of the *Margaret Garner* Steering Committee and training director for the Freedom Center, reports on Cincinnati Opera's formation of the Steering Committee charged with devising a strategic, preproduction campaign for *Margaret Garner* that Michigan Opera and Opera Company of Philadelphia also implemented. The Steering Committee anticipated that a higher percentage of African Americans from the metropolitan areas of the commissioning opera companies would be drawn to performances of the opera because of its focus on a historical enslaved African-American family; its premieres in northern cities with substantial black populations; and its world-famous African-American librettist. Carl B. Westmoreland, the National Underground Railroad Freedom Center's senior advisor and curator, makes the case that Morrison misses a key opportunity to resist racist stereotypes of black males as inept and absent when she curtails the life of the fictional Robert Garner in her libretto by depicting his lynching in act 2 during his family's run for freedom that culminates in Margaret's commission of infanticide. The historical Robert Garner survived the death of Margaret two years later. He reared their two sons and served in the Union army before dying in 1871.

Kristine Yohe, the local director for the Fourth Biennial Conference of the Toni Morrison Society that was held in Cincinnati concurrently with *Margaret Garner*'s premiere, gives an overview of the conference and discusses the public controversy that Maplewood Farm docent Ruth Brunings created when she alleged that Garner had had a consensual, adulterous affair with Archibald K. Gaines, her Kentucky enslaver. Brunings's ancestors lived adjacent to Maplewood during Gaines's ownership of the farm, Margaret Garner, and her children.

The remaining three essays align the libretto *Margaret Garner* with other works inside and outside its genre.

My own critical contribution to the volume, extending the thesis I forward in *Toni Morrison and the Idea of Africa* (2008), asserts that Morrison transfers from the novel to the libretto partially concealed esoteric features of Haitian Voudoun. My essay also firmly places Morrison's libretto within an African aesthetic that conceals and reveals and an African-American libretto tradition not fully known to performance experts that heretofore has not received critical attention by literary scholars.

Aimable Twagilimana, who works in the areas of Africana studies and world literature, discusses intertextual parallels that contemporary commentators drew between the tragic events surrounding Margaret Garner's radical actions and Livy's classical tragedy *Virginius*, popularized in America by James Sheridan Knowles's 1826 published version. Commentators also invoked Euripides's, Seneca's, and Pierre Corneille's versions of the Medea tragedy, as well as François-Benoît Hoffmann's libretto for Cherubini's opera *Médée* (1797), as earlier paradigms for Margaret Garner's real-life infanticide in order to explain her motive for the anti-maternal act.

And last, Helena Woodard, a specialist in Morrison's canon and African-American slave narratives, points out that Morrison alters the historical timeline of her libretto to juxtapose Margaret Garner's enslavement with the onset of the Civil War just as Christopher Hampton, the librettist for *Appomattox*, juxtaposes the final days of the Civil War with the post-1950s civil rights movement. The time conflations of both libretti "demonstrate opera's ability to locate critical, defining moments in the United States' vexed racial past and to call attention to social issues in the present that grew out of that tempestuous, racialized past."

The insights of each contributor in this volume provide an insider's perspective to an important historical moment in the literary and operatic worlds in the first decade of the twenty-first century. A work that centers on the libretto for *Margaret Garner* has been long overdue. Perhaps a critical study that treats the African-American libretti reclaimed above and throughout this volume will now appear.

## NOTES

1. Marc Scorca, interview with Toni Morrison and Richard Danielpour, "Meet the Margaret Garner Creative Team: On Stage with Toni Morrison and Richard Danielpour," Music Hall, Cincinnati, 15 July 2005.

2. Lawrence B. Johnson, "The Majestic 'Margaret' Sets Spirits Soaring: Morrison's Libretto, Emotive Performances Infuse Opera with Power and Eloquence," *Detroit News*, 9 May 2005.

3. Janelle Gelfand, "Breathtaking 'Garner' Chills, Inspires," *Cincinnati Enquirer*, 9 May 2005.

4. David Patrick Stearns, "'Margaret Garner' Worthy of Excitement It's Stirring," *Philadelphia Inquirer*, 11 May 2005.

5. Mary Ellyn Hutton, "'Margaret Garner' A Grand Debut/Highly-Anticipated Story of Runaway Slave's Sacrifice," *Cincinnati Post*, 9 May 2005.

6. Heidi Waleson, "A Tragic Opera Born of Slavery," *Wall Street Journal*, 11 May 2005.

7. David Gonzalez's libretto for *Rise for Freedom: The John P. Parker Story* (2007; Adolphus Hailstork, composer) and Talaya Delaney's *TRUTH, A New Folk Opera about the Life of Sojourner Truth* (2012; Paula M. Kimper, composer)—celebrating historical American enslaved subjects—followed *Margaret Garner*.

8. The University of Missouri's Labudde Special Collection, Kansas City, holds Duncan's libretto for *Gideon and Eliza*.

9. The program for Howard University's 1972 staging of *Slave Song: An Opera*, in addition to containing a list of the roles and their performers and synopses of the scenes and music, gives additional information about scenes' musical numbers, the technical crew, the production staff, and the opera's musical staff. The Library of Congress holds a program of the performance signed by the composer.

# Turning Words into Music

Toni Morrison's Libretto Margaret Garner *and*
*Its Musical Realization*

✳ MICHAEL HALLIWELL ✳

I have always felt that in any action that presents itself as a subject of opera there
should be an element that for its fullest expression demands music rather than toler-
ates it.—*David Malouf, Introduction to* Jane Eyre

W. H. Auden, a highly accomplished librettist, made the following rather contentious comment concerning the libretto: "The verses which the
librettist writes are not addressed to the public but are really a private
letter to the composer. They have their moment of glory, the moment
in which they suggest to him a certain melody; once that is over, they
are as expendable as infantry to a Chinese general: they must efface
themselves and cease to care what happens to them."[1] While Auden is
being somewhat facetious, there is truth in his comment.[2] The libretto
is a curious artifact, existing in a literary twilight zone similar to a film
script. Musicologist Stephen Benson describes the libretto as "a self-
consciously virtual text, in thrall to the real life it cannot attain."[3] A
particularly interesting dynamic occurs when the librettist is also the
author of the source work, an existing work that serves as a foundational
text for the later one. In operatic adaptation as in film adaptation, the
librettist (or screenwriter in film) might be the composer (which is rare,
but Wagner is the great model, with Carlisle Floyd and John Harbison
serving as more recent examples), but more frequently he or she is a
writer who has an interest and aptitude for the radical genre surgery
that transforming a literary work into a libretto requires. The case of
*Margaret Garner* is more complex, as the sources of the opera are varied
and the opera's libretto is certainly not simply an adaptation of Toni
Morrison's novel *Beloved* (1987), although elements of the novel are in

her libretto. Herein, I examine the libretto as a distinct genre with its own particular imperatives and characteristics, as a discrete genre that does not have an independent existence and only reaches its full potential through its musicalization. There are no set forms that a libretto adapted from a source work must take, yet frequently the nature of the source will determine the outcome so that the inevitable shortening that occurs is less problematic in the adaptation of a play than in the adaptation of a novel. The fundamental imperative is that the librettist provides both language and a dramaturgical structure that allow the text to be transformed into a textual/musical synthesis through operatic structures and a dramatic architecture that create situations of conflict, both physical and psychological, that are the essence of opera. Toni Morrison has provided composer Richard Danielpour with a skillfully constructed, poetically dramaturgical framework to which he has responded with a musical score that draws on a wide variety of musical idioms and styles. My discussion focuses on the dramatic representation of the central character of Margaret Garner and her enslaver, Edward Gaines, as embodying a successful synthesis of words and music. In the discussion of the music, I describe the vocal and orchestral music as a single entity unless otherwise indicated.

## Some Thoughts on the Libretto as a "Literary" Genre

Peter Conrad suggests that one should consider the similarities between the genres of opera and the novel rather than the more obvious connections between opera and drama:

> Music and drama are dubious, even antagonistic, partners and . . . opera's actual literary analogue is the novel. Drama is limited to the exterior life of action. . . . The novel, in contrast, can explore the interior life of motive and desire and is naturally musical because mental. It traces the motions of thought, of which music is an image. Opera is more musical novel than musical drama.[4]

With Conrad's comments in mind, one could argue that the "novelization" of a libretto occurs when the composer adds music to the text: a complex process comprised of interiorization and expansion. The issue of whether readers and critics should consider the libretto a "literary" genre or even a stand-alone artifact has occasioned some recent debate, whereas in the past when publishers would commercially distribute the libretti of celebrated writers such as Pietro Metastasio, these libretti would enjoy a long afterlife through frequent recycling by other composers subsequent to their first performances.[5]

At the heart of opera, whether in the comic or tragic vein, is conflict, and it is the librettist's task to construct situations and an overall dramatic structure that allow the composer to explore conflict primarily in the synthesis of vocal and orchestral music. Some would argue that musical form dominates and propels the dramaturgy given the framework in the libretto. Eminent musicologist Carl Dahlhaus maintains that "music does not alight from somewhere outside upon a drama that already has an independent existence, but rather that the music alone creates the drama, which is thus drama of a special kind."[6] Is the music subservient to the dramatic framework of the verbal text, or does the music actually embody the drama? However, the libretto is crucial in determining the final form of the opera as it is the first, and possibly the most important, "interpretation" of the source text if it is an adaptation of a preexisting work or a framework and blueprint for the composer if it is an original work.

Approaches to writing a libretto are varied. The librettist may use text as it stands in the preexisting work, a process known as *Literaturoper* (the German term literally translated as "literature opera"). In most cases, he or she has turned a play into a libretto, perhaps with just some shortening. Or the librettist may almost completely discard or imaginatively rework the source text as part of the transposition. The librettist must be aware of genre imperatives: a libretto is not a play script even if its source lies in a play, and however "faithful" the libretto is to its source, it must obey the musico-dramaturgic principles of the operatic genre, unless it is deliberately and self-reflexively seeking to overturn these, as in twentieth-century anti-opera.[7]

The libretto should provide opportunities for direct musical self-expression and expansion in the forms of arias and duets as well as uniquely operatic structures such as large ensembles and choruses so that there is aural variety in the musical response to the text. The collaboration between the composer and librettist determines the usage of these operatic structures. A character usually employs the aria for moments of internalized self-examination—or moments of individual reflection in an ensemble, which is, in effect, a series of arias occurring simultaneously when the action, or forward momentum of the plot, is halted. In traditional operatic forms the recitative sections move the plot forward, while arias and ensembles allow pause and emotional exploration. Essentially the libretto should map out characters' development both emotionally as well as behaviorally, and it needs to provide structures that facilitate dramatic momentum in music. It is then left to the composer to provide further expansion through the combination of the orchestral music in which the characters "exist" and their vocal expression.

Reviews of many recent "literary" operas criticize their lack of ensemble writing; this is particularly so for those that have stage plays as their source, which presents challenges to both composer and librettist to find a synthesis of musico-dramatic form.[8] Establishing conflict between characters in duets and larger ensembles works against the usual form of short, sharp exchanges in spoken drama because when characters sing together an emotional separation is hard to establish in terms of the audience's perception. Yet some of the great moments in opera occur in these ensembles where characters express conflicting thoughts and emotions within the context of an overarching narratorial voice: the orchestra. Fundamentally, a librettist must not be tempted to think of the libretto as a form of play script but as a form more akin to a film script.

While opera cannot and does not strive for the dramatic momentum of spoken theater or film, stimulating variety in the musical engagement within the textual framework is the task of the librettist as well as the composer. The librettist can determine much of the musical response through the dramatic structures he or she constructs, which then suggest possible musical strategies for the composer. The librettist's determination of musical response is an important element, as opera's inherently escalatory and anti-naturalistic nature can sometimes be in conflict with situations and events that the libretto maps out. That determination is also part of a tensional element observable in most operas between the striving for beauty and dramatic coherence in purely musical terms and the striving for dramatic effectiveness in theatrical terms.

The magnifying effect of music in opera might seem to distort both character and situation as music endows characters with more signifi-cance than they might have on the page or even on the spoken stage or screen. It conveys a ritualistic element due largely to the various time frames operating in opera. In drama and film, a real-time event might have a very short duration but it can be substantially extended in opera, which confers upon it this ritualistic quality. Just singing a text as op-posed to speaking it protracts time.

In opera the orchestral music "narrates" the action rather than ac-companies it, thus presenting the action in an unmediated form, as is the case in spoken drama. Opera's narrative mode might be regarded as primarily diegetic (in the literary sense of "telling") rather than exclu-sively mimetic ("showing" rather than "telling"): the audience, there-fore, experiences the singer not only as an autonomous character who "speaks" directly to it, but as part of a more complex narrative process. The music "tells" us about the characters, like a narrator in a novel, per-haps even more than the dramatic action "showing" us the characters in action, as in spoken theater. As novelistic characters exist only in the words on a page, so, too, operatic characters might be thought of as existing only through the music that surrounds and gives them life.

Musical characterization utilizing traditional musical devices achieves character individuality very effectively. The aural "presence" of characters despite their actual physical absence can be achieved in musical terms through devices such as leitmotif, reminiscence motifs, and a wide range of harmonic, melodic, and rhythmic musical ele-ments. The singer achieves character definition through both vocal self-expression, particularly in the aria, as well as through the orchestral music that surrounds the character and by means of which the audience gains insight into his or her psychic and emotional world. Musical char-acterization may vary enormously, but existing in this web of music, the operatic character is essentially and substantially different from his or her counterpart in the fiction, drama, or real life that is his or her source.

The choice of voice type—soprano, mezzo-soprano, contralto, tenor, baritone, or bass—also influences characterization, or role casting, in opera. These choices come freighted with a long tradition in which par-ticular vocal types evoke a specific response in an audience; the tacit role that voices play in opera in representing character types is important in understanding the ultimate meaning of the operatic work. In very simplified terms, the soprano is often the victim; the tenor the rebellious and romantic hero; the baritone a figure of authority; the mezzo a seductress, sorceress, or enchantress; and the lowest voices, the bass and the contralto, frequently inhabit an otherworldly realm. The voice-to-role-alignment is a very approximate typology with many exceptions where vocal casting goes "against the grain," but even in contemporary opera it is surprising how frequently these traditional or standard casting choices may perhaps even unconsciously still hold sway. Standard vocal casting and its subtle variation is an important aspect of characterization in *Margaret Garner*.[9]

Verbal style is important. Some libretti are too complex for a completely successful translation into a verbal and musical synthesis—the language might be too "dense" for easy comprehension by the audience. Or the dramatic architecture might be too convoluted for effective translation into the scenes of conflict on which opera thrives.[10] "As the text of a narrative-in-music," Benson observes, "the libretto contains both too much and too little verbal information."[11] A librettist (and composer) has to be aware that textual complexity is extremely problematic in opera; much of a relatively concise and "simple" libretto will still be lost to the audience in performance and librettist and composer must find musical solutions to these challenges. The libretto should consist of language that both shapes the dramatic situation and limits the verbal "music" in its own right, yet gives the composer space for the actual music. As composer Jack Beeson states, "We know the characters in an opera from their words, but we believe them because of what they sing. The music will appear to reflect them, as in an enlarging mirror; rather, as though the music were a magic mirror, it will appear to create them."[12] The advent of supertitles in opera has changed the dynamic of the interaction between stage and audience and the relationship of both to text and, in the view of some, has led to the detriment of the performance aspects of opera.

The libretto (and later the completed musical score) usually contains explicit dramaturgic instructions as to the staging of an opera. At what point these staging instructions enter the process will vary, but if they are part of the libretto presented to the composer they will undoubtedly influence the musical response. The composer, and later the director, can negotiate, rework, or even ignore these instructions, and many contemporary productions deliberately ignore the time frame and staging instructions contained within the libretto. There can also be the potential for conflict if the librettist's interpretation of the source does not accord with the composer's interpretation. A composer can ignore the philosophical underpinning of a libretto by composing music that suggests a radically divergent interpretation than the librettist posits. Opportunity for conflict potentially increases with the adaptation of a well-known literary source or historical event, which might provoke radically disparate interpretive views by librettist and composer; however, one would assume that a common perspective as regards the source would be agreed upon in the preliminary work on the libretto. A cursory glance at the history of librettist/composer collaborations throws up a picture of a variety of working relationships with a wide range of conflict as well as harmony. All in all, the role of librettist is complex and challenging.

## Margaret Garner—*The Libretto*

Toni Morrison's libretto for *Margaret Garner* has its primary source in an actual event, but both Morrison's novel and Jonathan Demme's film of the novel cast long shadows in terms of their influence on the final form of the opera as well as the possible expectations that an audience might bring to an operatic performance. Historical record well documents the facts surrounding the real-life figure that Morrison uses in her libretto even though the motivation of the imagined figure remains opaque. Considering the stature of Morrison as a novelist and the importance of *Beloved* in her oeuvre, it is understandable that readers and critics consider the novel as one of the sources, but there is a limited congruence between the novel and the libretto. In much the same way that Morrison reimagined and reworked the historical events surrounding Margaret Garner's story for her novel, so too has she reimagined both the novel and its historical background for the libretto. Critics have addressed the degree to which Morrison the librettist and Danielpour the composer are faithful to the known facts of the historical background as well as to the artistic inventions of Morrison's own novel.[13] However, fidelity to either is not necessarily their intention: Danielpour describes their project as follows: "Keep in mind that this is not a historical opera in the sense that everything is followed historically because as artists, we create sometimes an illusion in order to keep a greater truth and artists do this kind of thing. We take artistic license . . . [and] the gist of her story and of hundreds of stories that have in a way been assimilated into this work that we put together."[14] Morrison explains her fictive mediation of historical fact to achieve a greater truth:

> The crucial distinction for me is not the difference between fact and fiction, but the distinction between fact and truth. Because facts can exist without human intelligence, but truth cannot. So if I'm looking to find and expose a truth about the interior life of people who didn't write it (which doesn't mean that they didn't have it); if I'm trying to fill in the blanks that the slave narratives left—to part the veil that was so frequently drawn, to implement the stories that I heard—then the approach that's most productive and most trustworthy for me is the recollection that moves from the image to the text. Not from the text to the image.[15]

What is immediately striking in the printed libretto and score is that the musical numbers are laid out very explicitly within the overall musical discourse; it is apparent that this is a work in the tradition of "number opera" in the sense of having clearly defined stand-alone musical elements such as arias, duets, and larger ensembles as opposed to the ariosos or flexible recitatives that characterize much contemporary opera.

Morrison has constructed her libretto in terms of broad oppositions:

Margaret Garner—Edward Gaines
Robert Garner—Casey, the foreman
Cilla and Margaret's children—Caroline Gaines and George Hancock
The Slaves (aka, "Black Chorus")—The Townspeople (aka, "White Chorus") and Judges

Of course these oppositions reflect the binaries at the heart of the opera—black and white; enslaved and free. The synthesis of vocal and orchestral music characterizes each of these groupings, often in strikingly contrasting ways.

Structurally, act 1 of *Margaret Garner* has three scenes; and act 2 has four scenes with an intermezzo separating scenes 2 and 3, during which Margaret is alone on stage. Larger-scale, frequently choral scenes balance the scenes of intimacy and domesticity. However, moments of physical and psychological conflict often occur in both the intimate and the large-scale scenes. An epilogue concludes the opera, conferring a sense of musical closure and paralleling the opening scene of act 1, where the action emerges from darkness, and act 2, scene 4, where it returns to darkness at the opera's end.

Another striking aspect of the opera is that it has relatively few scenes, somewhat unusual in that many contemporary operas seek a scenic fluidity which approximates that found in film. What the slower-paced libretto of *Margaret Garner* allows is the creation of larger musical forms that need time to develop and resolve. Particularly notable is act 1, scene 3, a long scene characterized by a distinctive rhythmic structure, the waltz. The waltz remains constant, despite its subjection to a variety of "distortions." Within the opera there are many moments of reflection and introspection for the major characters. Benjamin Britten, certainly the most successful of post–World War II opera composers, felt that the opera audience needed these moments of lyricism in opera.[16] However, these lyrical moments do not annul a swift movement from one particular musical texture to another within the scene itself to create and sustain interest. Variations in musical texture are embodied in the striking use of the "divided" chorus, and signal the political aspect of the libretto. The librettist, as in many other celebrated operas, with Britten's *Peter Grimes* (1945) serving as a recent example, uses the chorus as a character in its own right to create a larger political and social dimension as backdrop to the representation of the more intimate personal conflicts while simultaneously achieving a wide range in musical texture and dramatic interest.

Another crucial choice Morrison makes at the construction stage of the libretto is to tell the story of Margaret Garner chronologically but with several alterations to the time frame of the actual historical events. The libretto unfolds in a linear fashion, in "present time," with no framing narrative or use of flashbacks, although there are some moments where characters recall the past in reflective moments as well as in instances in the dialogue that invoke memory. An opera occurs essentially in the present, thus the representation of memory that is central to *Beloved*'s narrative is problematic to depict in opera. However, not only through characters' words but also through music's ability to invoke the past and, even at moments, the future through the employment of a variety of musical devices,[17] the composer can project forms of representation subtly suggesting past recollection. These techniques are not systematically employed in the opera. It is in its execution of representing time that the libretto differs markedly from the novel with its constant welling up of memory for both Sethe and Paul D, the main protagonists in *Beloved.*

## Margaret Garner and Edward Gaines

Toni Morrison opens *Margaret Garner* in an undefined space. The orchestral music and the voices of the Slaves (aka, "Black Chorus") emerge out of the darkness as a musical prelude. The choral opening suggests that the libretto's central conflict will be as much about the community and the institution of slavery and its dehumanization of enslaved and enslaver as it will be about the unfolding events between Margaret Garner and Edward Gaines. Just as in some important libretto/operatic predecessors such as Modest Mussorgsky's *Boris Godunov* (1873) and George Gershwin's *Porgy and Bess* (1935) the chief protagonists are *both* the central characters *and* the folk of the community. The Slaves' chorus follows Margaret's first solo, and it soon becomes apparent that the musical structure will move between a solo voice and a choral group—a question-and-answer format—that the opera features repeatedly and which originates in the call-and-response of the African-American spiritual and sermonic traditions. The back-and-forth vocal pattern confers great energy and rhythmic drive that characterizes much of the vocal and orchestral music of the opera.

Morrison structures act 1, scene 1, as a triangulated exchange occurring among the Auctioneer, Edward Gaines, and the Townspeople (aka, "White Chorus"), whom she repeatedly delineates by a musical response verging on caricature. The words the Townspeople sing describing the Slaves are sung rapidly, often to rapid triplets, suggest their rapacity and lack of awareness of the humanity of the people that they discuss. The opening exchanges are musically fluid, approximating a naturalistic representation of the scene. Edward's first utterance, "Hold on!" (act 1, scene 1),[18] interrupts this rapid orchestral music, and it is immediately apparent that his jagged vocal line, characterized by large intervals frequently in the extreme upper range of the baritone voice, suggests an effort to conceal the violence at the heart of his nature. The vocal line of the singer is important in offering access to his character. In this case the powerful upper register of the baritone, in which the vocal effort is apparent, is a potent reminder of the position of power that Edward Gaines inhabits as a Southern white American male of means in a nineteenth-century antebellum agrarian society as well as a strong indicator of his potentially violent nature.

Jazz-inflected music frequently distinguishes Edward's vocal delivery, while the quality of much of Margaret's vocalizing—with its musical structures in ballad or spiritual form and delivered in the mezzo-soprano vocal range that exploits the color and depth of the female operatic voice—conveys her warmth and humanity as well as her strength.[19] The musicality of his singing rather than the words he sings suggests Edward's authority. As the Auctioneer attempts to quell Edward's interruption, not recognizing him as a Richwood resident of two decades earlier, Margaret's future owner sings, "I beg your pardon" (act 1, scene 1) with a sinuous vocal line: the smooth legato quality of his singing reinforces the sense of barely concealed danger and violence. As he reveals to those assembled his identity as the brother of the deceased whose property is up for auction, the Townspeople react in short, detached questions, and there is a distinct contrast between his suave vocal line and the disjointed and shallow musical response from the Townspeople that leads into his arioso[20] "I Was Just a Boy":

> I was just a boy
> When any of you last saw me.
> But I've been happily married
> With a daughter we both adored.
>
> Now I'm a widower, a man of means,
> A father with a child to raise.
>
> What my brother owned
> I have right of first offer to buy.
> Which I do now, friends.
> Which I do now.
>
> (ACT 1, SCENE 1)

Edward's "I Was Just a Boy" offers the first real moment of stasis in the libretto. He sings it "with swing"[21] and a rapidly moving, jazzy "walking bass" line under a syncopated brassy orchestral narration. His words are simple and direct, but the way in which his jazzy delivery insinuates itself into the music of both the Auctioneer and the Townspeople suggests his power. His vocal line and his rhythms completely dominate the orchestral music until he declares, "I want it all" (act 1, scene 1), thus claiming the Slaves and all of his brother's Maplewood estate as his rightful inheritance.

Margaret's vocal music frequently has elements of the folk song as well as qualities of the hymnal. Her first reflective moment is her arioso "I Made a Little Play Doll":

MARGARET

(*tenderly*)

I made a little play doll for my baby,
With button eyes and hair of yarn;
The lips are made of rose-colored thread.

(*Distracted, Edward looks up from his paperwork; he turns around and notices Margaret, who is wearing a red scarf. He is captivated, and grateful for his good fortune to have just purchased her.*)

One day she will love it;
I am waiting for her to love it

(*Edward turns around again, and finishes signing the contract. The businessmen extend handshakes of congratulations to him on the acquisition of Maplewood.*)

When she is old enough to hold it.

(*Margaret unties her red scarf. When one of the slaves brings in Margaret's infant daughter, wrapped in a white cloth, she drops her scarf on the ground in order to cradle the baby tenderly in her arms.*)

I'm watching this mystery called child.

(ACT 1, SCENE 1)

Her aria emerges out of the preceding rhythm "A Little More Time" and calms it down, but there is still a sense of the lilt that characterizes Edward's preceding "I Was Just a Boy." Like much of Margaret's vocal music, this brief aria has a folksy mood to it. However, musical wisps of the Slaves' "A Little More Time," which they sing when they learn they will not be sold and separated, persist in the orchestra even as her vocal line is smooth and calm, suggesting her heartfelt evocation of childhood arises out of her sense of community. Seamlessly this brief moment evolves back into the vocal and orchestral music of the Slaves, which ends with a vocal interjection from Margaret, and Robert (Margaret's husband), and Cilla (Robert's mother). In these instances, Danielpour creates a sense of individuality of character as well as the strong sense of the position in society of the character through varying his musical textures.

Left alone, Edward contemplates his scandalous actions that led to his leaving Richwood twenty years earlier; a few brass jazzy outbursts in the orchestra narrate his musings. As he recalls, "The girl was so young, / And from such a fine family" (act 1, scene 1), the orchestra provides jagged, unconnected motifs, suggesting perhaps his desire to rewrite his history. He reminisces in the aria "I Remember":

EDWARD

(*wistful, yet still optimistic*)

I remember the curve of every hill
The swans in the pond;
I remember them still.

I remember every tree:
Maple, birch, willows and pine.

I can see them now

Shading the drive,
Shelt'ring me from the heat.
Maple, birch and the odor of pine.

I remember every tree
But none of them remembers me.

The well, the creek,
Fishing by the lake.
Evenings of laughter
With girls who wanted to play.

I remember every tree
But none of them remembers me.

. . .

(*sotto voce*)

They won't forget me again!

(ACT 1, SCENE 1)

Here is the first substantial moment of revelation for Edward, and it is an abrupt departure from the swing that characterizes much of his singing to this point. Morrison gives him simple short lines structured very much as song lyrics in contrast to the more complex text she uses for expository passages. The rhythm of the lines is insistent, and Danielpour translates it into a waltz with a limpid, flowing movement that is beautiful but superficial, suggesting a lack of self-awareness in Edward's character. On the surface it has a folksy character, with other wind instruments accompanying an insistently wistful solo oboe, but there are occasional harmonic twists that slightly distort the simple, parlor-ballad, harmonic expectation and the peaceful, pastoral atmosphere evoked by the words, suggesting that this is as much fabricated past as true recollection, the orchestral music deliberately undermining the words in effect. His complaint, "I remember every tree / But none of them remembers me," loaded with self-pity, is set to a gradually descending vocal line and renders a sense of being a "constructed" rather than a deeply felt and sincere moment of revelation. The waltz rhythm identified with Edward here will characterize the whole of the third scene in the act as well as reemerge consistently throughout the opera. It often appears as a rhythm for nostalgia and memory, but it also strikes a contrast with the driving rhythms of much of the Slaves' choral music.

Morrison structures the second scene of act 1 with another choral opening moving through moments of calm and domesticity that Casey, the foreman of Maplewood, interrupts when he brings news of the impending forced separation of Margaret and Robert. A duet between the enslaved wife and husband, "Love Is the Only Master," a return to calm, completes the arc of the scene. The music that opens the scene, "O Mother, O Father, Don't Abandon Me!" led by Robert when the Slaves are returning to their quarters, once again has a strong rhythmic drive and is in the form of a work song with a shout-out by a soloist answered by the full Black Chorus. The vocal and orchestral music gradually evolves into a much calmer mode as Cilla welcomes Margaret and Robert to their cabin. Intricate figures in the woodwind section suggest the sounds of nature in the evening. The Garners' cabin segment in act 1, scene 2, strongly contrasts with the earlier depiction of the Slaves returning to their quarters and shows the intimate life of Margaret, Robert, and Cilla. Musically it has a strong lyrical element with a consistently warm orchestral narration. There are occasional moments of faster, rhythmic orchestral music, but it is predominantly slow and reflective.

Margaret then sings to her baby:

> Sad things, far away
> Soft things, come and play
>
> Lovely baby . . .
>
> Sleep in the meadow,
> Sleep in the hay
> Baby's got a dreamin' on the way.
>
> Bad things, far away
> Pretty things, here to stay
>
> Sweet baby, smile at me

Lovely baby, go to sleep.

Sleep in the meadow,
Sleep in the hay
Baby's gonna dream the night away.
Lovely baby, pretty baby
Baby's gonna dream the night away.

. . .

Sleep in the meadow,
Sleep in the hay
Baby's gonna dream . . .
Baby's gonna dream . . . (*softer*)
Baby's gonna dream . . . (*softer still*)

(ACT 1, SCENE 2)

Margaret's lullaby is set off from the preceding discourse, again emphasizing the "number" character of the opera despite the essentially through-composed score.[22] In the musical form of a ballad, the aria has a flowing melody with a gently rocking orchestral accompaniment including the occasional "bluesy" turn in the vocal line. The musical style here is strongly reminiscent of Gershwin's song "Summertime" from *Porgy and Bess* and illustrates the eclectic nature of Danielpour's musical response to Morrison's text.[23] There are also elements of folk song and spiritual present and verbal repetition reinforces the impression of a quasi–musical theater moment where stand-alone musical numbers, usually in the form of songs that essentially halt the forward momentum of the events, occur. Casey's entrance interrupts the calm, completely altering the scenic mood to one of confrontation. The lyricism of the preceding orchestral music evolves into a jagged and abrasive discourse.[24]

Morrison sets the third and final scene of act 1 in the "candle lit parlor at Maplewood Plantation" and contrasts it with the previous one, as the domesticity of the slave quarter exchanges gives way to an expansive choral scene. Her doing so reflects the tradition of situating a large-scale choral movement at the end of a central act. Scene 3 opens with the sound of a "parlor" piano wafting from the orchestra pit, providing the musical description of the events unfolding during Caroline and George's wedding reception. The abrupt change in the musical discourse provides a textural contrast with the lyricism of the previous scene through the vulnerable sound of the solo instrument as opposed to the full orchestra. Here it is musical narration that provides the backdrop for scene 3, and the sound of the piano in this instance creates an atmosphere of domesticity. When the full orchestra joins the piano, the orchestral music for the parlor scene morphs into a sentimental waltz. The smooth and slightly enervated rhythm of the waltz that characterizes the song of Edward Gaines's Guests (aka, "White Chorus") contrasts strongly with the earlier fiercely accented, vocally sumptuous, vibrant music of the Slaves. Edward Gaines assumes the waltz rhythm in his arioso:

> I promised Caroline's mother
> Two things.
> One, that I would stay
> A widower;
> Two, that I would see
> To our daughter's future care.
> Caroline has proven
> The rightness of those promises.
> She will inherit a sound estate—
> Which, I might add,
> Has grown from modest to grand.
> And her choice of husband
> Is everything
> Her mother would have wished for . . .
>
> (ACT 1, SCENE 3)

In a sense the smoothly flowing music "domesticates" him, at least briefly. The high-lying vocal line, which requires an obvious effort of control and reinforces the impression of the underlying power and violence of the man, undercuts his domestication. The tone in his words suggests long-standing resentments that are barely contained. The vocal effort required for that containment subverts the gently flowing waltz. The full orchestra accompanies the words "Has grown from modest to grand," musically underlining his sense of self-worth and pride in his economic achievements.

The waltz rhythm in its various guises dominates the entire parlor scene, subliminally characterizing it musically underneath the action. Seemingly alone when the reception's guests abruptly leave, Margaret picks up a glass, asking "Are there many kinds of love?" and begins a quasi recitative before her aria "A Quality Love." Hers is a slightly more disguised waltz rhythm with a rocking accompaniment under a series of solo obligato instruments:

MARGARET

(*looking at the glass*)
. . .
Only unharnessed hearts
Can survive a locked-down life.

Like a river rushing from the grip of its banks,
As light escapes the coldest star;
A quality love—the love of all loves—will break away.

When sorrow clouds the mind,
The spine grows strong;
No pretty words can soothe or cure
What heavy hands can break.

When sorrow is deep,
The secret soul keeps
Its weapon of choice: the love of all loves.

No pretty words can ease or cure
What heavy hands can do.
When sorrow is deep,
The secret soul keeps its quality love.

When sorrow is deep,
The secret soul keeps
Its weapon of choice: the love of all loves!

(ACT 1, SCENE 3)

The aria has a strong folk melody, finally breaking the stranglehold of the waltz that has musically characterized the scene. The music evolves into a compound rhythm that contrasts with the relentless waltzes. The words—mainly monosyllabic words typical of folk song, the musical form emphasized by its strophic structure—convey a sense of strength and fortitude. The melody of "A Quality Love" is strongly reminiscent of the Scottish traditional "Loch Lomond," a song about parting and loss, which has provoked some discussion about its role as a memory prompt and the use of what Danielpour has described as a "found object," a preexisting melody or style of music that facilitates memory.[25]

A sinister figure in the bass with sinuous, upward-moving chromatic line heralds a sudden break in mood as Edward advances on Margaret, forcing himself sexually on her as the curtain falls. The scene consists of a long, varied, and well-constructed sequence of actions; Morrison has skillfully created a framework for dramaturgic expansion through the music. Danielpour uses a range of distinctive musical styles to characterize his chief antagonist and protagonist: jazz-inspired riffs and a breezy vocal line predominate in the combination of the orchestral narration and Edward's vocal line, while the folk impulses in Margaret's aria is music distinctively hers.[26]

Morrison shapes the first scene of act 2 with a rising arc of tension that culminates in the separation of Margaret and Robert in order to run from enslavement in Kentucky to freedom in Ohio. There are moments of calm but no substantial reflective moments for Margaret or Edward. Ohio is the setting of scene 2, where the central event of the opera unfolds—Margaret's killing of her two children.[27] In her agony at being captured by the posse that Edward has organized, Margaret flings hot coals at him with her bare hands—an action alluded to symbolically at the end of the opera when Edward feels his own hands burning. The events move swiftly in both of these scenes, and there is little space for any of the characters' reflections.

An intermezzo starts in "total darkness" and gradually gives way to the figure of Margaret. The movement functions as another contextualizing moment in which the audience might distance itself in a Brechtian sense from the horror that it has just witnessed and dispassionately as possible consider the impetus and implications of her infanticide. Adagio doloroso (mournfully slow) marks the intermezzo with intensely warm orchestral music. Out of it arises the vocalizing of Margaret from the darkness:

MARGARET

(*consoling herself*)

Ah . . .
Like a river rushing
From the grip of its banks.

(*With defiant grandeur, Margaret embraces her life's circumstances.*)

Darkness, I salute you.
Reason has no power here,
Over the disconsolate.
Grief is my pleasure;
Thief of life, my lover now.

(*with quiet acceptance*)

Darkness, I salute you.

(*Fade to black.*)

(INTERMEZZO)

The operatic voice, here shorn of semantic connotation, is one of the most powerful elements in opera and it is as much the "grain of the voice" that contains the meaning as any words the character sings.[28] Carolyn Abbate argues that the power of the singing voice itself, stripped of all signification, contains moments that are disturbing because the sonority of the voice "pointedly focuses our sense of the singing voice as one that can compel *without* benefit of words. Such moments enact in pure form familiar Western tropes on the suspicious power of music and its capacity to move us without rational speech."[29] The verbal text may, in fact, be an impediment to the full expression of emotion, indicating, in a sense, the ultimate irreconcilability of words and music. Margaret's wordless vocalizing then becomes the brief aria "Darkness, I Salute

You." It is a slow, intense piece, accompanied by shimmering strings and open diatonic chords, conveying almost a feeling of transcendence and acceptance: *"With defiant grandeur, Margaret embraces her life's circumstances."* The scene gradually fades to black.

The large-scale, penultimate scene in the opera incorporates the Townspeople and a variety of individual characters. A brief, quiet introduction heralds the beginning of the court case. The three judges sing in identical rhythm and close harmony, suggesting the power of the forces mounted against Margaret. Thus begins the debate about the nature of her crime—murder of two human beings or theft and destruction of property. Occasionally the musical characterization of the Judges verges on the comical—as does the musical characterization of the Townspeople. Caroline and George plead with her father and the Judges not to view Margaret's killing of the children as a property matter, singing music of a simplicity and directness characterized by diatonic chordal movements in contrast with the chromatic, jazzy bluster of Edward and the straitjacketed harmony of the Judges. Caroline confronts the whole weight of the legal system epitomized by the Judges, whose music has a rhythmic, pounding bass under its quasi-unison vocal lines, as does Edward's and the Townspeople's music. When left alone, Edward sings an introspective arioso:

EDWARD

(*examining his hands*)

Nothing. I see nothing at all.
No wound, no rash.
Yet they burn.

What lights the flame?
Is it Caroline's kiss,
Or Margaret's coals of fire?

(*Edward steps forward a few feet—thereby "leaving" the courtroom—and moves to a dimly-lit area of the stage.*)

(*dismissing any questions of doubts from his mind*)

Damn it to hell!
I am approved.
Clearly what the world insists
I should be.
Law and custom endorse me.

(*reconsidering*)

Yet my only child
Looks at me with strange eyes;
Cold appraisal where naked adoration
Used to live.

(*aggressively*)

Am I not a legal man?
God's blueprint,
Flawed in merely ordinary ways?

(*assuming an aristocratic air*)

Hats still tip,
Gentlewomen dip their heads courteously
To me.

(*introspectively*)

And yet. And yet.
They sear like molten lead.

(*inwardly, glancing at his hands*)

(Look at them. Look at them!)
(*upon reflection*)

If the flaw is in the blueprint
Why must I choose?

If the flaw is in the blueprint—
Then I *must* choose.

(ACT 2, SCENE 3)

Edward's contemplation here is the most substantial moment of character revelation for him, with its powerful symbol of the lack of burn marks on his hands from the coals Margaret has thrust at him. The coals are emblematic of the whole destructive institution of slavery. An orchestral outburst shatters his introspection, and he attempts to remove his doubts and justify his actions, depicted in voice and orchestral music of violence and jagged harmonies. However, it is a solo oboe's plaintive melody that causes him to reassess the correctness of his position. The aria moves from doubt to certainty expressed in the rapidly changing musical response to the poetic text. Through the combination of the musical motifs in the orchestra as well as in the text he sings, the audience gains access to Edward's moral complexity. And it is the operatic synthesis of music and text that provides as much or more access to his thoughts than the words alone. He has lost all of the jauntiness and lilt that characterized most of his music up to this point.

The dominant rhythm of the aria is in a slow four beats to the bar, with the emphasis on the second beat creating a sense of disruption and unease; in a sense Margaret's music infiltrates his music, an aural symbol of the effect that she has had on him despite his denial. A sudden eruption of emotion occurs with the words "Damn it to hell!" (act 2, scene 3). The steady pulse of the music completely subverted, jagged outbursts from the orchestra punctuate Edward's words. When he thinks of Caroline, the original pulse starts again, but his words "Am I not a legal man?" interrupt it and the orchestral outburst recurs. But these subside as he looks at his hands and the steady, four-beat pulse continues relentlessly to the end of the scene with Edward's almost rhythmless interjections unconnected to the orchestral music. Musically there is a final lack of resolution mirroring Edward's sense of unrelenting moral and sexual guilt and parental uncertainty.

The last scene has the plangent sound of Cilla's soprano accompanying Margaret as she is led to the scaffold to be executed for the theft and destruction of Edward's property. The sound of her voice at the upper extreme of the range is a powerful expression of grief and despair. Edward rushes in with a document granting her clemency, ironically calling out, "Hold on!," just as he had at the beginning of the opera when he stops the public auction of his deceased brother's estate. Margaret sings a simple, repeated, rising phrase:

MARGARET

(*in a state of transcendence*)

Oh yes. I will live.
I will live.

I will live among the cherished.
It will be just so.
Side by side in our garden
It will be just so.

Ringed by a harvest of love.
No more brutal days or nights.

(*making eye contact with Cilla in the crowd*)

Goodbye, sorrow . . .
Death is dead forever.

I live.
Oh yes, I live!

(ACT 2, SCENE 4)

Her music has a simplicity supported by a strong pulse and ostinato bass line emblematic of her resolve and acceptance of her fate. The music achieves the impression of clarity and transparency with ringing brass chords suggestive of her transcendent state of mind. The final section is quieter, as she contemplates a life "side by side in our garden" (act 2, scene 4). To a rapidly undulating string and woodwind motif in the orchestra, she bids farewell and hangs herself, narrated by dramatic, jagged chords in the orchestra. Edward is left looking at his hands as he walks away with the realization that he will not find spiritual peace let alone moral redemption. His stunned posture invites the audience to consider that slavery has and will continue to affect psychically everyone—both black and white—that it touches.

The epilogue has all—the Townspeople, the Slaves, Caroline, George, and Cilla—without the orchestra join in a final chorus. The voices bring a solemn tone to the hymn they deliver. The orchestra's silence suggests that the opera's "narrator" has receded, allowing unadorned human voices to have the final impact.

Toni Morrison has constructed a libretto that has enabled a varied and eclectic response from Richard Danielpour. Textual variety as well as a scenic structure that offers many opportunities for conflict—the life's blood of opera—characterizes her libretto. Large-scale choral scenes contrast with intimate moments for the central characters. The central roles of Margaret and Edward dominate all, and Morrison explores their relationship within the unfolding larger political narrative leading to the tragic denouement. She presents Margaret as strong and unyielding, responding to each indignity with fortitude until she "breaks" at the prospect of recapture. She goes to her death with dignity, subtly and effectively conveyed through her deliberate actions, through the text she sings, and most powerfully, through the music that narrates her plight. Morrison nuances and multifacets Margaret's representation, and Margaret's music is strikingly powerful, showing the full capacity of the operatic mezzo voice.

Narratively and musically, Edward is the more interesting character. Morrison explores his thoughts and emotions in a series of introspective moments. From the swagger of his entrance and growing sensual awareness of Margaret to his conflicted paternal relationship with Caroline, he is a complex character. His final aria reveals the divided nature of the man, plagued by guilt resulting from his immoral, inhuman actions and anger at being frustrated in dominating those around him. In the libretto as well as through the music, Edward psychically evolves in his social consciousness. While a jazz-inflected music, rhythmically varied and ever changing, characterizes his bluff, potentially violent presence in the opening scene, in later scenes his appropriation in particular of the ubiquitous waltz rhythms shows a man uncomfortably attempting to accommodate himself to the upwardly elitist Kentucky agrarian society in which he finds himself. However, both Edward's vocal and orchestral music assume many of the characteristics identified with Margaret, suggesting a growing closeness and even respect for her despite the physical and psychological conflict that characterizes their relationship. Edward's final aria reflects his evolving emotions in rapidly changing music with frequent rhythmic disruptions and a tortured vocal line.

Both the libretto and its musical response are, in the positive sense of the word, conservative. Morrison and Danielpour use traditional operatic structures rather than opt for a possibly more radical approach to representing the historical story. Of course some commentators have criticized the musical idiom of *Margaret Garner*.[30] However, because of rather than despite the eclecticism of the score, the music well serves Morrison's tightly structured and poetic libretto. The composer represents the Southern society that functions as a backdrop to the central events in a wide range of stylistically varied musical idioms that gives vitality and variety to their representation but still focuses on the central conflict between Margaret and Edward while not obscuring the larger political dimension of the opera.

## NOTES

1. W. H. Auden, *The Dyer's Hand and Other Essays* (London: Faber, 1975), 473.
2. In broad terms, one of the neglected aspects of much scholarship dealing with contemporary opera is the libretto itself. Its neglect can be particularly noted in the critical and popular receptions of new opera, where the libretto is usually glossed over in a line or two, if at all, in the reviews. How different it was in earlier opera where the "poet" was frequently accorded more importance than the composer, and the libretto would be separately published with the poet's name much more prominently displayed than the composer's name.
3. Stephen Benson, *Literary Music: Writing Music in Contemporary Fiction* (Aldershot: Ashgate, 2006), 46.
4. Peter Conrad, *Romantic Opera and Literary Form* (Berkeley: U of California P, 1977), 1.
5. See Arthur Groos and Roger Parker, eds. *Reading Opera* (Princeton, NJ: Princeton UP, 1988). Groos notes that as adaptations of preexisting literary works, "libretti pose questions of intertextuality, transposition of

genre, and reception history; as verbal artifacts, they invite the broad spectrum of contemporary reading strategies ranging from the formalistic to the feminist; and as texts for musical realization, they raise issues regarding the relation between the two media and their respective traditions. According to such perspectives, libretti are not 'beneath contempt as literature,' but very much within the purview of contemporary humanistic scholarship" (10). Regarding the often undervalued status of the libretto, see Benson, *Literary Music*, 41–42.

6. Carl Dahlhaus, "What Is a Musical Drama?," trans. Mary Whittall, *Cambridge Opera Journal* 1.2 (1989): 95. Dahlhaus states that it is character that determines the actual dramatic structure of opera. He notes that while commentators regard the dialogue as being fundamental to the nature of Western drama, it is "not decisive in the creation of drama by musical means." He observes that it is important to look at "the configuration of characters amongst whom a drama occurs as the fundamental structure of opera. Conflicts between a group of characters do not have to be expressed in dialogue if they can be manifested in an interrelating system of arias: the connection between the affects represented musically in the arias is dramatic insofar as it reveals the fundamental emotional structure concealed under the surface of the action. . . . Presenting a configuration of characters in a drama of affects is the stylistic principle opera imposes on the action represented, just as expressing human conflicts in dialogue is the stylistic principle of a play" (96).

7. Anti-operas explicitly interrogate and often overturn the conventions of the genre that have developed over four hundred years and include works such as John Cage's *Theatre Piece* (1960) and György Ligeti's *Le Grand Macabre* (1978), a work written in response to what commentators have considered the defining example of the development of anti-opera, Mauricio Kagel's *Staatstheater* (1971).

8. A lack of ensemble writing is a criticism that has been leveled against André Previn's operatic adaptation of Tennessee Williams's *A Streetcar Named Desire*. Severe restrictions on changes to the source text were imposed by Williams's estate. See Ralph V. Lucano, "Guide to Records: Previn," *American Record Guide* 62.2 (Mar.–Apr. 1999): 192–93; David Schiff, "We Want Magic," *Atlantic Monthly* 284.3 (Sept. 1999): 92–96; Terry Teachbout, "Brand-Name Opera," *American Jewish Committee* 106.5 (Nov. 1998): 56–59.

9. There is an irony with the vocal casting of Cilla (soprano) and Margaret

(mezzo) with the older character having the higher voice, thus reversing the traditional expectation.

10. Reading the libretto before the performance has been standard practice in the past, but current operagoers have largely allowed the practice to fall into abeyance.

11. Benson, *Literary Music*, 50.

12. Quoted in Elise K. Kirk, *American Opera* (Urbana: U of Illinois P, 2001), 251.

13. See the contrasting views of Catherine Gunther Kodat, "*Margaret Garner* and the Second Tear," *American Quarterly* 60.1 (Mar. 2008): 158–71; and Leon James Bynum, "Toni Morrison and the Translation of History in *Margaret Garner*," in "Opera and Translation," special issue, *Doletiana* 3 (2010–2011), www.fti.uab.cat/doletiana/English/Doletiana3-e/Doletiana3e. html.

14. Carl B. Westmoreland, "The Music, Story, and Significance of *Margaret Garner*," interview with Richard Danielpour, transcription of Cincinnati Opera's "Opera Rap Lecture and Performance," 19 Feb. 2004.

15. Quoted in Bynum, "Toni Morrison and the Translation of History in *Margaret Garner*."

16. See Benjamin Britten, "Mapreading: Benjamin Britten in Conversation with Donald Mitchell," in *The Britten Companion*, ed. Christopher Palmer (London: Faber and Faber, 1984), 87–96. Britten acknowledges the inherently "unrealistic" element of opera in an interview with Mitchell: "The audience needs the tunes, it needs the lyricism of the aria and the ensemble, rather than the realistic side of perpetual recitative. . . . One should enjoy it *because* it is opera" (90).

17. These include all the musical effects such as leitmotif and reminiscence motifs that can suggest memory as well as bring past events to life or even foretell future events.

18. Toni Morrison, *Margaret Garner: Opera in Two Acts*, composed by Richard Danielpour (rev. ed.; New York: Associated Music, 2004). All references to the libretto are to this edition.

19. Interestingly, Margaret, the principal female protagonist of the opera, is not a soprano that might have been the obvious choice. Of course, there are many factors at play in the choice of voice type, including the desire for particular singers, but as I stated earlier in the essay, the soprano in opera is often the victim and it would seem that Morrison and Danielpour did not wish to present the title character in this way despite her tragic story.

20. Danielpour makes a distinction in the score between arioso and aria. Arioso suggests relatively brief melodic moments of reflection as opposed to recitative. The arioso is generally shorter and less strictly structured than the aria.

21. Richard Danielpour, *Margaret Garner: A New American Opera*, vocal score (New York: Associated Music, 2005), 47.

22. Although the music flows seamlessly within each scene, there are moments that are set apart musically from the ongoing discourse. These moments can be categorized as musical "numbers" (and can easily be extracted from the score to be performed as solo pieces). In this sense the opera can be classified as a "number opera" although the music is through-composed in the sense that there are no obvious breaks in the flow of the music as one might find in musical theater.

23. One can trace a variety of influences in Danielpour's music, but there are strong echoes of Michael Tippett's great oratorio composed between 1939 and 1941, *A Child of Our Time*, in which Tippett, in masterly fashion, weaves a series of spirituals throughout the musical texture of the work.

24. An interesting aspect of the vocal casting here is that the role of Casey calls for a tenor, which in a sense goes against the "normal" casting option, since the tenor voice is usually, but of course not always, employed for more romantic characters.

25. Danielpour describes his process of assimilating these elements: "I will take an idea that may resemble another composer's or have the equivalent of a found object to a visual artist, and I'll kvetch and mull and agonize over it until it no longer resembles the object I have found. Hopefully, it becomes something else." Quoted in Robert Fallon, "Music and the Allegory of Memory in *Margaret Garner*," *Modern Fiction Studies* 52.2 (Summer 2006): 532. See Kodat, "*Margaret Garner* and the Second Tear," 168, for a critical view of the eclecticism of the music of the opera.

26. As Fallon notes: "By characterizing Edward with jazz and Margaret with a Scottish song, Danielpour exchanges their cultural heritages. Rather than rigidly separating music along color lines, he reminds us that the components black and white require each other to create their binarism" (534).

27. The opening of act 2, scene 2, has the sound of an offstage trumpet lending a quasi-military feel to its events. It is significant that the setting of the scene has been shifted to a few days before the opening of the Civil War on 12 Apr. 1861, of which the trumpet is a traditional yet still potent aural military reminder of the imminent war.

28. The "grain of the voice" formulation is that of Roland Barthes, *Image-Music-Text*, trans. Stephen Heath (New York: Fontana, 1977), 179–89.

29. Carolyn Abbate, *Unsung Voices: Opera and Musical Narrative in the Nineteenth Century* (Princeton, NJ: Princeton UP, 1991), 10.

30. See Kodat, "*Margaret Garner* and the Second Tear," 169, and Bynun, "Toni Morrison and the Translation of History in *Margaret Garner*," 7, for contrasting views. The reviews of various productions of the opera also reveal a wide range of critical responses. See Heidi Waleson, "Opera's New (York) Season: 'Lucia' and 'Margaret Garner,'" *Wall Street Journal*, 27 Sept. 2007; and Anthony Tommasini, "A Runaway Who Paid a High Price for Freedom," *New York Times*, 13 Sept. 2007.

# "Dangerous Territory"

*The* Margaret Garner *Opera and the Margaret Garner Case*

\* STEVEN WEISENBURGER \*

For archaeological purposes it is registered as site 15Be483 and described in the records as "the ca. 1850 plantation of Archibald [K.] Gaines," known as Maplewood, a place of "some notoriety because of its association with the Margaret Garner story, made famous in the book *Beloved* [1987][1] by Toni Morrison and subsequent motion picture"—and, we should add, as setting for Richard Danielpour's 2005 opera *Margaret Garner*, for which Morrison provided the libretto.[2] In their work at Maplewood beginning in 1998, lead archaeologists Kim A. McBride and M. Jay Stottman documented various extant or partly extant structures. Their teams excavated around and near those buildings, confirming an 1850 newspaper report that fire had destroyed the farm's main residence, which was then rebuilt that year. They did not locate a slave quarters for Mr. Gaines's fifteen human properties, including Margaret Garner and her four little children. A midden gave up sundry finds—an 1845 penny, pottery shards, a broken fine china plate bearing an English coat of arms, handmade nails, broken buttons, arrowheads—things handled by Maplewood occupants, free or enslaved, and perhaps signifying historically relevant understandings about their lives in the Richwood community.[3] Among those pieces now stored in cabinets, the Indian arrowheads are rather enigmatic. Perhaps it was only coincidence that they appeared under or alongside trash deposited by later, nonnative Kentuckians, or perhaps a Maplewood resident—an enslaved African American plowing Massa's fields or Squire Gaines walking his demesne—had found them. Yet how and why would such interesting artifacts wind up in the midden? Perhaps the arrowheads simply signify that any people, their artifacts and their histories, are subject to disposal, mere loss, and vanishing.[4]

But perhaps we ask such things to say more than they can. The "desire to make contact with the 'real'" in contemporary historicism, indeed its widely acknowledged push for material culture studies and the history of everyday life, particularly the lives of subaltern peoples whose cultures have been shattered and dispersed, is a striving to see through objects and into the lost worlds of which they are synecdoches. In short, to make the objects speak and represent. But such a project becomes theoretically problematic, Bill Brown cautions, with the necessary recognition that *things* are not *objects*. Shards, broken buttons, and lost arrowheads exist prior to the order of objects and do not in themselves signify. External to schemas of symbolic and discursive ordering and narrativizing, unavailable as such to the museum, they may be numbered and consigned to the long darkness of archaeological cabinet drawers, yet they will not satisfy desires for them to be windows on the past. They cannot unfold the history of domination and diaspora imputed to them.[5]

It is somewhat the same, but different, with the physical sites where historical events have occurred. The mid-October 1998 release of Jonathan Demme's film *Beloved* produced occasions—including the *Oprah Winfrey Show* episode celebrating the film and its historical context—when a mass audience could learn about the Maplewood property where Margaret Garner had lived and from which, in January 1856, she and her family fled for Ohio and freedom. Since 1998 that farm has become, using Pierre Nora's terminology, a prominent *lieu de mémoire*, or "site of memory."[6] Shortly after the film's debut, preservationists filed paperwork to have Maplewood designated a state historical site—a presently stalled effort. Today, the National Underground Railroad Freedom Center in Cincinnati kindly provides interested tourists directions to Maplewood. So does the Kentucky Commission on Human Rights website in its pages on Margaret Garner; as does an article in the November 2010 *Kentucky Monthly*, which ranks Maplewood third among the Bluegrass State's nine must-see "Storied Places."[7]

As early as 1998, busloads of students, professors, and cultural tourists began visiting Maplewood and the Richwood Presbyterian Church, whose records note Margaret's baptism there but nothing more. The former plantation itself had passed (in the 1980s) from the estate of the last A. K. Gaines relative into the hands of Cincinnati businessman George Budig, who graciously opened Maplewood to archaeological research as well as to limited tours of the grounds. By late 1998 a former Richwood resident, Ruth Brunings, who descended from Archibald K. Gaines's brother, attorney James Gaines, and from a prominent nearby family (the Bedingers) who played mere bit parts in the Garner story, began using the presumed authority of her lineage to guide some of those Maplewood history tours, especially with the July 2005 Cincinnati debut of the *Margaret Garner* opera. During these years Brunings aggressively made her way into Garner-related forums, speaking not only on her family but on the history of slavery. Discounting plain evidence of A. K. Gaines's emotional volatility and violence against his enslaved laborers—at the Garners' fugitive slave hearing Margaret testified that Gaines had inflicted the injury that left the scar visible on her face— Brunings pressed her case for the general benevolence of Kentucky slavery and her ancestors' slaveholding Christianity in particular. In her telling, an A. K. Gaines still distraught from the accidental death of his first wife (years earlier, when she was pregnant) and beleaguered by the responsibilities of running Maplewood and overseeing its enslaved laborers, had lost his mental balance.[8] Thus recuperating "white man's burden" ideology of the previous century—of Dunning School historians (ca. 1910–1950), and of *Gone with the Wind*–style popular fantasies about American slavery—Brunings's account also had to conjure a Garner family that bolted for freedom and a Margaret who tried to kill all four of her children and then take her own life, not because enslavement at Gaines's Maplewood farm was for her a form of social death and terror, but instead because Margaret was also irrational, mentally imbalanced, and volatile—a characterization lurching toward racist stereotype. Such efforts are problematic enough.

Yet even before Brunings took the stage to uphold her Gaines ancestors on those terms, independent Ohio writer/researcher and documentary filmmaker Joanne Caputo was already (in early October 1998) guiding news reporters around Maplewood, clutching to her breast as she did so a handmade "Margaret doll" while displaying the shrine she had constructed beside a dilapidated outbuilding. Caputo was considering a screenplay and writing a book, subsequently entitled *Margaret Garner: Diversity and Depth of Love*, later self-published online. And although at times diligently researched, this text's ultimate authority or witness is none other than Margaret Garner's murdered two-and-a-half-year-old daughter Mary, understood as reincarnated in Caputo herself and thus helping to guide visitors around Maplewood and the gnarled historical narrative seen as growing from its fecund soil.[9]

Pierre Nora's original work on "sites of memory" argues for their rising popular significance in a contemporary, postcolonial context. Decolonization's wake, he argues, has left humanity nothing of *milieux de mémoire,* the "real environments of memory," composed and dearly held in living communities in spite or because of the traumas attending their domination. Instead, left behind in the aftermaths of diaspora and decolonization are mere sites within or remnants of that greater but now devastated cultural memory. So we latter-day people—offspring of colonizers and colonized—nostalgically and variously "consecrate" these places, Nora argues, precisely because the shared memory that was once alive there has passed, unrecorded, into oblivion. As formerly eventful places, often sites of great wrong, they would seem to be richly significant for a proper historiography. Emptied, however, of practically all except its proper name ("Maplewood"), a site of memory typically exists in relation to a near vacuum. Although the site of a very real wounding, it resists scholarly work on the agents, actions, means, and purposes of that violence and thus remains "forever open to the full range of . . . possible significations." That openness is precisely the issue. Story and storytellers may flood into it, but if they cannot predicate narrative on a critical, evidence- and archive-based historiography, then they also cannot achieve the ethical bearing or purchase in regard to these places where the customs and laws of state power have been manifested. So Nora cautions us about the quite limited or even absent signifying powers of these sites. Practices that imagine or use the *lieu de mémoire* as a window, or regard it as a speaking *physis* will tend to deploy it as a means (a fetish) for projective fantasy, for affective cathexis. That projective tendency is similar to what Bill Brown cautions in regard to the *thing.* But more so, for the still greater presence and, indeed the spatiotemporal extent of the site of memory have the effect of clothing it in the regalia of a special, compelling witness—not only a *physis* where the past unfolded but even a gnosis, or "knowledge"—an already-given cognition of the past. Our affective investment thus magnified, the popularly identified *lieu de mémoire* morphs into a busy intersection of under-processed psychological and sociopolitical interpretations and uses, a terrain traversed by professional historians, history buffs, reenactors, reincarnated spirits, and, yes, ghosts. Ruth Brunings's Southern nostalgia and Joanne Caputo's Kentucky gothic are instances of the extensive record growing from and around "Maplewood" as an exemplary instance of such a space.[10]

But what about archives, too, as a kind of textual territory? Theory has also compelled us to realize the problematics of recovering and working respectfully and responsibly with the witnessing stored in archives, because archivization itself is involved with state power. Seen as an *economic* edifice wherein archons daily enact the state's *oikos nomos*, or "household law," chiefly by regulating memory, the archive is for Jacques Derrida a bureaucracy dedicated to admitting, classifying, and preserving the recollection and knowledge required for the state to reproduce its authority through generations. In *Archive Fever* he specifically compares that project to the maintenance of blood purity—as a means for regulating the patrilineal transmission of status and property—to Freud's view, in *Civilization and Its Discontents*, as a force of law essential to the racialized project of "civilization." (Such was the presumptive source and project of Ruth Brunings's authority.) And thus interpreted psychoanalytically as bureaucracies of anxious patriarchy, Derrida calls us to understand archives as, Freud would insist, institutions for *repression*. Tasked to regulate or efface upstart and illicit sociocultural desires, expressions, and understandings, archival work is genealogical in the sense that it regulates the record of civilization's adulteration and bastardization. (And such was the main challenge Margaret and her children posed to the Gaines family and to its heirs.) Derrida does not develop this argument vis-à-vis the politics of race. Still anyone working on the history of race in a former slaveholding and segregated republic like the United States understands as a matter of ordinary practice the barriers to scholarship of an archive deeply complicit for centuries in policing "miscegenation" and the "shadow families" and societies it produced. The Garners stood in 1856 and afterward as an exemplary case: Margaret was a "mulatto" woman; her murdered daughter "practically white"; the child's paternity unclear. The Garner family's acts of resistance and rebellion, seen as reactions to the anarchy of *someone's* illicit desire, needed to be repressed and, indeed, rewritten, mainly as symptoms of inherent ("negro") malignity and/or madness, which is how countless news writers depicted her in 1856. So the Garner case exemplifies what Derrida names "archive fever": as a state's Others contest with it for self-assertion, rights, and being itself, state bureaucracies deploy their greatest resources and authority to erase, repress, and negate those upstart efforts. Mindful of Derrida's critique, historians have learned to regard archives not only as sites for triumphal remembering but also as regimes for an implicitly violent, repressive misremembering. Ethical work on a case like the Garner infanticide required the use of archival materials with methods guided by postholocaust and postcolonial critiques.[11]

For US historians working in slavery studies, Derrida provides a theoretical purchase on a familiar problem: the constraints of a selectively limited and implicitly untrustworthy archive. But another prior constraint that operated on a personal or subjective level magnified that institutional or objective constraint. The public silence of slaves—masters' total ban against their chattel's access to civic discourse in oral or print media—was a constitutive fact of their existence. Few cases—consider also the Nat Turner rebellion—illustrate the double constraint better than the Garner infanticide. In the winter and early spring of 1856, a multitude of pro-slavery and antislavery voices, nearly all white, filled the near absence of testimony from the Garners themselves, speaking for and about them from all manner of vantage points. These included Squire Gaines, from Maplewood. During Reconstruction those dinning voices passed into a long dormancy, then resumed with the critical reception of *Beloved*.

In his trenchant critique of that print record, Mark Reinhardt's 2002 essay "Who Speaks for Margaret Garner?" argues for the historiographical necessity of *refusing to fill in* the silence, the near absence of Garner voices. Instead he calls all who encounter the story, in the words of philosopher Giorgio Agamben, to "bear witness in the name of the impossibility of bearing witness." Agamben's dictum seems counterintuitive for humanists because it appears to disrespect practices and objectives researchers and the consumers of that research venerate the most: using archival evidence to infer and thus to tell true—which is to say—whole stories. But Reinhardt argues that adhering to Agamben's dictum means being true to a greater ethical calling. In doing so we accept, he argues, that while scholarship on a historical account such as the Garner case will be "offering no redemption and repairing no injury," at least it will mean no disrespect and commit no further harm. The imperative against doing no more harm is logically clear. Stated in the terms offered here, if our representations and analyses treat the Garners as *things*—as windows on their world, or telephones transmitting their speech and thought—then uncannily our work comports with the very regime that commodified them. Moreover, we will have hazarded that work on basic errors of critical practice because we will have slighted analytical suasion and depended instead on the compulsions of affect and fantasy. Thus Reinhardt sets an eloquently defended, difficult, necessary standard. Doing so, he rightly criticizes the end of my 1998 book *Modern Medea*, which, while otherwise striving always to speak of and for the Garner case using the historiographically responsible subjunctive mood, breaks down in the epilogue and, in narrating details of the typhoid fever that evidently took Margaret's life, ventriloquizes for her in declaratives.[12] For which: mea culpa. I take this lapse as a reminder of the strength of that nostalgic pull that Nora also cautions historians and literary critics to resist.

Finally, though, one's work on a case such as the Garner infanticide has to employ the archive, however fraught it is, and despite its offering no records of the Garners' unmediated speech and even precious few instances of their *edited* discourse. Undoubtedly new evidence will yield itself up to research; indeed some already has appeared.[13] An example, from the Gaineses' side of things: during the July 2005 meeting of the Toni Morrison Society celebrating the Cincinnati premiere of *Margaret Garner*, an opera company employee called my attention to a document that John Gaines, a distant nephew of Archibald K. Gaines (and like Ruth Brunings also interested in defending the family name), believed that I should have consulted and which he used as one item evidencing my having misrepresented various things, in this instance the relation between Margaret Garner and John Gaines's distant relatives. The recently discovered document from the Kentucky Historical Society archives that John Gaines referred to was a copy of a 1947 typed transcript made by Nashville resident Louis Farrell, excerpting a December 22, 1901, letter penned by Mrs. Elizabeth Ann Gaines Burke. Elizabeth was the niece of A. K. Gaines and about fifty-nine years old in 1901; in 1856 she had resided for at least six years with the B. F. Bedingers, some distance from Maplewood. She provided personal recollections of Margaret, of her escape, and of her infanticide. Of the discursive context for her 1901 letter (its addressee, and the situation moving Elizabeth to provide her anecdotes), Farrell says nothing.

In the excerpt, Burke uses Margaret's diminutive name "Peggy" and recalls her as a "fine looking woman" whom the "children liked," and as "Grandma's pet servant" despite her having "a violent temper." So, could one use Burke's claims, which are after all presented as those of an individual who knew "Peggy" before the 1856 events, to support a narrative (like Brunings's) in which Margaret's volatile temperament explains the infanticide? In which the Gaines family may be represented as beneficent and loving Christians? First, though, how much of Burke's witness can be taken as factually creditable, when the excerpt is otherwise filled with error, rumor, and likely misremembering? It repeats a gaffe widely circulated among Cincinnati area whites after the Civil War, to the effect that "the 'Peggy' case" (of 1856) provided the "basis" for "Mrs Stowe's Uncle Tom's Cabin" (published in 1852). Burke also reiterates a bit of local legend circulated among pro-slavery writers as early as winter 1856: that Margaret "was run away by her husband and two Underground Railroad emissaries"—as if her own agency was nil. Burke also shares an anecdote found nowhere else in the record, about "the scars on [Peggy's] back" resulting from her fighting with another Gaines slave, Nellie, using "switches," which sounds like an errant version of the family's alibi to counter Margaret's courtroom testimony about Gaines being responsible for putting the *scar on her face.*[14]

In his later work on the Garner case, Reinhardt rightly concludes that "the letter is thoroughly unreliable."[15] To a greater or lesser degree, we would say the same about countless other documents and texts produced in the aftermath of the Garner infanticide: innumerable newspaper stories, accounts of northern Kentucky and Cincinnati witnesses, and especially the spate of poems and historical fictions that retold old or invented new rumor and speculative misinformation. The complexity of that print archive is why the Garner escape and infanticide—almost unstudied for 130 years—needs the eyes and wisdom that a range of scholars can bring to it, as was necessary for reclaiming the facts of the Nat Turner rebellion.[16]

Following quickly on the opera's May 7, 2005, world premiere in Detroit, the opera's July 2005 Cincinnati debut certainly rekindled that 1998–1999 debate which followed *Beloved*'s cinematic release. Once again, Gaines descendants defended the family with vigor, and at times with outrage. In a moment recalling the Thomas Jefferson descendants who had been battling for the third US president's reputation against new interpretations of his relationship with the enslaved Sally Hemings and the shadow family she gave to him, John Gaines offered to provide genetic material so that it could be checked against that of a Garner descendant, if one could be found (a risk-free offer, doubtless, because they all had died or vanished), thus to put at rest claims (in 1856, and in 1998) that A. K. Gaines may have fathered some of Margaret's children. Thus Maplewood became again a hotly contested site of racial and sexual politics. But in Cincinnati, this time, an array of African-American and European-American scholars from local universities and the year-old National Underground Railroad Freedom Center countered with lectures and presentations on historical contexts and issues. Also stepping in were longtime civil rights activists representing African-American communities still recovering from the city's April 2001 race riot, which had erupted after a white police officer shot and killed an unarmed nineteen-year-old black man during a chase. The opera's debut gave them opportunities, forums, to seek redress for that violence, perhaps to heal decades of ineffectually answered charges of police racism and brutality in the city, and to ensure that another violent episode in US race history would not be trampled under. All of these voices—those of the Gaines descendants, scholars, activists, opera stars, and Morrison herself—made for engaging and theatrical debate over history even before one attended Music Hall to take the opera's imaginative historical journey.

During one Cincinnati Opera–sponsored Maplewood tour, Ruth Brunings and John Gaines played prominent roles, expressing concern over potential "stereotypes" (reverse racism, they thought) in the opera's depiction of Margaret Garner's owner. Michael Mayes, white cover for the role of Edward/Archibald K. Gaines, somewhat allayed their concern when he took John Gaines "aside to talk about the portrayal of his ancestor" and to give him assurances that in the opera his great-great-great uncle would "come off as both a villain and a victim."[17] Together, Morrison and Danielpour also made their first-ever visit to Maplewood. Morrison later told a reporter of her initial reluctance to compose the libretto because she believed revisiting *Beloved*'s subject matter would draw her back into "dangerous territory." Morrison stated, "I was averse to putting myself at risk emotionally." She went on to say that while sharing John Gaines's concern "about stereotyping," it had been "an even greater challenge transforming Margaret's tragic tale into a dramatic work of art: making her story one of hope rather than despair, and in the process making a parable of love, not hate." The opera's director for the Detroit, Cincinnati, and February 2006 Philadelphia stagings, Kenny Leon, similarly offered, "We have not healed and grown from slavery, and I think *Margaret Garner* can make a difference in this country."[18]

"Dangerous territory," indeed: for what is at stake ethically in representing Archibald K. Gaines as "both a villain and a victim"? And what is at stake ethically in figuring the Garner case as a "tragic tale" and the infanticide thus as sacrificial violence posing triumphal potentials—"hope rather than despair," in a "parable of love, not hate"? As Morrison's dichotomized value-terms indicate, her *Margaret Garner* libretto had summoned deeply conflicted but powerful desires. It also attempted, in critic Catherine Gunther Kodat's apt words, "to do a lot of work for a lot of people, and for reasons that seem both inflated and mundane."[19] Morrison's comment represented these purposes as growing *from* an affectively and politically contested "dangerous" Maplewood that the dramatic work of art should transcend. Then it would land again on earth and offer, in Leon's phrasing, a healing balm for the cultural-political schisms that race and white supremacy created "in this country."

Given that people want to believe that the supposed nature of things, sites, and archives sponsors metaphysical and even supernatural uses of them, we have good reasons to urge caution in the face of claims for the libretto and the opera *Margaret Garner*'s aesthetically transcendent powers. Fastened by thin threads to the unstable, contested ground of "Maplewood" and amid a welter of representations (including Toni Morrison's own) and the sociocultural work they were supposed to do, Morrison's libretto accomplishes a striking revision of subject matter she treated in the novel that made her famous. In its title especially, but also in its characters, setting, and transformation of actual events (such as the drama of a courtroom trial), the libretto signals an *apparent* shift from the supernatural to the real. From *Beloved*'s uses of the Garner infanticide only as enigma sparking Morrison's psychological novel and its revenant namesake, she sought to offer in *Margaret Garner* a more fully historicized representation, most of it situated at Maplewood, thus a story seemingly attending to the real even while it works within operatic demands for compression and melodrama.

Many of the revisions Morrison made are truly minor. The historical Gaines's given name Archibald becomes Edward because the latter name is more singable, and the characterization of Robert's mother, Cilla, is admittedly fictional. Other changes are more significant. For instance, the libretto's characterization of Robert nicely realizes the man who emerges from the print archive—willful, strong, forceful, a leader in his demeanor and deeds—and baritone Gregg Baker portrayed him with extraordinary grace and power. On the other hand, Robert's lynching (two-thirds of the way into the opera) stands very much at odds with historical fact (he survived into the 1870s, at least), as does the libretto's representation of a Margaret with two children, both of whom she murders. The historical Margaret had four, was pregnant with a fifth when she fled Maplewood, and succeeded in killing only one in Cincinnati when the slave catchers arrived at the house where the family had taken sanctuary. These revisions were undoubtedly scripted for the sake of compression and tidiness, leaving none of those loose ends from the actual Garner case. Indeed, the libretto's conclusion completes the Garner family holocaust with Margaret's incredible hanging/suicide, probably unknown in the annals of American slavery. The opera thus ends with guilty white folks arrayed onstage. Moreover (and most daring of all historical revisions), the libretto ends with a repentant Edward who is no longer a villain in his daughter Caroline's eyes. Thus the curtain falls with an Edward ensconced once more as sovereign patriarch of his intact white household. And the libretto's sequential logic implies that this restoration—which another of its remarkable historical revisions situates in March–April 1861, the time spanning Lincoln's inaugural and the outbreak of the Civil War—can only occur *after* the complete erasure of that shadow family. Importantly, that shadow family *may have been the consequence* of Edward/Archibald first raping Margaret (at the close of act 1), then forcing her into four years of concubinage when she used to warm his bed ("Remember . . . Remember?" he implores her in act 2, scene 2), and when Edward *may have fathered* her second child.[20]

But Morrison's script opens the door on miscegenation without ever decisively going through it. Throughout, characters never mention skin color and repeatedly refer to Margaret's offspring neutrally as "the children." Robert never uses the singular or plural possessive ("mine" or "ours"); and once, only, does Margaret (in act 2, scene 2) refer to them as "our children." As for Edward, before the Judges (in act 2, scene 3), he names them "Two children, both mine" but then tellingly amends his claim: "I mean, both my *property*." Thus in trying to be faithful to the incomplete archival record, the libretto leaves paternity wholly unresolved and its audience at odds. Critic Robert Fallon, in "Music and the Allegory of Memory in *Margaret Garner*," writes that "Edward has been raping Margaret for years; she has borne two children by him," which cannot be true; her first was born before Edward, after a twenty-year absence, returns to Maplewood.[21] And Catherine Gunther Kodat surprisingly states that the libretto "closes the door" on any possibility of an interracial offspring, thus exonerating the melodrama's villain, who confesses (in act 1, scene 1) that he previously assaulted a local girl, "so young, / And from such a fine family" because he was "a boy with an appetite" and "Things got a little out of hand."[22]

In the July 14, 2005, Cincinnati premiere of *Margaret Garner*, the key event in scene 3 ending act 1 unfolded differently than the libretto directs: "*Edward overpowers her [Margaret], and drags her forcibly out of the parlor. The curtain falls slowly.*" Instead that night Edward wrestled a resisting Margaret to the floor and pressed himself full length upon her, whereupon the curtain, malfunctioning, stubbornly and incredibly refused to budge. So as baritone Rod Gilfry and mezzo-soprano Denyce Graves, who performed the respective roles, lay in a violently sexualized interracial tableau, the audience gazed and squirmed in the seats for an inordinate length of time, the staged rape and its attendant theme of slave concubinage riveting itself in each onlooker's mind. That telling revision to the script and especially the remarkable happenstance, only amplified Edward's villainy. The effect of that night's stubborn curtain left a lasting impression on viewers as they next pondered act 2's unwillingness to resolve clearly the enigma of whether or not Edward fathered Margaret's second child, the kind of matter that the actual, silenced, enslaved Garners were banned from speaking into the archival record but that their imaginatively realized counterparts certainly would address with grammatical consistency and clarity, especially while alone together. In other words, the curtain glitch of the evening highlighted that the libretto lets Edward off the paternity hook.

In what sense, then, may we read Edward as a "victim?" The libretto's conclusion in act 2, scene 4, further muddles a response to that question when Edward races in to stop Margaret's hanging, "*excitedly waving a document*" granting her clemency. Amid hugs and handshakes, daughter Caroline and son-in-law George Hancock exclaim, "Thank God. Thank you [to Edward]," as Cilla also thanks "Sweet Jesus." With the gallows rope encircling her neck, Margaret, "*in a state of transcendence*" (according to the stage direction), then proclaims, "Death is dead forever" and orchestrates her own hanging on the scaffold, making herself a Christlike sacrifice. Afterward, Caroline takes from her father's coat pocket the same red scarf of Margaret's that he had slowly tied "around her neck" just before the rape that ends act 1, then she *"reverently ties it around Margaret's waist."* Thus the libretto ascribes or "ties" rape and concubinage to Margaret's motive for suicide, signaled in her words—"No more brutal days or nights"—intoned just before her death drop. Moreover, Edward's running in with the clemency document in his hand and Margaret's red scarf in his *"front pocket" may imply* that his recognition of culpability for sexually (and otherwise) brutalizing Margaret is what compelled his volte-face successful plea for her life. The problem is that other than the red scarf's metonymic tie, the libretto gives us nothing by which to reckon Edward's practically instantaneous conversion. Edward's moral conflict takes place offstage, in the hiatus between the third and fourth scenes of act 2, between his saying "Law and custom endorse me" and wondering if—even though he has always understood himself as "God's blueprint" for "a legal [white] man"—"The flaw is in the blueprint." Since act 1, scene 1, *Margaret Garner* has figured slaveholding white supremacy persisting socially and politically in the United States because, in the Auctioneer's words, which the Townspeople echo, it is a matter of "powers invested" and "customs ingested" in sum, and ideology fully *naturalized*, in body, mind, and spirit.

African-American thinkers like Frederick Douglass and William Wells Brown, and even devoted European-American Quaker abolitionists like John Jolliffe, Margaret Garner's attorney during her January–February 1856 incarceration and fugitive slave trial, had all learned the hard way that rarely would moral and theological persuasion miraculously awaken slaveholders to the evils of slavery. They lived smugly in the dominion of a white supremacist, pro-slavery Christianity. As for Edward's conversion, it must also leave behind his bedrock white supremacist belief in blacks' irremediable ontological debility: "How could love exist in a slave?" he asks in dialogue with Caroline. "Passion, perhaps. / But how would she know the difference?" (act 1, scene 3). We have a still harder time crediting that conversion when the struggle with his better angel occurs offstage in the lacuna between the libretto's last two scenes. The audience knows only that his daughter and son-in-law's expressed threat of abandoning him if he does not plea for

Margaret's life precedes Edward's conversion: "Don't fail me. / It's all in your hands," Caroline warns. As such Edward's instant conversion to liberal republicanism—to a new view of African-American humanity, and freedom's universality—seems a desperate, last-minute retreat intended to keep his own nuclear family together. And our unease deepens because of Morrison's structure for the libretto's ending, an ending that secures a future for the white Gaines family while completing the eradication of the black Garner family. For Margaret's hanging/suicide completes the family holocaust that commenced (in act 2, scene 2) with the burning coals which remind Edward of the "bed warmer" she formerly used to run over his sheets at night, but that Margaret uses now in this scene in revenge, gathering a handful and lunging toward Edward in a futile assault. Moments later, with Robert abruptly lynched, she kills both children, "Never to be born again into slavery." It is a swiftly moving, powerful scene, the opera's most sobering and in many ways its thematic climax—followed by the intermezzo played in "total darkness" as a supposedly inferior, passional, and irrational Margaret sings of slavery's illogic: "Reason has no power here." During these moments, Edward recalling Margaret warming his bed is the closest *Margaret Garner* will come to acknowledging its historical namesake's concubinage, her white master's possible paternity of children she birthed, and the horrors of white-on-black violence committed in the name of law.

To those considerable thematic burdens the libretto's final scenes (set two days "in early April") add still more. Edward insists in act 2, scene 3:

> Damn it to hell!
> I am approved.
> Clearly what the world insists
> I should be.
> Law and custom endorse me.

Thus he asserts a combined ontological, juridical, and cultural claim to an identity staked to slaveholding democracy. Caroline contrarily stakes hers to the principles of liberal republicanism, and concludes:

> We are so at odds
> In these past few years.

Our land will not survive
This violent test.

Consider the dual reference of those pronouns. Caroline's "we" clearly indicates her father, with whom she has been disputing slavery since act 1, set in 1856 and 1858. But the phrase "our land" widens the scope of her claim against him. It analogizes the domestic white nuclear family to the national household, then ("in early April 1861," according to the scene's headnote) just days or even hours from the onset of civil war—at 4:30 a.m. on April 12, 1861.

Morrison carefully pegged the libretto's structure, and the Garner case, to that chronology and its world-historical significance. Act 1, scene 3, is set in evening "in the early summer of 1858," when Abraham Lincoln gave his famous "House Divided" speech (the evening of June 16, in Springfield) accepting the Republican Party nomination to run against the Democratic incumbent, Senator Stephen Douglas. The link will be confirmed in act 2, scene 2, set nearly three years later, and two weeks after Lincoln's March 4, 1861, inauguration. Robert, having taken his family to Ohio, references the 1858 speech, telling Margaret he's heard that "this new president / Doesn't hiss like a snake; / That he talks like a man" in addressing the slavery debate and admonishing Americans "That a house divided / Cannot stand. / And that the Union is sacred." Margaret replies: "That means war . . . / You better make your spirit ready." In fact the prior scene, scene 1 of act 2, makes explicit reference to another key moment in that run-up to war. Set (the headnote tells us) on "Sunday, February 24, 1861, in the early evening," the date of scene 1, and the date following Lincoln's secretive February 23 arrival in Washington, DC, which concluded his triumphal railroad sojourn from Springfield, contextualizes events in this part of the libretto. In Philadelphia, Pinkerton agents had picked up word of a plot to assassinate Lincoln in Baltimore, then quietly arranged an alternate route. That Sunday was President-elect Lincoln's first full day in the capital. He attended services at St. John's Episcopal Church, sat for portrait photos at Matthew Brady's DC gallery, received various people at the family's Willard Hotel suite, and, that evening after a Marine Band serenaded them from the plaza below, briefly thanked them and the assembled crowd, pledging himself to save the Union.[23]

That chronology, so momentous because of the looming war, rationalizes the temporal setting provided for each scene of the opera, from act 1, scene 3, until it ends. The Lincoln-centered plot shadows the action, which extends from the "House Divided" speech to the brink of the Civil War, and beyond. Anyone who picks up the shadow plot's main thread in Robert's allusion will have in mind Lincoln's eventual assassination, prefigured by events of February 23–24, 1861. In this way the libretto seeks to backlight the Garner family's destruction and Margaret's self-sacrifice with the nation's great trauma and Lincoln's martyrdom. Also, and equally important, it seeks a paradigm for the reconstruction of Edward Gaines's representative white supremacist American manhood in the racial politics of the dedicated but doomed antislavery president. To do this cultural work, to suggest in other words that an Edward Gaines might slough off his identity as villain of the libretto, requires the audience to recognize and bear in mind quickly Abraham Lincoln's status as an all-American icon of universal freedom and liberal humanism.

Here then is a way to reckon how the libretto's thematic burdens tend to overstress the structure of its timeline, which so notably recasts actual 1856 events. By pegging scenes to the looming war, Morrison's libretto puts a much more profound world-historical weight on the Garner case. Moreover, Morrison's revision of that 1856 history in order to backlight the opera heroine's transcendent martyrdom with the glow from an assassinated president, and in order to recuperate her libretto's villain, requires an iconic "Lincoln" who may not withstand the burdens of a historical Lincoln. Yet what happens if one considers even momentarily the historical Lincoln we know from *after* the "House Divided" speech. On June 16, 1858, the presidential nominee had acknowledged famously that the nation would have to either abolish slavery or agree to its extension nationwide. He warned that the latter condition had become much more likely because key figures in the judicial, legislative, and executive branches had been conspiring to make it so. He specifically named "Stephen, Franklin, Roger, and James"—Stephen Douglas for pushing through Congress the 1854 Kansas-Nebraska Act eliminating the ban on slavery north of the Mason-Dixon line, Roger Taney for writing the Supreme Court's *Dred Scott* decision eliminating the ban against slave owners taking their human chattel into free-soil states (a ban that was very much at stake in the 1856 Garner fugitive slave hearing), and presidents Franklin Pierce and James Buchanan for ensuring obedience to these dictates.[24] That evening Lincoln craftily argued that *Dred Scott* nullified the right of voters to settle the slavery question within their state or territory, or in other words, nullified pro-slavery thinkers' hallowed states' rights doctrine. His speech, though, was antislavery by implication only. After claiming the Union had to be one thing or the other, Lincoln only inferred that in having to conspire for it to become *their thing*, pro-slavery forces had practically admitted dwindling support for slavery. Douglas fought back using tried and true racist laws, as that summer's Lincoln-Douglas debates gave Illinois voters and the nation a chance to learn much more about the Republican candidate's convictions.

Waving off the conspiracy charge against him, Douglas concentrated on what abolition, from a white supremacist view of it, would "quite obviously" mean. It would give freed blacks the vote and thus (in his view) destroy a US government "made by the white man, for the benefit of the white man." He argued destruction was inevitable because blacks were irremediably inferior, the lowest of the "dependent races." Any "mixture or amalgamation with inferior races" would, he argued, destroy American "civilization" just as it already had in the hemisphere's "Spanish-American states."

These then were the terms—black inferiority and "amalgamation" phobias—with which Lincoln had to deal as the two debaters crisscrossed Illinois that summer. These historical debates contextualize the parlor debate at Maplewood in act 1, scene 3. Lincoln labored hard and long, resisting Douglas's efforts to box him in as a negrophile and as an "amalgamator" while knowing full well that the vast majority of Illinois voters accepted white supremacy and viscerally disliked interracial intimacies. In fact he shared their view. Lincoln repeatedly rejected the "counterfeit logic that, because I do not want a black woman for a *slave* I must necessarily want her for a *wife*. [He maintained,] I need not have her for either, I can just *leave her alone*." At every debating stop Lincoln proclaimed his belief in white supremacy and blacks' providential inferiority ("God gave him but little, that little let him enjoy"). Lincoln did assure voters that he had "always hated slavery," but also sketched his pinched view of a post-slavery America: give freedmen *natural* but not *citizenship* rights, otherwise abandon them. Or worse: agreeing with voters that "a physical difference . . . will forever forbid the two races living together," Lincoln floated the idea of recolonizing freedmen, perhaps to Africa.[25]

Now, the decades-old defense of Lincoln's clearly stated and at times bluntly eliminationist white supremacy is that he expressed it out of political expediency, placating racists while binding them over to free-labor Republicanism. Recent scholarship rejects the excuse, which George M. Fredrickson names the "he didn't mean what he said school" of Lincoln idolizers who cannot admit that the Great Emancipator was a "convinced believer in white supremacy." Michael Lind further shows that white supremacist ideology took Lincoln into his presidency's least defensible moments, such as an 1862 model scheme for colonizing free blacks on a Caribbean island, where a third were soon dead. And we have Lerone Bennett Jr.'s devastatingly brief *Forced into Glory* (2007), which rakes through the same Lincoln archives that historians had consulted for decades but locates in them a racist white man with an "almost obsessional fear of Black violence and slave insurrections," a Lincoln who privately delighted in "Coon Jokes," who mocked the speech and gait of "his imaginary Negroes," who began thinking seriously about deporting all black people from the United States as early as 1852, and who during the Civil War's nadir even asked Congress to divert huge sums from the war effort in order to commence that deportation effort.[26]

In Morrison's and Danielpour's defense, these revisionary efforts are altering Lincoln scholarship without affecting the popular view, and Bennett's *Forced into Glory* was published two years after the debut of *Margaret Garner*. Nonetheless, scholars' ongoing challenges to our understanding of Lincoln spotlight the libretto's problematic uses of "Lincoln" as an icon of racial liberalism. Certainly these efforts trouble the libretto's model of what an ethically rehabilitated Edward Gaines might think and do. For operagoers who processed these brief yet weighty allusions, "Lincoln" must also stand in for the ways individuals may see "American History" as triumphally redressing the manifold injuries done to "Margaret," chiefly (one supposes) by Lincoln's Emancipation Proclamation (January 1, 1863). Even for operagoers knowing some of the new Lincoln scholarship, the fact of emancipation may erase the warts of Lincoln's white supremacy, in which case "Lincoln" anchors the libretto's melodrama to an instantly recognizable Good White Man, in contrast to Bad Edward, which is to say, Edward *before* his belated and hasty turnabout.

But *after* Edward's moral epiphany, does the libretto's tight structuring make room for Edward as "victim"? Certainly audiences were not going there, for they booed Edward and Casey, the foreman of Maplewood Plantation, during curtain calls.[27] Indeed probably the only way one might imagine a victimized Edward would be to recall the Auctioneer's chant in the opening scene, and to suppose Edward wronged "by the powers invested / And by customs ingested"—that is, by white supremacist custom and belief, what Edward (in act 2, scene 3) calls a bad "blueprint." But who would want to go down that ethically perilous slope? Letting a wrongdoer plea-bargain that ideology made him commit crimes against humanity such as rape or lynching surely would be a boon to Klansmen and Nazis alike. It would annul justice. For if, as Charles Mills incisively argues, white supremacist practice rests on "an epistemology of ignorance," an oxymoronic knowledge for misknowing the human world and for advantaging one's own white self by harming others, then the "ideology made me do it" plea amounts to an ignorance-of-the-law defense.[28] Logic and justice disallow that defense, otherwise courts would have to take their hands off the wrongdoer and punish—by some metaphysical or fabulous means—the Bad Knowledge his mind "ingested."

Writing for the Summer Festival program distributed at the Cincinnati premiere of *Margaret Garner,* Toni Morrison recalled the making of *Beloved* as a five-year effort "to do justice to the historical characters involved while exercising the license [she] needed to interrogate the dilemma Margaret both presented and represented." Writing the libretto furthered that prior effort. Of it she could say in 2005: "Finally, to the real people who lived this tale, I trust we have done them, their heirs, and their spirits justice."[29] Those remarks went straight to the heart of the matter. They compel us to ask if in fact it would have been wiser to have taken up the Garner case with a less finalizing goal—that of offering "no redemption, and repairing no injury." Was it that such a project would fail the tragic conventions of opera seria? Or that folks believed it could not be sold to popular audiences? In this essay I have attempted only a theoretically and historically informed critique of the libretto. Here the aim was to understand better those stress points in *Margaret Garner* that reviewers have underscored, thus to realize thematically, structurally, and ethically why the libretto cracks under the burdens of trying to do justice to the living and the dead. I have wondered if we hear Morrison nodding to those difficulties in her program remarks. For the libretto staged and published under her name, we must remember, was actually a corporately produced artwork revised, during the fall and winter 2004–2005, in a politically and culturally fraught environment, with a number of interested individuals, groups, and business entities pitching into the fray. Morrison's revising *Beloved*'s subject matter in the libretto was a return to "dangerous territory," for sure. And the little that we know from the public record suggests that privately held texts—revised libretto scripts, correspondence, notes from meetings and rehearsals—will be a rich field for scholars to excavate, one day.

NOTES

1. Toni Morrison, *Beloved* (New York: Knopf, 1987).

2. David Pollack, ed. *The Archaeology of Kentucky: An Update*, vol. 2 (Frankfort: Kentucky Heritage Council, 2008), 1004.

3. Kim A. McBride and M. Jay Stottman, "In Search of Margaret Garner: Preliminary Archaeological Investigations at Maplewood, 15Be483, Boone County, Kentucky," in *Current Archaeological Research in Kentucky*, vol. 8, proceedings of the 17th Annual Kentucky Heritage Council Archaeology Conference, March 26–27, 2000, ed. Sarah E. Miller et al. (Frankfort: Kentucky Heritage Council, 2007), 237.

4. "Dig Dates Farm to 'Beloved' Slave," *Cincinnati Enquirer*, 19 Nov. 1998, B1. See also Cameron McWhirter, "Boone Farm Confirmed as Slave Home: But Building's Authenticity Isn't Known," *Cincinnati Enquirer*, 9 Oct. 1998, A1.

5. Bill Brown, "Thing Theory," *Critical Inquiry* 28.1 (2001): 15 and passim.

6. Pierre Nora, "Between Memory and History: Les Lieux de Mémoire," trans. Mark Roudebus, *Representations* 26.1 (1989): 7–24. Also see Thomas W. Laqueur, "Spaces of the Dead," *Ideas: From the National Humanities Center* 8.2 (2001): 3–16; and Marianne Hirsch, "Past Lives: Postmemories in Exile," *Poetics Today* 17.4 (1996): 659–86.

7. "Great Black Kentuckians, No. 49. Margaret Garner," Kentucky Commission on Human Rights, http://kchr.ky.gov/about/gallergreatblack.html; "Kentucky's Storied Spaces," *Kentucky Monthly*, Nov. 2010, 26–30.

8. Brunings's essays "Slavery in Kentucky" and "Slavery and the Tragic Stories of Two Families—Gaines and Garner" are available on the Boone County (Kentucky) Heritage Council website with the proviso that they "do not reflect the views" of that organization.

9. Caputo offers her book, *Margaret Garner: Diversity and Depth of Love* (Yellow Springs, OH: JoJo Beanyhead, 2008), for sale on her website: www.boonecountyheritage.org/History/Research.asp. Her early involvement with the Maplewood site is detailed in "A Remnant of Slavery's Horror," *Cincinnati Enquirer*, 2 Oct. 1998, A1, 5.

10. Nora, "Between Memory and History," 7–9, 22–23. After the *Margaret Garner* opera premiered in 2005, John Gaines, "a great-great-great nephew" of Archibald K. Gaines, joining Ruth Brunings, also spoke at Cincinnati Opera–sponsored events at Maplewood and nearby Richwood Presbyterian Church. He complained of "stereotyping" and complemented Brunings's narrative version of the Garner case.

11. Jacques Derrida, *Archive Fever: A Freudian Impression*, trans. Eric Prenowitz (Chicago: U of Chicago P, 1995), 28–29, 62–64, 90–91.

12. Mark Reinhardt, "Who Speaks for Margaret Garner? Slavery, Silence, and the Politics of Ventriloquism," *Critical Inquiry* 29.1 (Fall 2002): 81–119.

13. Ruth Brunings's essays mentioned above provide some new and previously unavailable genealogical information on the Gaines and Bedinger families, and on local history, for example on Richwood and the Richwood Presbyterian Church.

14. Mark Reinhardt, in *Who Speaks for Margaret Garner? The True Story That Inspired Toni Morrison's "Beloved"* (Minneapolis: U of Minnesota P, 2010), 263–64 , reprints Louis Farrell's excerpt of the 1901 Elizabeth Ann Gaines Burke letter, housed at the Kentucky Historical Society archives in Frankfort, Kentucky.

15. Ibid., 263.

16. On early narrative versions of the Garner case, including journalistic, poetic, fictional, and artistic texts, see Steven Weisenburger, *Modern Medea: A Family Story of Slavery and Child-Murder from the Old South* (New York: Hill and Wang, 1998), 232–80. For the reclamation of facts surrounding the Nat Turner rebellion, see Albert E. Stone, *The Return of Nat Turner: History, Literature, and Cultural Politics in Sixties America* (Athens: U of Georgia P, 1992).

17. Kathleen Doane, "A Song for Margaret," *Cincinnati Magazine*, July 2005, 95.

18. Ibid., 94–95. As *Margaret Garner* was in early production and up until its Cincinnati debut, stories and editorials in the *Cincinnati Enquirer* from this period reported a similar range of views, concerns, and hopes regarding the work and its impacts.

19. Catherine Gunther Kodat, "*Margaret Garner* and the Second Tear," *American Quarterly* 60.1 (2008): 164.

20. Toni Morrison, *Margaret Garner: Opera in Two Acts*, composed by Richard Danielpour, rev. ed. (New York: Associated Music, 2004). All references to the libretto are to this edition.

21. Robert Fallon, "Music and the Allegory of Memory in *Margaret Garner*," *Modern Fiction Studies* 52.2 (Summer 2006): 527.

22. Kodat, "*Margaret Garner* and the Second Tear," 167.

23. Among the many sources on Lincoln's day-to-day life I am indebted here to Stanley P. Kimmel, *Mr. Lincoln's Washington* (New York: Coward-McCann, 1957), 15–23.

24. Abraham Lincoln, "'House Divided' Speech at Springfield, Illinois, June 16, 1858," in *Lincoln: Speeches and Writings 1832–1858*, ed. Donald E. Fehrenbacher (New York: Library of America, 1989), 428, 431.

25. Douglas and Lincoln quoted, respectively, in Paul M. Angle, ed. *Created Equal? The Complete Lincoln-Douglas Debates of 1858* (Chicago: U of Chicago P, 1958), 19, 23; and 39, 82.

26. On Lincoln's racial beliefs see also George M. Frederickson, *Big Enough to Be Inconsistent: Abraham Lincoln Confronts Slavery and Race* (Cambridge, MA: Harvard UP, 2008), 15–16, 81–82; Michael Lind, *What Lincoln Believed: The Values and Convictions of America's Greatest President* (New York: Anchor, 2005), 201–5; and Lerone Bennett Jr., *Forced into Glory: Abraham Lincoln's White Dream* (Chicago: Johnson, 2007), 87–112.

27. The audience for the Cincinnati premiere booed Edward the loudest; and so did the New York City audience in 2007, for which see Fred Cohn, review of *Margaret Garner, Opera News* 72.6 (Dec. 2007): 63–64.

28. On white supremacy as an "epistemology of ignorance" see Charles M. Mills, *The Racial Contract* (Ithaca, NY: Cornell UP, 1997), 18 and passim.

29. Toni Morrison, "Notes on *Margaret Garner*: From Toni Morrison, Librettist," *Cincinnati Opera: 2005 Summer Festival* (Cincinnati, 2005), 21.

# Rendering *Margaret Garner* Accessible

*The Preproduction Outreach Campaign*

✳ DELORES M. WALTERS ✳

The creators and coproducers of *Margaret Garner* intended, from its inception, that the newly commissioned American opera be accessible to both traditional and nontraditional operagoers. It was this collectively held mission that motivated Cincinnati Opera's board of trustees, once it agreed to share the opera's commission with Michigan Opera Theatre and Opera Company of Philadelphia,[1] to assemble in late 2003 the *Margaret Garner* Steering Committee comprised of leaders from the private and public sectors.[2] Seeking to commemorate the new millennium and the upcoming first anniversary of the National Underground Railroad Freedom Center in 2005, the same year as the opera's world premiere, these leaders actively pursued partnerships with the Freedom Center and other artistic, educational, philanthropic, cultural, and religious institutions in Greater Cincinnati. Their efforts led to the formulation of an extensive strategic, collaborative outreach campaign that the other two opera companies also implemented.[3] These partnerships designed and executed a remarkable array of public programs that successfully attracted African Americans and other underrepresented groups such as Native Americans and Arab Americans that had little prior exposure to the musical performance genre. The Steering Committee anticipated that a higher percentage of African Americans from the metropolitan areas of the commissioning cities would be drawn to performances of the opera because of its focus on a historical enslaved African-American family, its premieres in northern cities with substantial black populations,[4] and its world-famous African-American librettist, the Nobel laureate and Pulitzer Prize–winning author Toni Morrison. Even with these advantages, to draw nontraditional operagoers of African-American descent the committee had to overcome Cincinnati's distant past of excluding the very group the planners now sought to include. Historically, musical performances were segregated in the northern city. It was not until the 1950s, during the early civil rights movement, that African-American singers and musicians were welcomed into Music Hall, the performance home of Cincinnati Opera, located in the Over-the-Rhine section of downtown Cincinnati and the nation's second-oldest opera company, which in 2005 would celebrate its eighty-fifth anniversary.[5]

The *Margaret Garner* Steering Committee and its partners carefully identified churches, public schools, libraries, and universities willing to serve as culturally appropriate venues for programs aimed at familiarizing preproduction audiences with the historical Margaret Garner and the imaginative representation that Toni Morrison's *Margaret Garner: Opera in Two Acts*, the libretto for Richard Danielpour's opera, depicted. The preproduction programs effectively increased the awareness of the Garners' specific story of enslavement in the mid-nineteenth century for Cincinnati residents; for Boone County, Kentucky, residents where the Garners were enslaved; for history, opera, and musical theatre aficionados and performers; and for readers of twentieth-century American literature and the literary canon of Toni Morrison. The programs also rendered the Garners' story accessible to first-time operagoers whom the newly commissioned work attracted, bringing the contested topic of slavery before a significantly wider group of attendees and discussants. And, because of Toni Morrison's decision to modify events of the Garner story rather than to adhere strictly to the historical record, the programs assisted in widening the public's historical grasp of American enslavement as an institutionalized practice rather than viewing the Garners' experience as a singular, individualized occurrence. Ultimately, to promote community involvement and public dialogue about race and slavery in the United States the Steering Committee deployed a strategic, preproduction campaign that entailed reaching out to local performers, students and community residents, and the national and local public to render Richard Danielpour's *Margaret Garner: A New American Opera* accessible to new and old opera constituents.[6]

At its outset, the Steering Committee faced a major challenge: how to raise the general public's awareness concerning the history of Margaret Garner and her family when so little was known about her or them? Few

African Americans and fewer European Americans, including Northern Kentucky University students who had grown up in Boone County, had been exposed to the history of the region's courageous freedom seekers that the operatic production commemorated. Most of the histories of African Americans who successfully freed themselves were transmitted orally if at all, leaving little to reference in the written record. Consequently, the story of Margaret Garner's desperate solution to the horrors of slavery lay dormant for over a century until Toni Morrison's Pulitzer Prize–winning novel *Beloved* attracted artistic, scholarly, and public attention in 1987, and talk show hostess and media mogul Oprah Winfrey bought the rights to the novel and enlisted Jonathan Demme to direct its cinematic adaptation, which Touchstone Pictures and Harpo Films released in 1998. The Steering Committee strategically elected to collaborate with the Freedom Center, which had recently opened in 2004, to offer the local communities an opportunity to reexamine slavery of nineteenth-century America in order to restore substantial local history to its residents in the twenty-first century.[7]

Despite its eschewing historical accuracy, Toni Morrison's transformation of the Garners' story into a fictional adaptation for the opera ultimately proved a superb vehicle for conveying the unspeakable tragedy and heroic resistance by women such as Margaret Garner. Yet, whether the libretto for *Margaret Garner* could transcend historical accuracy was an unresolved question when the *Margaret Garner* Steering Committee began its preproduction outreach programs in Cincinnati. Since the story had been forgotten in the public memory and overlooked in the written record, members of the committee were concerned that for individuals who were unfamiliar with the 1856 historical basis for the opera the imagined events that the libretto outlined would become the "true" narrative retained in historical memory for future generations. In short, the true story of the Richwood Station, Kentucky, fugitive slave woman who succeeded in killing one of her four children in an attempt to murder them all before slave catchers apprehended her and the seven members of her family in a Cincinnati safe house, while no longer forgotten, would be misremembered.

For example, one of the libretto's major imaginative divergences from history was the lynching of Robert Garner, Margaret's husband. Attendees of the preproduction workshop and rehearsal in Detroit in August 2004, which brought together historians, literature scholars, performing artists, and members of the *Margaret Garner* Steering Committee, noted during the opera preview an altered fate for him, leaving no doubt about the opera's departure from history. Some members of the Steering Committee were uneasy with his lynching in act 2 when a slave posse surprises the Garners as they are camped in Ohio en route to a free life. The reworking was a significant departure from the historical Robert Garner's surviving Margaret's death in 1858, serving in the Civil War, and returning to Cincinnati and dying there a free man in 1871.[8]

In a February 2005 panel discussion at Cincinnati's Hebrew Union College entitled "Margaret Garner and the African American Family," Carl B. Westmoreland, curator of the National Underground Railroad Freedom Center, and I, as facilitators, emphasized the relevance of portraying to a black community Robert Garner's role in his family's flight, his life after the death of Margaret, and his liberation, both in historical and contemporary terms, particularly to the Cincinnati neighborhood surrounding the opera house where *Margaret Garner* would be performed. His profile as a strong and devoted African-American husband and father stood in stark relief to police violence perpetrated against black men perceived as menaces to society and to the riots protesting racial profiling that had headlined local and national news coverage in the decade preceding the opera's July 2005 Cincinnati premiere. A number of shootings involving the police killing unarmed underage and adult black males had plagued the city. The police shooting death of nineteen-year-old Timothy Thomas in 2001, for example, was "the fifteenth man killed by police since 1995—all of them Black."[9]

Addressing the imaginative divergences in the libretto, Toni Morrison, in a 2005 preview interview, provided the most direct and eloquent outreach statement to assist audiences in understanding the historical departures:

> There are so many Margaret Garner stories, even in that [the historical] story. There's Margaret Garner from the point of view of Robert Garner, and Margaret Garner from the point of view of the children who survived. Then there's purely the legal Margaret Garner. . . . And then there's Margaret Garner the ultimate mother—mother destroyer, mother nurturer. I hope somebody does all of them over time. You can't just nail it down. They were complex human beings. And that's what's exciting about her narrative and there must be thousands of

others from that period. It's a whole virgin territory now before the imagination.[10]

*Margaret Garner*'s strong emotional appeal based on its combination of an imaginative libretto and broad-based music score was apparent to members of the Steering Committee even prior to the premieres. Yet without the outreach to promote *Margaret Garner* and to prepare audiences for the opera's historical divergences in Cincinnati and the other co-commission cities, it is doubtful that an overwhelmingly positive response would have occurred. *Philadelphia Inquirer* critic David Patrick Stearns acknowledges the role that the preproduction campaign played in cementing *Margaret Garner*'s success: "Long before the curtain went up on the hotly anticipated Toni Morrison/Richard Danielpour opera *Margaret Garner*, the Michigan Opera Theatre premiere on Saturday [May 7, 2005] was a public-relations triumph. . . . Dramaturgical lapses are there, but the strengths of *Margaret Garner* are so considerable and wide-ranging that the piece is legitimately destined to make new friends for opera without alienating old ones."[11]

When mezzo-soprano Denyce Graves, for whom Richard Danielpour had composed the title role, made her pitch in 1999 to David DiChiera, the General and Artistic Director for Michigan Opera Theatre, to consider *Margaret Garner* in the company's future, he indicated that he had been searching for an opera that would pay homage to African-American experience and appeal to an ethnically diverse metropolitan area. His affirmation emboldened Graves to speak with representatives from Cincinnati Opera and Opera Company of Philadelphia, petitioning them to join the coproduction of *Margaret Garner*. For DiChiera, who green-lighted the opera, it would be the first world premiere on the Detroit Opera House stage.[12]

DiChiera first met with prominent members of a largely African-American advisory group in Detroit—a city whose population in 2005 was, and still is, more than 80 percent black—to coordinate an appropriate launching of the opera. Initially, black community leaders in Detroit opposed the selection of *Margaret Garner*, advising a contemporary focus instead of "old history" for a new opera. Still, DiChiera "was convinced the story of Margaret Garner had merit and needed to be told. It was also a way to get more blacks into an opera theatre."[13] Furthermore, he noted, "All of us who have been involved with 'Margaret Garner' take special pride in having created an opera that directly addresses Detroit's African-American community. . . . Diversity is essential for the arts in our country. Building bridges to the community is as important as the art itself."[14]

## The Prelude: Reaching the Public in Detroit

As a prelude to the three-state tour of *Margaret Garner* that would begin in Detroit in May 2005 and end in Philadelphia in February 2006, the three commissioning opera companies jointly created an official *Margaret Garner* website to help future audience members prepare for the opera. Directly linking its website to the *Margaret Garner* website, Michigan Opera Theatre collaborated with the state's public schools by providing a database containing an index of electronic educational links for social studies teachers and their students on the topic of American slavery. The website featured extensive lesson plans for elementary, middle, and high school students and contained interactive programming that educated its young visitors about the evolutions of slavery in America and the Underground Railroad in Detroit, the latter from a study which Dr. Norman McRae Jr., the former Detroit Historical Commissioner, compiled. It also included historical information about Margaret Garner, a display of the texts of the Declaration of Independence and the Constitution, an outline of the Underground Railroad in Michigan, and a timeline of the abolition of American slavery.

To further expose the youth of Detroit to opera and to demonstrate its commitment to diversifying interest and participation in a performance genre that has been historically thought of as European and the artistic preserve of the white elite, Michigan Opera Theatre implemented two highly visible public strategies aimed at capturing the attention of the next generation of American operagoers and their families and placing racial and ethnic inclusion as the central topic of discussion for the nation's opera companies. First, it inaugurated a one-act show entitled *No Doubt*, a musical revue that toured local schools prior to *Margaret Garner*'s world premiere. Based on Sam Swopes's award-winning book of the same name, *No Doubt* is a humorous and endearing story of diversity and tolerance told through opera that targets children between five and twelve years of age but appeals to all ages. Second, Michigan Opera Theatre offered to host OPERA America's 2005 conference in Detroit with the contingency that diversity with respect to race, ethnicity, gender, and sexual orientation in opera be the guiding theme of the meeting. The conference, *Diverse Voices*, which took place in May 2005 in the days leading up to the *Margaret Garner* premiere, which all of its conveners attended, held workshops to compile ways to build diversity in audiences and among staff and stage performers. As a follow-up to the meeting, OPERA America introduced *Diversity in Performance*, a new event to be continued annually for African-American, Native-American, and Arab-American communities. It also presented *Diversity in Performance* in sign language to demonstrate that opera was also a viable musical art for the hearing impaired.

## Cincinnati's Preproduction Campaign: Reaching Local Performers, Students, and Community Residents

The Cincinnati Opera staff, with the support of the Steering Committee and local arts and cultural organizations, collaborated with African-American singers from the opera's chorus to encourage local artists' participation by informing them of audition opportunities and requirements. In the process of identifying and auditioning local operatic talent, Cincinnati Opera and collaborating organizers developed relationships with community groups and local houses of worship. Thus, opera staffers and their collaborators also coordinated opportunities for young black artists from the region to gain valuable experience as guest performers and soloists for the community programs that would launch the opera.

Yearlong programming leading up to Cincinnati Opera's opening included a family/youth celebration, *Oh Freedom! A Musical Portrait Honoring the African American Quest for Freedom from Slavery through the Civil Rights Movement*, and a benefit concert, *Opera from a Sistah's Point of View*, slated for two performances. *Oh Freedom!* used spoken stories and songs to teach the history of African-American enslavement and freedom. It incorporated a wide range of musical expressions—spirituals, secret songs of the Underground Railroad, music of the Harlem Renaissance, and anthems of the civil rights movement. Singers also performed excerpts from *Margaret Garner*. In *Opera from a Sistah's Point of View*, opera singer Angela M. Brown, who sang the role of Cilla, Margaret Garner's mother-in-law, performed selections from various operas. Its two engagements—held on June 15, 2005, at Princeton High School and on June 17, 2005, at Southern Baptist Church—included gospel, jazz, and spiritual selections.

Previews, lecture series, and study guides formed the breadth of educational programs that prepared traditional and nontraditional audiences. Exposing students and community residents to opera proved very effective through "Introducing *Margaret Garner*," a performance and dialogue highlighting the story of Margaret, that targeted schools, churches, and community centers in order to provide them with a substantive live trailer of the opera. Composed of seven free concerts featuring arias and duets from the opera and presented at the Freedom Center, the Mercantile Library, and four other community venues, these performances featured a cast of five singers: mezzo-soprano Tracie Luck, baritone Michael Mayes, baritone John Fulton, soprano Adrienne Danrich, and tenor Mark T. Panuccio. Local award-winning actress Burgess Byrd narrated the concerts, and the Freedom Center facilitated post-performance dialogues. The Steering Committee and opera staff also developed a *Margaret Garner* lecture series exploring the multiple dimensions of the Margaret Garner story—operatic and historical versions—for a wide range of audiences in Greater Cincinnati and offered a Margaret Garner youth study and program guide for the season's performances. Leading up to the Cincinnati premiere, a free dress rehearsal provided a special opportunity for regional high school and Northern Kentucky University students to consider the opera genre as a work in progress.[15] Tickets for the opera were also heavily discounted for high school and college students.

A focus on adult education was also a primary consideration of the preproduction campaign. Prior to the performance of *Margaret Garner* in Cincinnati on July 14, 2005, the University of Kansas and Northern Kentucky University sponsored a seminar for high school teachers that demonstrated approaches to teaching the work and to connecting it with the Civil War. Janelle Gelfand, who covers Cincinnati's performing and visual arts with a focus on classical music for the *Cincinnati Enquirer*, designed a course for the Institute for Learning in Retirement at the University of Cincinnati in which one segment focused on the relevance of the *Margaret Garner* opera for today.

Because of the current popularity of book reading groups, the campaign directed publicity at members of book clubs. Book groups were encouraged to prepare for *Margaret Garner* by reading and screening Toni Morrison's *Beloved* in their private meetings or by attending a Cincinnati Opera–sponsored Freedom Center screening and reading that occurred in March, facilitated by Kristine Yohe, a Northern Kentucky University professor. Members of the community were also invited to see Thomas Satterwhite Noble's painting *Modern Medea* (1867), which depicts Margaret Garner's capture, also on display at the Freedom Center.

The Toni Morrison Society held its Fourth Biennial Conference under the watchful care of its local codirector, Kristine Yohe. The public was invited to attend the conference held July 14–17, 2005, at the Hilton Cincinnati Netherland Plaza. In conjunction with the opera's premiere in Cincinnati, the conference featured a plenary session entitled "Music and the Echoes of Memory," which focused on the African-American traditional songs, literature, opera, and jazz in the story of Margaret Garner. Columbia University professor Robert O'Meally moderated the event, which Cincinnati Opera, the Ohio Humanities Council, and the College-Conservatory of Music at the University of Cincinnati sponsored on July 16. Bernice Johnson Reagon, who discussed slave songs and oral transmission, was among the invited speakers who presented at the Conservatory's Corbett Auditorium. Toni Morrison attended the event. The Toni Morrison Society also sponsored "Meet the Margaret Garner Creative Team: On Stage with Toni Morrison and Richard Danielpour" on Friday, July 15, 2005, at 8 p.m. in Music Hall Auditorium the day after the opera's Cincinnati premiere. The librettist and composer engaged in "a conversation about their inspiration, their artistic collaboration and their journey to create this new American opera."[16] OPERA America president and chief executive officer Marc Scorca moderated the event and Channel 9 WCPO's Clyde Gray hosted it. At the Toni Morrison Society's July 15 Authors' and Editors' Recognition Luncheon, held in the University Ballroom at Northern Kentucky University, Steven Weisenburger, author of *Modern Medea*, gave the keynote address. Earlier in January, he had also contributed to the inaugural preproduction campaign by giving a lecture at Cincinnati's Xavier University.

Finally, of the three opera companies that commissioned *Margaret Garner*, Cincinnati Opera was the most directly connected to the opera's reenactment of historical events because of the city's centrality in the nineteenth-century Garner saga. Perhaps as a consequence, it is in Cincinnati that the opera has had its most resounding impact. On July 19, 2005, at 7 p.m. in the Freedom Center's theater, members of the Ohio Chapter of the American College of Trial Lawyers presented free to the public "A Mock Trial: *The State of Ohio v. Margaret Garner*," a murder trial based on legal precedents of the mid-nineteenth century but one that never occurred. The only trial Margaret Garner and her family received was a hearing before a federal commissioner to decide whether they should be returned to their respective Kentucky slave owners, Archibald K. Gaines and James Marshall, or freed in opposition to the Fugitive Slave Law of 1850. The commissioner ordered her and the other captured runaways returned to their owners. While abolitionists later managed to have a warrant issued for Gaines to return Margaret Garner to Ohio to stand trial for murder, she could not be found to be served the warrant because Gaines moves her from city to city in Kentucky. After the mock trial, the Honorable James L. Graham and local attorneys led a panel discussion with historians.

Televised segments on the *Oprah Winfrey Show*, CBS's *Sunday Morning*, PBS's *NewsHour*, and BET contributed to informing the national public of the opera's performances. At the local level, however, two televised films disseminated information to the surrounding viewing area. Cincinnati Opera partnered with Media Bridges, Cincinnati's Community Media Center, to promote and educate the public about the opera. A documentary directed by Mustapha Hasnaoui on the making of *Margaret Garner* aired on WCET and WKET. A second film, *The Journey of Margaret Garner*, produced and directed by Alphonzo Wesson III, explored the local and national significance of the story. It aired on WCPO-TV Channel 9 on July 12, 2005. Wesson's documentary, according to Mary Ellyn Hutton, "was the highest rated locally produced show in the station's recent history."[17]

## Margaret Garner: *Attendance Exceeds Expectation*

Between 2005 and 2006, the span of time that the opera was performed in the three cities, *Margaret Garner* attendance goals exceeded the Steering Committee's expectations. The opera was consistently well attended, often sold out, and received exhilarating standing ovations from audiences in the commissioning cities as well as in the cities where the next productions appeared.[18] DiChiera reported that the turnout in Detroit was "the largest, most successful ticket-generating work in the last five years—more than 'Boheme' or 'Aida.'"[19] In Cincinnati, *Margaret Garner* completely sold out—the first for an opera in its recent history.[20] Furthermore, reviewers observed that the operatic story, albeit a new artistic form for many, was particularly resonant among black operagoers.[21] Michigan Opera Theatre had the country's highest percentage of African Americans in its audiences at 12 percent, but DiChiera asserted that the company had been "aiming much higher"[22] because of Detroit's more than 80 percent black population. Typically, only 4 percent of opera audiences nationally are people of color.[23] In Cincinnati, 11 percent of Cincinnati Opera's audiences were people of color—African American, Asian, and Latino—in 2005 during the run of *Margaret Garner*.[24] While 45 percent of the city was African American in the 2010 United States Census, the Over-the-Rhine neighborhood surrounding Music Hall is predominantly African American at 78 percent.

The objective of the preproduction campaign to stimulate a public discussion about the real Margaret Garner, thereby raising public awareness about the Garners' compelling history and attracting new operagoers, was realized. The work of the *Margaret Garner* Steering Committee in Cincinnati had a significant impact on the success of the opera. Patricia Beggs, Cincinnati Opera's general director and chief executive officer, remarked that "Cincinnati Opera would like to see more people of color in the audience all the time and not just when it mounts operas such as *Margaret Garner*." She and the company's leaders recognize that the incentive for greater participation and attendance by people of color occurs when they see people like themselves onstage.[25] Beggs expresses an eagerness that Cincinnati Opera "become more reflective of the city, the community, and the world we live in."[26]

According to Beggs, Cincinnati Opera laid the groundwork in the 1990s for what became the *Margaret Garner* Steering Committee's multitude of community programs. In the past two decades, Cincinnati Opera's annual open dress rehearsal held in Over-the-Rhine has become a tradition. Recent investment by the city of Cincinnati in revitalizing Over-the-Rhine has resulted in the predominantly African-American neighborhood's transformation from a run-down, inner-city space with abandoned buildings and a high crime rate to a vibrant arts community unparalleled in the city. Beggs maintains that a diversity committee such as the one that initiated the outreach for *Margaret Garner* has now become obsolete, as Cincinnati Opera ensures that diversity is considered for every performance and in the makeup of every cast, committee, and board. She points out that the last performance of *Aida* sold out to a very diverse audience as confirmation of the opera company's success in achieving diversity and inclusivity in its performances and administration.

Cincinnati Opera was first recognized for its commitment to engaging African Americans in November 2005 when the company received the prestigious Post-Corbett Award in the Extraordinary Event category following the spectacular Cincinnati premiere of the *Margaret Garner* opera in July of that year. Indeed, the award was an acknowledgment of Cincinnati Opera's noteworthy achievement in promoting the opera and educating the public about the Garners' story, real and imagined.[27] "For their extraordinary efforts in building connections to the African American community," the National Association for the Advancement of Colored People (NAACP) recognized Cincinnati Opera with its prestigious community outreach partnership award in 2007, and in the following year the NAACP honored both the Cincinnati Opera and Beggs for extraordinary efforts in building connections to the African-American community.

The preproduction outreach campaign for *Margaret Garner* in Cincinnati has had a lasting postproduction impact largely through its appeal to nontraditional operagoers whose high numbers in the metropolitan area warranted it. Following the opera's success, Cincinnati Opera commissioned another opera with an African-American focal point, *Rise for Freedom: The John P. Parker Story*, performed in 2007, and the company is in the planning stages of yet another African-American–themed opera.[28] An enduring result of *Margaret Garner* is a particularly noteworthy collaboration between Cincinnati Opera and the African-American community called "Opera Goes to Church," which began in 2006. African-American opera singers such as Angela M. Brown and Adrienne Danrich perform gospel, jazz, and classical music with the choirs of black churches in their Sunday morning and weekday evening services. Allen Temple A.M.E. Church, St. Barnabas Episcopal Church, College Hill Presbyterian Church, and Christ Church Cathedral presently host the annual event. "Opera Goes to Temple" debuted at Rockdale Temple in Amberley Village, ten miles northeast of Cincinnati, in 2012. Like *Margaret Garner, Rise for Freedom* in 2007 and the musical programs appearing annually in Cincinnati houses of worship provide continuity and context for the historical and contemporary lives of the city's residents. In support of such programs, Beggs argues that "the only way for opera to have a wider appeal is to draw a parallel between our lives and what is being produced onstage."[29] Toni Morrison's libretto for the opera reclaims the realities of the morally untenable institution of slavery from America's past and connects contemporary audiences to the remembrance of the historical Margaret Garner and the regional and national racial politics that have informed their lives. The preproduction outreach campaign ensured that *Margaret Garner* would have a wide and lasting impact on diverse peoples and their communities.

## NOTES

1. In 2013 Opera Company of Philadelphia changed its name to Opera Philadelphia.
2. As a member of the *Margaret Garner* Steering Committee, the author served as a public historian, a role which complemented my training, scholarship, and teaching as a cultural anthropologist. The author also facilitated several of the *Margaret Garner* community involvement programs based on a careful analysis of culturally appropriate public venues focused particularly, but not exclusively, on engaging black community groups.
3. For a description of the community outreach conducted by Michigan Opera Theatre and Opera Company of Philadelphia, see the National Arts Policy Database, Project Profile: *Margaret Garner*, Americans for the Arts, 1 Jan. 2006, and note that particularly at Michigan Opera Theatre outreach included Native Americans and Arab Americans.
4. See Anastasia Tsioulcas, "'Margaret Garner' Gets National Buzz," *Cincinnati Post*, 8 July 2005.
5. Because of Cincinnati's musical segregation, Gelfand states, "a parallel classical music scene flourished in the black community alongside white musical institutions" through the 1930s and '40s. She poses the probabil-

ity that the inability to attract greater black participation in contemporary Cincinnati Opera programs may be due to lingering effects of this segregated past. The alternate music scene included the illustrious Paul Robeson in 1942 prior to appearances by such great African-American opera singers as Marian Anderson and Estella Rowe with the Cincinnati Symphony Orchestra in 1952; and Leontyne Price and William Warfield as part of the black musical festival in 1956. See Janelle Gelfand, "Songs Amid Segregation," *Cincinnati Enquirer*, 2 Feb. 2005; and "One-color Classics," *Cincinnati Enquirer*, 14 May 2007, C1. The Metropolitan Opera House in New York City at Lincoln Center is the oldest, founded in the 1880s, and the largest—with 3,800 seats—of the current total of 125 opera houses in the United States. Cincinnati Opera Associated inaugurated its founding on 27 June 1920 to a sold-out performance of *Martha*. For fifty years the company staged performances at the Zoo Pavilion. In 1972 Cincinnati Opera moved from the Zoo Pavilion to Music Hall, a 3,412-seat theater with National Historic Landmark status. Placido Domingo, Beverly Sills, and Roberta Peters are a few of the performers who have frequented Cincinnati Opera's stage.

6. Naomi Hoyt, Director of Education, and Julie Maslov, Director of Public Relations at Cincinnati Opera, spearheaded this extraordinary outreach during *Margaret Garner*'s run in Cincinnati.

7. The National Underground Railroad Freedom Center recounts the stories of enslavement-era heroism as well as those in modern times.

8. "A Reminiscence of Slavery, The Slave Mother Margaret Garner. Her Tragic Sacrifice of a Child in This City. Interview with Her Husband, Subsequent History of the Family," *Cincinnati Chronicle*, 11 Mar. 1870. Rpt. in Mark Reinhardt, *Who Speaks for Margaret Garner? The True Story That Inspired Toni Morrison's "Beloved"* (Minneapolis: U of Minnesota P, 2010), 236–40. The author wrote to Professor Morrison who did not attend the workshop, describing Robert Garner's relevance to black communities in the Cincinnati area. She did not respond in writing to my letter petitioning for his survival, which had been supported by colleagues at Northern Kentucky University and the Freedom Center, but she remembered my appeal when I spoke with her during the opera's run in Cincinnati. Despite Robert Garner's early demise in her libretto, his legacy persists throughout the opera. Although Steering Committee members, including myself, initially responded critically to witnessing his lynching that was not in accordance with history, it was apparent, even in the previews that

the opera's emotional intensity would succeed in captivating viewers.

9. See also "Patterns of Police Violence," *New York Times*, 18 Apr. 2001; and Dan Horn, "The Trigger: Shooting 'Ignites Furious Response,'" *Cincinnati Enquirer*, 30 Dec. 2001.

10. See Gelfand, "When Art Doesn't Imitate Life," *Cincinnati Enquirer*, 10 July 2005, D4.

11. David Patrick Stearns, "'Margaret Garner' Worthy of Excitement It's Stirring," *Philadelphia Inquirer*, 11 May 2005.

12. The following articles detail select community outreach efforts in Detroit and Cincinnati for the opera. See Kimberly Hayes Taylor, "The Changing Face of Opera: Directors Increasingly Cast Minorities in a Push to Attract Broader Audiences" (*Detroit News*, 3 May 2005). Taylor reports on David DiChiera's massive role in organizing the tri-city sponsorship of the opera in Detroit, Cincinnati, and Philadelphia. For a more extensive profile of DiChiera's contributions to Michigan Opera Theatre, see the National Arts Policy Database, Project Profile: *Margaret Garner*, Americans for the Arts, 1 Jan. 2006. She also discusses the mock trial of Margaret Garner. See also Kristine Yohe, "Toni Morrison and Sites of Memory: The Fourth Biennial Conference," *"Word-Work": The Toni Morrison Society Newsletter* 11.1 (Spring 2006): 14; and "Detroit Opera: 'Margaret Garner,' A Powerful Story of Slavery," *Detroit Free News*, 7 May 2005, 10A.

13. Ted Shaw, "Slavery: Opera Puts Face on Controversial Story," *Windsor (Ont.) Star*, 7 May 2005, B1.

14. Lawrence B. Johnson, "MOT Steps into the Spotlight; World Premiere of 'Margaret Garner' Tells the Tragedy of the Kentucky Slave," *Detroit News*, 30 Apr. 2005, 1D. Also see Shaw, "Slavery," B1.

15. Cincinnati Opera's Director of Community Relations, Tracy Wilson, coordinates this annual tradition of open dress rehearsals held in Over-the-Rhine attracting thousands of children and families.

16. C. Denise Johnson, "*Margaret Garner*: Art and Reality Converge," and "Cincinnati Opera Announces Series of Community Events Celebrating 'Margaret Garner' Premiere," *Cincinnati Herald*, 9–15 July 2005, B5.

17. Mary Ellyn Hutton, "Opera 'Margaret Garner' Box Office Bonanza," *Cincinnati Post*, 14 July 2005.

18. The opera was revived in Charlotte, North Carolina (2007), New York (2007), and Chicago (2008).

19. Janelle Gelfand, "Breathtaking 'Garner' Chills, Inspires," *Cincinnati Enquirer*, 9 May 2005.

20. Janelle Gelfand, "Roaring Ovations, Capacity Crowd at 'Garner' Premiere," *Cincinnati Enquirer*, 15 July 2005.

21. Gelfand, "Breathtaking 'Garner' Chills." Also see Taylor, "The Changing Face of Opera."

22. Shaw, "Slavery," B1.

23. Taylor, "The Changing Face of Opera."

24. Janelle Gelfand, "Morrison Contributes to Diversity in Opera," *Cincinnati Enquirer*, 8 May 2005. In the latest 2011 survey of subscribers and single ticket buyers, Ashley Tongret, Director of Public Relations at Cincinnati Opera, states that 9 percent of Cincinnati Opera's audience, not including participants in community and educational programming, identified themselves as people of color.

25. Gelfand, "One-Color Classics," *Cincinnati Enquirer*, 14 May 2007.

26. Patricia Beggs, telephone interview, 9 May 2013.

27. In 1975 the *Cincinnati Post* and the *Kentucky Post* started the Post-Corbett Award in honor of Patricia and Ralph Corbett, patrons of the arts, to encourage sustainable arts communities in Greater Cincinnati and Northern Kentucky. It has now become the Post-Scripps Award.

28. John P. Parker purchased his freedom, then led numerous daring recues of other enslaved individuals across the Ohio River. He became a business owner and inventor whose children were college educated. David Gonzalez wrote the libretto for the opera and Adolphus Hailstork composed its music. Premiering in a smaller theater than Music Hall, the opera's performances were also sold out.

29. Patricia Beggs, telephone interview, 9 May 2013.

# Who Speaks for Robert Garner?

The Historical and the Libretto Representations

* CARL B. WESTMORELAND *

On March 11, 1870, a reporter for the *Cincinnati Chronicle* interviewed Robert Garner—a former Richwood Station, Kentucky, slave—in the office of Colonel F. M. Moore, a Cincinnati attorney. Reminiscing about the events of his life during his enslavement in Kentucky in the 1850s that were mixed with both triumph and defeat, Garner detailed his masterminding of a run for freedom from Richwood Station in January 1856 that included his pregnant wife, Margaret, their four young children, and his parents. To facilitate his family's liberation, he stole a rusty pistol, a sleigh, and the best horses belonging to James Marshall, who owned him and his parents. The proprietor of the neighboring farm, Archibald K. Gaines, owned his wife and children. With the undocumented agreement of Margaret and to lay the groundwork for his plan, Garner had taken advantage of an 1855 trip to Cincinnati, in the free state of Ohio, where Marshall had sent him for the purpose of selling pigs at one of the city's stockyards. The Cincinnati court testimony, recorded after the family's capture, documents that he made contact with Joseph Kite and his son Elijah Kite, the uncle and cousin of Margaret, who were free men of color, to gain their assistance in helping his family escape to Canada. Because Marshall routinely sent him on work-related errands to Cincinnati, Garner knew that the tollbooths between Richwood Station and Cincinnati, across the Ohio River, would probably be unattended the Sunday evening of January 27. And if the booths were occupied at one or two locations, he was reasonably certain that after late evening their attendants would be asleep. It was on the Ohio Valley's coldest night in several decades that Robert Garner, after passing the toll checkpoints undetected, abandoned the sleigh and horses outside a livery stable[1] at least one mile from Covington, Kentucky, and led his wife, children, and parents to the frozen Ohio River and crossed it on foot. The family walked another three miles to the west side of Cincinnati, headed for a safe house where food and shelter awaited them and where an agent of the Underground Railroad would conduct them to a securer location.

What had gone on in the rolling countryside of Richwood Station, Kentucky, in Boone County, sixteen miles south of Cincinnati on adjoining farms where corn, soybeans, and pigs were raised for the market in Cincinnati, which was then America's largest meat distribution center? Why would eight members of two black families made one by marriage and ranging in ages from three years to more than fifty choose to flee from Kentucky to Ohio following a snowstorm of several inches on one of the coldest nights of the mid-1850s? The answer is physical violence and sexual bondage.[2] One would think that the enormity of the responsibility for the lives of seven people would have overwhelmed a young husband and father barely in his mid-twenties. And perhaps a less mature man would have bolted for freedom alone.

Who were Robert Garner's teachers? And who were his predecessors in constructing a plan to liberate an entire family? How was an enslaved man with no formal education able to organize and implement a plan that would have been difficult to execute even in temperate weather and with accomplices on the road leading to the Ohio River? One of his sources of support and assistance was his father, Simon Garner. Much of what Robert knew about Simon Garner, whom Marshall had sold almost twenty-five years earlier and whom he had only recently repurchased, was based on the positive remembrances that his mother, Mary, recounted. The willingness on the part of the elder Garners to surrender to his guidance in such a major undertaking, an undertaking that would allow Robert and Margaret to make their separated family one on free soil, is a tale of mutual trust, love, and respect.

While narratives of the lone fugitive slave have become standard reading fare for students in English departments and American and Africana studies programs in the last quarter of a century—the narratives of Frederick Douglass and Harriet A. Jacobs are fine examples[3]—there are few recorded accounts readily known and taught in the academy in which enslaved men and women, husbands and wives, made a bid for freedom together. There are fewer still that chronicle the run for freedom of an entire family with a husband and father as the organizer of the liberating plan. Mark Reinhardt, in *Who Speaks for Margaret Garner? The True Story That Inspired Toni Morrison's "Beloved,"* underscores the anomaly that the Garners' escape represents:

> [The Garners] stood out for escaping as a family. About 80 percent of runaways were young men seeking freedom alone. Often these men had no wives, or at least no children. Most male runaways who were married or had children left their families behind. Women, more strongly tied to children, were less likely to run (and typically slave girls had begun having children by their late teens). Few fugitives were as old as Simon and Mary. Few were as young as the Garner children. Very few parties were families. And even when families did escape together, they tended to do so in smaller clusters, not groups of eight, spanning three generations.[4]

In the husband-and-wife-runaway category, Ellen and William Craft's story, which they recorded in *Running a Thousand Miles for Freedom* (1860), heads the dearth of narratives in which an enslaved married couple outwitted slave patrollers. In December 1848, Ellen Craft, whose skin was very light, cut her hair and posed as a white man traveling by train and steamboat from Macon, Georgia, to Philadelphia, while her husband William posed as "his" slave valet. To hide the fact that she was illiterate, Ellen tied her arm in a sling so that she would not be expected to sign travel documents. Robert Garner, during one of his work-related errands to Cincinnati, may have heard of the Crafts' story, which was widely retold on the abolitionists' lecture circuit. The Crafts published their narrative four years after the Garners' escape.

The courageous escapes of Josiah Henson (1789–1883) and Lewis Hayden (1812–1889) with their wives and children preceded the Crafts' joint freedom flight. At the age of twenty-two, Henson married Nancy, with whom he had four children while they both were enslaved in Charles County, Maryland. During the course of his enslavement, Isaac Riley, their owner, entrusted him with delivering eighteen slaves by foot to his brother in Daviess County, Kentucky. Later, when Henson attempted to buy his freedom, Riley cheated him out of his money and made plans to sell him in New Orleans. In the summer of 1830, Henson fled with his wife and children, carrying two of them in a bag on his back. Passing through Ohio and New York, the family settled in Dresden, Ontario, Canada. Josiah Henson's narrative, *The Life of Josiah Henson, Formerly a Slave, Now an Inhabitant of Canada, as Narrated by Himself* (1849), to which Harriet Beecher Stowe contributed a foreword in the 1850 and 1879 editions, starts with the brutal abuses his parents suffered and their cruel separation. He returned to the United States, leading others to freedom on the Underground Railroad.[5]

Enslaved in Lexington, Kentucky, Lewis Hayden self-emancipated his family and became a Boston abolitionist. His first wife, Esther Harvey, and son were sold to the US senator Henry Clay, who later sold them farther south. Hayden never saw them again. In 1842 he married Harriet Bell. Two years later, they, along with their son, Joseph, escaped with the help of the Underground Railroad. Covering the adult Haydens' faces with flour and hiding young Joseph under the carriage seat, conductors transported them to Ohio. Their ultimate destination was Canada. By January 1846, the Haydens had settled in Boston. Like Josiah Henson, Lewis Hayden and his wife aided numerous escapees on the Underground Railroad, giving them shelter in their home. William and Ellen Craft were among their most famous boarders. The Lewis and Harriet Hayden House, a site on the Black Heritage Trail in Boston's Beacon Hill but not open to the public, commemorates their contributions to American freedom.

In the novel *Beloved* (1987), the imaginative literary precursor to the libretto *Margaret Garner: An Opera in Two Acts*, Toni Morrison includes the story of a husband who runs for freedom without his wife and the story of an expectant father who distracts slave catchers so that the woman carrying his unborn child can escape with a family whose fictional description parallels the historical Garners. Baby Suggs, whose enslavement loosely resembles Mary Garner's experiences and who in the novel is the mother-in-law of Sethe, the fictional analogue to the historical Margaret Garner, has had eight children but only one remains—Halle Suggs—the fictional equivalent of Robert Garner. Earlier in her life Baby Suggs makes an escape agreement with the husband whose name she bears that if either one of them gets the chance to run for freedom independent of the other, then he or she will take it. His chance comes; hers does not. The African Sixo, whose nocturnal wanderings lead to obtaining information about the Underground Railroad, is the shaker and mover behind the plan to escape from Sweet Home, a

Kentucky plantation owned first by Mr. Garner and then by his brother-in-law, schoolteacher. Halle and his wife, Sethe, who is pregnant with their fourth child, agree to take part in the plan. Halle fails to escape from Sweet Home with his family, and thereafter the narrative depicts him as a psychically broken man whose life terminates in a mentally deteriorated state. Sixo also does not escape from Sweet Home, sacrificing his own freedom for the escape of Patsy, pregnant with his child, who represents the seventh generation of his lineage and his continuance in the circle of life. Patsy's nickname, the Thirty-Mile Woman, indicates the distance Sixo must walk at night to visit her on a distant plantation. Because she is now fourteen and bound for sexual use by those who wield power over her, he acts quickly. They forgo a planned marriage ceremony in a wooded sanctuary in order to consummate their love for one another immediately. The Thirty-Mile Woman conceives Sixo's child before her master can impregnate her. After successfully coordinating the escape of several Sweet Home slaves, Sixo dies defiantly and triumphantly. As schoolteacher and the slave catchers burn him at the stake, he interrupts his victorious laughter to call out, "Seven-O! Seven-O!," the name of his unborn, free offspring.[6]

## The Lynching of the Libretto Robert Garner

In February 2005, as part of the pre-opera educational programming and public outreach for *Margaret Garner: A New American Opera*, Delores M. Walters, director of a history-training program at the Underground Center, and I facilitated a panel discussion at Cincinnati's Hebrew Union College entitled "Margaret Garner and the African American Family." Both she and I asserted that the opera first and foremost missed a key opportunity to resist racist stereotypes when the plot of Toni Morrison's libretto depicts the slave catchers lynching Robert after they surprise him, Margaret, and their two children in a wooded hideout in Ohio. During his lynching in the imaginative version, Margaret kills the two children. The subsequent trial takes place in Richwood Station and not in Cincinnati as the historical trial did. If the historical Robert was the architect of his family's successful flight to Cincinnati, how can he be rightly remembered if death silences his imaginative namesake just as he is gaining a voice and before he realizes his greatest success? Reinhardt accuses past and present figures of ventriloquizing Margaret Garner. Does Robert's untimely death in the libretto's representation equally deprive him, or at least his actions, of historically speaking for himself?

Robert Garner's premature death also buries the heroic acts that he performs during the remainder of his life. The historical Robert Garner in the years immediately after Margaret's death, which occurred two years following their escape, reared alone Thomas, their oldest child, and Samuel, whom Margaret's white enslaver may have fathered. Shortly after the Cincinnati trial that returned the Garners to Kentucky and slavery, Robert, Margaret, and the two boys survived a riverboat crash on the *Henry Lewis* that claimed the life of the fourth child, Cilla, an infant who drowned during the accident. Archibald K. Gaines had quickly booked the family's passage on the steamboat departing from Louisville in order to send them downriver to Arkansas to their new owner, his brother Abner LeGrand Gaines, a former cotton broker, to avoid Margaret's extradition to Ohio to be tried for murder. The warrant's server was unable to locate her because Gaines moved the Garners between Kentucky cities to evade him. Their new owner ultimately took them to New Orleans, where they worked for a short time before he sold them to Judge Dewitt Clinton Bonham of Tennessee Landing, Mississippi. Thus Robert and Margaret were together with Thomas and Samuel when she died of typhoid fever in Issaquena County, Mississippi, in 1858.

Obtaining his freedom in the early 1860s, Robert Garner fought for the Union army in the Civil War and, following his honorable discharge, reconnected with Thomas and Samuel before returning to the Ohio Valley. The 1870 United States Census verifies that Samuel Garner, age eighteen, was still a farm laborer residing in Issaquena County with a post office address of Vicksburg, Mississippi, when Robert Garner met with Colonel F. M. Moore and a *Cincinnati Chronicle* reporter fourteen years after the Garners lost their bid for freedom first through escape and then in the Cincinnati court. Seeking to file a suit against the owners of the *Robert Burns* for rib injuries sustained while working onboard the Cincinnati steamboat, Garner went to the law office of Moore just before the spring of 1870. He died the following year.[7] And as was the case for most African-descended peoples whose lives ended in Cincinnati in the nineteenth century, he was most likely buried with the city's poor and nameless in a potter's field.

Because Edward Gaines (Archibald K. Gaines renamed in the libretto) and a posse of slave catchers lynch Robert Garner in act 2, scene 2 of the libretto,[8] the operatic and historical profile of a strong African-American husband and father would not reach and inspire first-time operagoers in communities in Detroit, Cincinnati, and Philadelphia where the opera premiered, and in subsequent performances in Charlotte, New York City, and Chicago.

Foremost, Robert Garner's life is a profile of courage. First, he demonstrated that he was adept at successfully planning and executing a sophisticated stratagem and thus resisting enslavement. Second, choosing not to run alone, he demonstrated the utmost romantic, paternal, and filial love and respect, respectively, for Margaret, their children, and his parents. And he does not run ahead of them, leaving their fate uncertain. Third, wanting to save his wife from emotional pain and physical violation, the real-life Robert Garner took action to liberate her from sexual tyranny. And while some may argue that it is not certain that Gaines sexually violated Margaret Garner, it is certain that the bodies of men and women who were the property of others had no protection under the law and that their owners could submit them to any heinous and immoral act without fear of legal penalty or redress. And last, joining the Union army, he participated in safeguarding not only his own liberty but the nation's liberty and solidarity. His positive, historical profile counters stereotypical representations of black men as anti-intellectuals, abandoners of their families, misogynists, and anti-Americans. These negative representations collectively strip them of social masculinity.

Independent of each other and prior to the panel we facilitated, both Delores Walters and I had drafted letters to Toni Morrison making the case for Robert Garner's survival in her libretto. As members of a contingent that was invited to Detroit in August 2004 to preview a run-through of the opera scenes before its premiere, both of us noted the departure from history and strongly felt that Robert Garner's early demise undercut the positive impact he made on re-imaging black men. Walters sent her letter, dated November 17, 2004, to Morrison. And while she did not receive a written response from her, she reported that she spoke of her concern with Professor Morrison sometime later. I did not fully complete and send my letter, dated November 30, 2004. In it, I request that the libretto follow the historical events of Robert Garner's life to dispel prevailing antiheroic, anti-familial stereotypes of black males:

> Margaret and Robert Garner created a family in a society that was and continues to be hostile to the notion of a Black nuclear family, and he lived to tell their story. He gave clarity and power to a love story for the ages. I hope you will use your creative powers to mine the historical record, refine it, clean it of the dust of the neglect of time when for too long the world has seen Black men as inept [and] absent. Robert Garner was not lynched; he outlived many of the people who impacted his family's life.[9]

At the close of my letter I reiterate my respectful call to allow Robert Garner's fate in the libretto and thus in the opera to adhere more closely to the facts of his life:

> I understand that you have artistic and intellectual license to develop the libretto for the opera absent any outside interference. I am trespassing on your good will in a spirit of respect for your towering intellect and the awesome power of your work. I hope that you will give consideration to reviewing the copy of *Modern Medea* . . . and let the historic[al] record become a part of the opera so that this time America won't forget Margaret, her husband Robert, and their family.[10]

### The Historical Robert Garner's Life Speaks

At an early age, Robert Garner and his father, Simon Garner, were subjected to the instability that came with domestic slavery in America. Apparently, because of their owner's financial difficulties, James W. Marshall sold Simon to a Boone County planter, George Anderson, in the nearby town of Florence, Kentucky, where he would remain for almost two and a half decades. In 1849, Robert Garner and Margaret Kite Gaines, whom John Pollard Gaines enslaved on an adjoining farm named Maplewood located one-quarter of a mile southwest of the Marshall property, made it known to their respective owners that they wanted to marry. Marshall and John Pollard Gaines agreed to allow the fifteen-year-olds to enter into a slave marriage. The following year Margaret gave birth to her first child, Thomas.

When Thomas was born in March 1850, Archibald K. Gaines, the younger brother of John Pollard Gaines, had taken possession of Maplewood. Under his ownership, Margaret had three children, with each "notably lighter than their brother Tom" and arriving a few months after the births of Archibald and Elizabeth Gaines's children.[11] In *Honor and Violence in the Old South*, Bertram Wyatt-Brown identifies the practice of slaveholders requiring enslaved women to perform as sexual surrogates during and after their wives' pregnancies, a period referred to as the "gander months." Many white, Southern men regarded it an act of gallantry to excuse their wives from their conjugal duty during this period. The practice often resulted in enslaved women giving birth to light-skinned babies in the months following their owners' wives delivering offspring.[12] Elizabeth Gaines gave birth to a daughter, Margaret Ann, in November of 1852. In the same year, the month unknown, Margaret gave birth to her second child, Samuel. Margaret's third child, Mary, arrived in May 1853. Elizabeth delivered her second child, William LeGrand in November 1854. Less than five months later, in April 1855, Margaret's forth child, Priscilla (Cilla), was born. Elizabeth Gaines was expecting a third child when Margaret, pregnant with a fifth child, ran for freedom with the Garners on January 27, 1856. Elizabeth Gaines gave birth to a daughter, Jane, in late March. The birth and fate of the child Margaret was carrying when she was captured and jailed are unknown. Also, under the younger Gaines's ownership, Margaret had conceived and given birth during stretches of time that James Marshall had leased Robert for work assignments to planters residing outside of the Richwood area.

Based on the "notably lighter" skin of Samuel, Mary, and Cilla and the occurrences of each of their births several months after the births of the Gaineses' children, it is questionable that Robert Garner was the biological father of all three of the children who were credited to his paternity after Thomas. In *Modern Medea*, a recounting of Margaret Garner's life, Steven Weisenburger states that her newly born son Thomas was listed as "Black" in the 1850 United States Census. The *Cincinnati Daily Gazette* and other newspapers at the time of the Garners' capture referred to Margaret's son Samuel, who was less than four years old, as "Mulatto"; to Mary, the two-and-a-half-year-old whose throat Margaret cut as slave catchers surrounded the Cincinnati safe house to which they had fled, as "almost white"; and to Cilla, a nine-month-old infant, as "much lighter in color" than her mother.[13]

As was the case for many enslaved men who had wives, mothers, and daughters who were vulnerable to planters' licentiousness in American slavery, Robert suspected that Gaines was demanding sexual service from Margaret. Mary Garner, Robert's mother, had experienced the same institutionalized, systematic rape. When interviewed on February 10, 1856, by the Reverend P. S. Bassett from Cincinnati's Fairmount Theological Seminary while she was held in confinement during the court hearing that followed the Garners' capture, Mary Garner stated that she was the mother of eight children whom Marshall had sold with the exception of Robert. She volunteered that her husband, Simon, had been separated from her "twenty-five years," during which time she did not see him. She went on to say that could she have prevented it, she would never have permitted her husband to return because she did not want him "to witness her sufferings."[14] Robert, who was little more than a year old when his father was sold, had witnessed the children she gave birth to after him auctioned off, never to be seen again.

In addition to information gathered from the Garners after their capture, the statement of Lucy Stone, a nationally known abolition activist who had spoken with Margaret Garner in confinement, would identify sexual abuse and the iron control of both Gaines and Marshall as catalytic agents creating ugly insight into the horror of one human being owning another. Stone alluded to the sexual exploitation that Margaret had experienced by stating that the skin color of her children attested to it. After the court's adjournment and the Garners and the federal commissioner John L. Pendery, who would decide the case, had left the courtroom, she was allowed to address the spectators who remained to hear her remarks. Archibald K. Gaines was among them: "The faded faces of the negro children tell too plainly to what degradation the female slaves submit. Rather than give her little daughter to that life, she killed it. If in her deep maternal love she felt the impulse to send her child back to God, to save it from coming woe, who shall say she had no right to do so?"[15]

John Jacobs—the younger brother of Harriet A. Jacobs—described the powerlessness that haunted most enslaved black men who were unable to shield their women in antebellum American from the "woe" to which Stone alludes:

To be a man, and not be a man—a father without authority—a husband and no protector—is the darkest of fates. Such was the condition of my father, and such is the condition of every slave throughout the United States; he owns nothing; he can claim nothing. His wife is not his; his children are not his; they can be taken from him, and sold at any minute, as far away from each other as the human flesh-monger may see fit to carry them. Slaves are recognized as property by law, and can own nothing except by the consent of their masters. A slave's wife or daughter may be insulted before his eyes with impunity. He himself may be called on to torture them, and dare not refuse.[16]

Jacobs's statement—along with his sister's narrative, *Incidents in the Life of a Slave Girl, Written by Herself* (1861)—clearly describes the ugly "insults," sexual coercion and rape, perpetrated against enslaved women.[17] John Jacobs's observations reflect the sense of helplessness that Garner experienced knowing that his wife Margaret was defenseless against the sexual demands of Gaines, who not only owned her labor but also her body, and, through the de facto tradition of white male privilege, could and did take sexual advantage of her despite the fact that she was married to a black male who by law and social custom in the antebellum era, and well into postbellum America, had no say in the matter. These de facto traditions, and the trauma that they engendered, continued well into the twentieth century under slavery by another name. A senior resident of Cincinnati recounted to me a haunting example of its continuance when he was a boy growing up in the South.

Jacob McCants, a resident of Cincinnati's predominantly Black West End, when discussing his unwillingness to visit the National Underground Railroad Freedom Center, angrily told me that he, who at the time of our conversation was in his early seventies, still had disturbing memories from his life as the son of a sharecropper in rural Georgia in the 1930s: "Being there was just like being in slavery. We all picked cotton. We all hoed. If you couldn't carry a bag, you drug it. On Sunday the white man, the boss, would drive up and tell my uncle to take us fishing. He had come to see *his* woman, my aunt." Mr. McCants's open anger, three-quarters of a lifetime and several hundred miles north of where he witnessed his aunt's and uncle's degradation, was palpable. As Mr. McCants walked away, he said, "White been doin' to our women since slavery."

Robert Garner, young, energetic, and trusted by his owner to walk almost twenty-five miles one way to sell livestock and return with every penny of the proceeds, had absolute control over his master's business of livestock trading. However, like too many black men of his generation, both North and South, he had very little impact on the lives of those closest to him—his wife, his children, his parents. Robert Garner apparently had the maturity of an older, wiser man, possibly an intergenerational maturation based on what he'd learned from older men of African descent. Cincinnati newspapers reported that Garner loved and trusted his wife and regarded the persons who enslaved them as the source of unacceptable torment endured by black people. He thus determined that, working with other enslaved and free black people, he would free his wife from sexual tyranny, remove his parents from the site where they had experienced it, and ensure that the little girls who were in his care were not touched by it when they began to develop into young women. In the March 11, 1870, *Cincinnati Chronicle* interview recalling the Garner court case, the reporter writes that Robert Garner faced the reality that he, his wife, their children, and his parents belonged to James Marshall and Archibald K. Gaines and that he had "no control over or duties in regard to them. But his desire to exercise such rights and privileges led him to hitch up two of his master's horses to a sleigh in the dead hour of night, and, putting his old father and mother and his own family therein, drive rapidly to the river."[18]

When Robert Garner left Maplewood farm on the night of January 27, 1856, he was not only headed to the home of Joseph and Elijah Kite, located on the north bank of the Ohio River at the point where Mill Creek joins it, but he was also headed toward America's sixth-largest city, with a black population that would be supportive of the arrival of the Garner family. Any reader of *Beloved* or viewer of its cinematic adaptation will remember that the fictional narrative is based on the real-life escape of Robert Garner (Halle Suggs); his parents, Simon and Mary (Baby Suggs, who is liberated before the escape); his wife, Margaret (Sethe), and their four children, Thomas (Howard), Samuel (Buglar), Mary (the "crawling-already?" girl whose throat Sethe cuts and who returns as the revenant Beloved); and Cilla (Denver, who is born during the escape). The *New York Tribune* and Boston and Philadelphia newspapers reported to the world that the Garners' attempt to secure assistance in Cincinnati from the Quaker abolitionist Levi Coffin was unsuccessful, and before the family could be taken to another location, agents for Marshall and Gaines were able to track the Garner family to the Kites' residence. Robert Garner and his father, with a stolen pistol, were able for a short time to hold off Gaines; Thomas Marshall, who was present on his father's behalf, a US Marshal; and eight men deputized to pursue them. While bullets flew, one of which struck one of their pursuers, John Patterson, in the mouth, Margaret, using a knife belonging to the Kites, cut Mary's throat, almost decapitating the two-and-a-half-year-old, and wounding two of her three remaining children in an attempt to kill all four of them and herself, pregnant with a fifth, rather than have them returned to slavery. Once the fugitives had been subdued, the unseemly response of Gaines to the discovery that little Mary, a child described in the *Cincinnati Daily Gazette* as having "rare beauty,"[19] had been killed suggests that his relationship to the toddler was more than that between owner and property:

> Before Menzies [the city coroner] arrived, however, a strange scene unfolded. One of Kite's neighbors, a white laborer, named Sutton, saw Archibald Gaines appear on the front porch of the house carrying little Mary's body and sobbing uncontrollably over her corpse. From his almost incoherent phrases, deputies realized that Gaines meant to leave Cincinnati on horseback with the corpse. They had a difficult time persuading the distraught man to put down the child's body and stay at the Kites' house. . . . When the coroner arrived Gaines still refused to release Mary's body and insisted on carrying it inside by himself.[20]

The *New York Daily Tribune*, then noted as an abolitionist newspaper edited by Horace Greeley, published excerpts in its September 22, 1862, edition from a letter received from Robert Garner, stating that he was free and no longer enslaved in Mississippi. At that time he was aboard the USS *Benton*, a Union gunboat. He also asked if his mother, who had been enslaved in Kentucky, was still alive. He informed the *Tribune* that Margaret had died on May 14, 1858, and that Thomas and Samuel were still living. He ended by saying that he would come north soon.[21]

The next and final time the public would hear from Robert Garner was in the 1870 *Cincinnati Chronicle* interview. Robert's return to Cincinnati was an act of defiance, of triumphal return from the jaws of death and humiliation, of knowing that neither he nor any man of his standing and race could be in control of anything or anyone, including himself, prior to the ending of the Civil War. He proudly talked of the free life he had built after leaving the Bonham plantation at Tennessee Landing, Mississippi.

In a paternalistic Western culture, Robert Garner and most men of African descent in the 1850s had absolutely no power to protect the women in their lives, or the children that they fathered, or any members of their extended family. Any effort on the part of black males to assert themselves verbally or physically would result in their being separated from their communities and families through sale or death. Robert Garner emerges in history as neither a broken man—the psychological state of his fictive counterpart in Morrison's novel—nor as a lynched one—the fate of his biopic analogue in her libretto—but as a skillful strategist who successfully led his wife, his children, and his parents to a Cincinnati safe house on free soil. The part for which he was responsible in their run for freedom was done. In the 1870 interview, he alleged that subterfuge had precipitated their capture,[22] but we who now inspect the record will never know. How radically different our present discussion of the Garners might be, or there might not be a discussion of them at all, if, "like the four Maplewood slaves who followed them," escaping four days later, "on January 31, they could have disappeared without a trace."[23]

## NOTES

1. In *Modern Medea: A Family Story of Slavery and Child-Murder from the Old South* (New York: Hill and Wang, 1998), Steven Weisenburger writes that Robert Garner's abandonment of Marshall's horses outside a livery stable "says something . . . about the man: his spite was for the slave master, not the man's nonhuman chattels: Having sorely taxed Marshall's horses, Robert left the pair in the likeliest place for them to get much-needed care" (59).

2. Mark Reinhardt, "An Extraordinary Case?," introduction to *Who Speaks for Margaret Garner? The True Story That Inspired Toni Morrison's "Beloved"* (Minneapolis: U of Minnesota P, 2010), 14–15.

3. Douglass wrote three autobiographies: *Narrative of the Life of Frederick*

*Douglass* (1845); *My Bondage and My Freedom* (1855), and *The Life and Times of Frederick Douglass* (1881), which he revised in 1892. His first slave narrative was and still is the most popular of the three. A Boston company "Published for the Author" Harriet A. Jacobs's *Incidents in the Life of a Slave Girl* (1861). Jacobs's slave narrative first appeared in serial form over a number of months in the *New York Tribune*. In 1835, at the age of twenty-two, Jacobs, who took the pseudonym of Linda Brent in the text, went into hiding for seven years in her grandmother's garret in Edenton, North Carolina, to avoid the sexual harassment of her underage owner's father, Dr. James Norcom (Dr. Flint in the text), the town's prominent physician. Her not wanting to leave her two young children, fathered by a white attorney whom she deliberately chose to foil the doctor's plan of sexual exploitation, informed her seven-year reluctance to go to the North. Ultimately, Jacobs fled to New York without them.

4. Reinhardt, "An Extraordinary Case?," 15–16.

5. Josiah Henson, *The Life of Josiah Henson, Formerly a Slave, Now an Inhabitant of Canada, as Narrated by Himself* (Boston: A. D. Phelps, 1849).

6. Toni Morrison, *Beloved* (New York: Knopf, 1987), 226.

7. For a discussion of the death of Robert Garner, see Reinhardt, *Who Speaks for Margaret Garner?*, 301–2.

8. Toni Morrison, *Margaret Garner: Opera in Two Acts,* composed by Richard Danielpour, rev. ed. (New York: Associated Music, 2004). All references to the libretto are to this edition.

9. Carl B. Westmoreland, unsent letter to Toni Morrison, 30 Nov. 2004, draft.

10. Ibid.

11. Reinhardt, "An Extraordinary Case?," 14. Margaret herself was lighter than her purported father, the enslaved Duke Kite, who was the husband of her mother, Priscilla, indicating that she, too, may have been an interracial offspring. On the other hand, one might argue that Margaret's own parentage and the vagaries of dominant and recessive genes may have been responsible for her children's light complexions.

12. See Bertram Wyatt-Brown, *Honor and Violence in the Old South* (New York: Oxford UP, 1986), 113.

13. See Reinhardt, "An Extraordinary Case?," 38; and "The Fugitive Slave Case," *Cincinnati Daily Gazette*, 11 Feb. 1856. Rpt. in Reinhardt, *Who Speaks for Margaret Garner?*, 97.

14. P. S. Bassett, "From the American Baptist: A Visit to the Slave Mother

Who Killed Her Child," *National Anti-Slavery Standard*, 15 Mar. 1856. Rpt. in Reinhardt, *Who Speaks for Margaret Garner?*, 216. Bassett wrote the Sunday, 10 Feb. 1856 interview on 12 Feb. 1856.

15. Weisenburger, *Modern Medea*, 173, 242–43.

16. John Jacobs, "A True Tale of Slavery," *The Leisure Hour: A Family Journal of Instruction and Recreation*, 7 Feb. 1861, 476.

17. Harriet Jacobs's narrative also records an account of a young, rich, bedridden, male slave owner's sexual exploitation of a male slave named Luke: "As he lay there on his bed, a mere degraded wreck of manhood, he took into his head the strangest freaks of despotism; and if Luke hesitated to submit to his orders, the constable was immediately sent for" to flog him with a cowhide. "Some of these freaks were of a nature too filthy to be repeated. When I fled from the house of bondage, I left poor Luke still chained to the bedside of this cruel and disgusting wretch" (192).

18. "A Reminiscence of Slavery. The Slave Mother Margaret Garner. Her Tragic Sacrifice of a Child in This City. Interview With Her Husband, Subsequent History of the Family," *Cincinnati Chronicle*, 11 Mar. 1870. Rpt. in Reinhardt, *Who Speaks for Margaret Garner?*, 237.

19. Weisenburger, *Modern Medea*, 157.

20. Ibid., 75–76.

21. "The Case of the Garner Fugitive Slave Family." Rpt. in Reinhardt, *Who Speaks for Margaret Garner?*, 236.

22. Robert Garner suspected at the time of their capture that Elijah Kite had betrayed them. He believed that Kite, who did not return on the morning of January 28 before daylight from the Underground Railroad agent Levi Coffin with instructions for their next move, had conspired with his owner to have his family apprehended.

23. Reinhardt, "An Extraordinary Case?," 16. See also Weisenburger, *Modern Medea*, 127.

# Confronting *Margaret Garner* in Cincinnati

*The Opera, the Toni Morrison Society Conference, and the Public Debate*

✳ KRISTINE YOHE ✳

Ohio is right on the Kentucky border, so there's not much difference between it and the "South." It's an interesting state from the point of view of black people because it is right there by the Ohio River, in the south, and at its northern tip is Canada. And there were these fantastic abolitionists there, and also the Ku Klux Klan lived there.
—*Toni Morrison, 1977 interview with Robert B. Stepto*

In 2005, the consciousness of the citizens of Cincinnati, Ohio, grew with respect to the deep roots the northern city has in the history of American slavery. Local residents became more aware that Cincinnati's distinctive geographical location on the Ohio River had given it a powerful political role as a border city between North and South, between freedom and slavery, and between the complicated racial relations, power dynamics, and conflicting viewpoints that prevailed during the antebellum era. Many learned that year that competing perspectives on the morality of chattel slavery—which European settlers initiated in colonial America in the seventeenth century and which continued until the end of the Civil War in 1865—were surprisingly still evident. For some, even 140 years after the last enslaved people of African descent had officially gained their court-decreed freedom, American slavery was still a morally defensible institution. For many Cincinnatians, this long-backgrounded history came to the forefront because of media coverage leading up to the July 14, 2005, Cincinnati premiere of Richard Danielpour's *Margaret Garner: A New American Opera*, for which Toni Morrison wrote the libretto. The plot and geographical trajectories of Morrison's libretto, inspired by the 1856 events of the historical enslaved woman of its title, depict a desperate mother choosing to kill her two children when Kentucky slave catchers pursue the fugitive Garner family across the Ohio River into Cincinnati—the sixth-largest city in the nation in the free state of Ohio.[1] While the plot of the libretto may appear the stuff of sensational fiction, it actually mirrors fact. The historical Garner managed to kill one of her four children before a slave posse apprehended her.

The disturbing facts of Garner's mid-nineteenth-century life often emotionally challenge twenty-first-century learners of that history. In 2005, political tensions came to a head in the weeks before the opera's premiere when a local woman, Ruth Wade Cox Brunings, publicly alleged that an "adulterous" relationship between Margaret Garner and her enslaver, Archibald K. Gaines, had led Garner to kill her daughter in 1856. Many local residents—as well as members of the cast and creative team for the opera—vehemently disagreed with Brunings's speculation, maintaining that enslaved women had neither the liberty to select their sexual mates nor the power to refuse any white man sexually. Therefore, white men's forcibly having sexual relations with enslaved women—without their consent or as a requirement of their domestic service—constituted rape. In short, much of the Cincinnati community in 2005 became aware that residual racial biases from earlier centuries had the power to color and distort contemporary views.

## Background

Cincinnati residents' knowledge about American slavery expanded even before 2005 because of programming related to the opening of the National Underground Railroad Freedom Center in 2004, which the presentation of *Margaret Garner: A New American Opera* was chosen in part to commemorate. The reason the city is the site of this important center affiliated with the Smithsonian Institution, however, goes back to the eighteenth and nineteenth centuries, as it was a main corridor of escape for persons of African descent fleeing slavery. Its location on the Ohio River drew escapees up that waterway en route to freedom in Canada, especially after 1850, when the Fugitive Slave Law rescinded freedom for persons who fled north of the river. Because it was a border city during slavery and a region of tremendous political conflict and transition during the Civil War, Cincinnati is fraught with a record of racial tensions. The majority of its antebellum civic leaders was staunchly pro-slavery, while Levi Coffin and other abolitionists worked there feverishly to end the inhumane system. In fact, local hero John P. Parker, a very active and successful African-American conductor on the Underground Railroad who helped hundreds of fugitive slaves to escape, in an interview in the 1880s called the region along the Ohio River the Borderland: "The Borderland on the Ohio reached the top of the riverbank, while the Kentucky limits extended across the state even into Tennessee, in fact there was no southern limit. It was through this Borderland that enslaved persons made their way to Canada."[2] While Parker was based primarily in Ripley, Ohio, forty-three miles upriver from Cincinnati, he worked throughout the region on behalf of the cause of abolition, as the Greater Cincinnati region was a crossroads for escapees.[3]

In a 1953 scholarly article about Margaret Garner, New York lawyer Julius Yanuck argues that Cincinnati in 1856 evinced "a marked antipathy towards abolition." He notes that in 1855 newly elected Ohio governor Salmon P. Chase, a confirmed abolitionist, won the statewide election *in spite of* southern Ohio's overwhelming hostility to his candidacy, as almost 80 percent of the votes cast in the Cincinnati region were for his pro-slavery opponents, Governor William Medill and former governor Allen Trimble. The complex, seemingly contradictory dynamics of the city were clear, yet, as Yanuck argues, "In spite of its strongly anti-abolition electorate, Cincinnati's geographical location and its efficient abolitionist organization made it a main starting point on the Underground Railroad." Yanuck goes on to describe the political climate in the region during Margaret Garner's trial, showing the extreme tensions between state and federal sovereignty concerning whether Ohio's antislavery position would prevail, or the Fugitive Slave Law would remand enslaved runaways to Kentucky, where slavery was still the law of the land. Yanuck asserts that the Cincinnati conflict over the case was but a preview of discord to come: "It was out of cases such as that of Margaret Garner that friction between free states and the national government grew into increasingly bitter hostility," leading not long thereafter to the Civil War.[4]

Cincinnati's volatile racial climate has been demonstrated numerous times since the close of the Civil War, and race-based segregation in many sociopolitical arenas persisted well into the second half of the twentieth century. A sustained, sometimes tense, racialized environment has continued in recent decades, most especially evident in 2001, when the city was roundly criticized following white police officer Stephen Roach's killing of an unarmed nineteen-year-old African-American man, Timothy Thomas. Judge Ralph E. Winkler of Hamilton County Municipal Court later acquitted Roach in a trial that did not include a jury. Four days of unrest and protest followed Thomas's killing, and many individuals and groups, including performers Bill Cosby and Smokey Robinson, participated in a boycott of the city for approximately a year thereafter.

When I moved to Greater Cincinnati in 1997 to teach at Northern Kentucky University, which is just south of the Ohio River, I told friends and family that I was moving to *Beloved* country, as this area is where Toni Morrison set her 1987 Pulitzer Prize–winning novel of that name also inspired by Margaret Garner's local history. Learning that Margaret Garner had lived approximately twenty miles from Cincinnati when she was enslaved in Richwood, Kentucky, and that she and her family had crossed the frozen Ohio River at Covington, Kentucky, on their attempt at freedom, I was eager to learn more about the region's conflicted antebellum history. Having read in *Beloved* of the Licking River—where the character Stamp Paid in the novel works as an Underground Railroad conductor similarly to the historical John P. Parker—I traced the smaller river by car to see where it fed into the mighty Ohio and to ponder the difficult, transformative, and awe-inspiring route that so many escapees from enslavement took. In fact, Baby Suggs, the character who is the mother-in-law to Sethe, the Margaret Garner figure in Morrison's novel, realizes that she possesses her own heart and hands during her crossing of the Ohio.[5]

In spring 2003, members of Cincinnati Opera, including Patricia K. Beggs, Julie Maslov, and Tracy L. Wilson, approached me after they had learned that I was an active member of the Toni Morrison Society. Beggs informed me that Morrison was writing the libretto about Margaret Garner for an opera that Grammy Award–winning composer Richard Danielpour would score and that Cincinnati Opera, along with Michigan Opera Theatre and the Opera Company of Philadelphia, had co-commissioned. For the opera's July 2005 Cincinnati premiere, they requested that I invite the Toni Morrison Society to attend. I conveyed Cincinnati Opera's invitation to the Toni Morrison Society officers at its June 2003 conference in Washington, DC. Carolyn Denard, the Toni Morrison Society board chair and founder, and Maryemma Graham, the organization's president at that time, accepted and subsequently decided to convene the Society's Fourth Biennial Conference in Greater Cincinnati from July 14 to 17, 2005, concurrent with the opera's premiere on July 14, and asked me to be the local director of the conference. Shortly thereafter, with the help of a committee composed of colleagues at Northern Kentucky University and members of the Toni Morrison Society, I began planning the conference. In addition, Beggs and Maslov at Cincinnati Opera enlisted me as a member of the *Margaret Garner* Steering Committee, which included my attending the opera's Detroit rehearsal performance and workshop on August 28 and 29, 2004.

The Toni Morrison Society planning committee for the Fourth Biennial Conference, intending to take participants on a tour of the Underground Railroad sites in the area, considered Ripley, Ohio, but its resounding preference was to take conveners to Maplewood Farm in Richwood, Kentucky. To lay the groundwork for the visit, in February 2005, I accompanied Delores Walters, who was then a professor at Northern Kentucky University, and her Underground Railroad anthropology class to Maplewood. It was on this occasion that I first heard Ruth Brunings share her Margaret Garner "adultery" theory, apparently supported by the Reverend Jean Frable, pastor of Richwood Presbyterian Church. Brunings speculated that Margaret Garner had escaped from slavery in early 1856 and subsequently killed her child because of her guilt over having engaged in an extramarital relationship with Archibald K. Gaines after joining the Richwood Presbyterian Church in 1855. On that day, Brunings prohibited Walters from speaking to share an alternative account.[6] At the end of the February visit, Brunings and I spoke about the Toni Morrison Society participants visiting Maplewood during its upcoming Cincinnati conference, which at that point was less than six months away, and she tentatively affirmed a group tour.

Ruth Brunings's centrality in overseeing visits to Maplewood Farm had evolved after the appearance in 1998 of Steven Weisenburger's seminal work on Margaret Garner's 1856 flight from enslavement, entitled *Modern Medea: A Family Story of Slavery and Child-Murder from the Old South*. Following its publication, interest in Margaret Garner and her local roots sharply increased, in part because Weisenburger's *Modern Medea* includes both maps and detailed descriptions of Maplewood

Farm, where Margaret Garner spent twenty-two years of enslavement;[7] of Northern Kentucky, through which her family escaped; and of the Mill Creek area of Cincinnati, where slave catchers apprehended them.[8] Weisenburger's book catapulted Brunings, a member of the Boone County Historical Society, into the position of docent or tour guide for Maplewood Farm, with the cooperation of the property's present owner, George J. Budig, a member of a prominent local family and a Greater Cincinnati businessman whose holdings include transportation and trade-show companies. In the capacity of docent, Brunings became the contact person for anyone wanting to visit the still-extensive farm, which, according to Weisenburger, was originally approximately three hundred acres, while Brunings wrote in 2004 that it was 221 acres during Margaret Garner's time.[9]

In 2002, the president of Northern Kentucky University, James C. Votruba, obtained George Budig's permission for Northern Kentucky University students and other academic groups to visit Maplewood as a learning experience, with Ruth Brunings serving as the intermediary who would arrange visits. Faculty members—particularly Delores Walters and leaders of the Northern Kentucky University Institute for Freedom Studies—took conference groups, students, and colleagues to Maplewood Farm on Underground Railroad tours by scheduling these visits with Brunings. While the access and protocol for these tours of Maplewood and another site—Richwood Presbyterian Church, where Margaret Garner had worshipped and where Archibald K. Gaines is buried—were clear initially, the visiting terms changed over time. Early on, visitors' access to the church's cemetery had been open, but it soon became restricted. Later, before granting access to Maplewood, Brunings required visitors to listen to her prepared talk, which, at times, Rev. Jean Frable and others supplemented with their own presentations. Walters reported that Brunings began to limit and censor the discussions that she and her students conducted about slavery, eventually telling her that her anthropology classes could continue to come to Maplewood but only if Walters did not speak. Presently, the statement on the Boone County Heritage website regarding visits to Maplewood reads: "To protect the property and insure historical accuracy, presentations are given by a designated member of the Boone County Historical Society. Questions by visitors are welcome."[10] Brunings also initiated the requirement that all visitors receive copies of various versions of an essay that she had written which postulate her interpretations of the circumstances of Margaret Garner's pregnancies and escape. These versions include her 2004 article published in *Northern Kentucky Heritage*, as well as a shorter, unpublished essay.[11] Walters stated that she continued to take university students to Maplewood, even with the censoring of her discussions with them, so that her students could observe firsthand that American history continues to be filtered, even silenced, particularly when one believes that his or her family heritage or honor is at stake.

## Pre-Opera Educational Programming and Public Outreach

In the months leading to the local premiere of *Margaret Garner* in July 2005, Cincinnati Opera presented educational programming and public outreach to familiarize the community with the historical context of Margaret Garner. On the Cincinnati Opera Raps schedule were "free community lectures, book chats, films, art exhibits, and performances celebrating the 2005 Season."[12] Steven Weisenburger's January 2005 public lecture on Margaret Garner's history, held at Xavier University in Cincinnati, began the slate of educational programming.

A panel discussion followed in February, at Cincinnati's Hebrew Union College, entitled "Margaret Garner and the African American Family," which was facilitated by Carl B. Westmoreland of the National Underground Railroad Freedom Center, and Delores Walters. Westmoreland and Walters argued that the opera missed a key opportunity to counter racist stereotypes, because the historical Robert Garner, Margaret's husband, raised as his own the sons that her white enslaver most likely fathered, and he also fought for the Union in the Civil War.[13] They lamented that the profile of a strong African-American father and husband would not have the opportunity to inspire the community, since in act 2, scene 2, of the libretto slave catchers, counter to history, lynch Robert.[14]

Several *Margaret Garner*–related activities occurred in March, with two standing out as significant. Cincinnati Opera sponsored a screening of the movie *Beloved* at the National Underground Railroad Freedom Center, followed by a discussion of its connections to Margaret Garner, which I facilitated. And later in the month, Northern Kentucky University was the site of a panel discussion, "History, Memory, and Representation," which included Kenny Leon, director of the tri-city production of *Margaret Garner*; Tiffany Hinton, an English professor at Northern Kentucky University; and Janelle Gelfand, classical music and arts writer for the *Cincinnati Enquirer*.

Concurrent with these Opera Rap programs, Cincinnati Opera also brought a musical performance, "Introducing *Margaret Garner*," to community venues in the area, including the Mercantile Library, Northern Kentucky University, and the National Underground Railroad Freedom Center. In it, singers performed arias and duets from *Margaret Garner* to familiarize the public with the new American opera. Although the singers did not include the primary, original cast members for *Margaret Garner*, these preview performances, of which there were seven, did feature Tracie Luck as Margaret, a role she covered in Detroit, Cincinnati, Philadelphia, and Charlotte in 2005 and 2006, and in which she starred when the opera premiered as a New York City Opera production at Lincoln Center in 2007.[15]

To prepare for their performances, the cast for "Introducing *Margaret Garner*" visited Maplewood Farm in February 2005, where members spoke with Ruth Brunings, Rev. Jean Frable, and John Gaines, a descendant of Margaret Garner's enslaver Archibald K. Gaines, as well as Philip Naff, a descendant of the Marshalls, the family that enslaved Robert Garner. During this visit, Rev. Frable stated: "Margaret was baptized in the church, very close to the time that she made her decision to seek her freedom. We think that had something to do with her decision, that she was a Christian now and she could not continue living the way she had been living."[16] Also during the preview cast's visit to Maplewood, John Gaines acknowledged his ancestors' participation in the slave trade: "It's kind of upsetting and weird (to know) that they were involved in the slavery issue, but the wrong side of it . . . [Margaret Garner] and I might share the same DNA. Which is kind of weird, but I have no problem with it. It did happen 150 years ago. It's way past being corrected."[17] And Naff shared his own curiosity about the practices of his ancestors: "It's always been a suspicion of mine (that the Marshalls owned slaves) since I started doing research. Everything's been sort of a puzzle for me, maybe because I never knew anything about the Margaret Garner story. It's interesting to see the real story, To have some blanks filled in and to see a narrative of what was going on here."[18] Tracie Luck commented that she felt fortunate to visit Maplewood and to "witness and be a part of the legacy of . . . [her African-American] ancestors," whose strength she exalted.[19] Overall, several of the cast members noted their personal family histories and connections to slavery, which performing in the opera preview and visiting Maplewood Farm brought powerfully to life.

## Maplewood Farm, Summer 2005

A culminating experience for the 2005 activities preceding the opera and the Toni Morrison Society Conference occurred on June 27 when, with the exception of titular mezzo-soprano star Denyce Graves, baritone Rod Gilfry (Edward Gaines), and librettist Toni Morrison, the primary cast members of *Margaret Garner*—Gregg Baker (Robert Garner) and Angela M. Brown (Cilla)—and its creative team, which included Richard Danielpour along with Cincinnati Opera board members and staffers, visited Maplewood Farm.[20] Also present were a dozen members of the local and regional media, some of whom were there to film a segment of a documentary entitled *The Journey of Margaret Garner*.[21] As a part of their tour, the cast and creative team listened to presentations in the Richwood Presbyterian Church by Rev. Frable, Brunings, Naff, and Anne Butler, director of the Center of Excellence for the Study of Kentucky African Americans at Kentucky State University. Frable discussed the history of Richwood Presbyterian Church, and Brunings spoke on the history of the Gaineses and their neighbors, the Bedingers, who are her ancestors.

Although both the Gaineses and the Bedingers owned slaves, Brunings stated that her relatives also were "abolitionists and emancipationists," asserting that they "accepted slavery as the social order" of the day, while they also opposed it. Brunings spoke of what has been written about Margaret Garner in recent decades, stating that "most is fiction, even if it is said as fact," and she praised the representation of emotions in Morrison's novel *Beloved*. Of the *Margaret Garner* opera, which she had attended in Detroit, and its libretto, Brunings said she believed it had "wonderful music" and the libretto was "a compelling story," but she saw the narrative as being more about "the institution of slavery" than about the historical Margaret Garner; thus the story's emotional impact was more impressive to her than its accuracy.

Anne Butler then spoke of her research into American slavery and her work with the archaeological dig at Maplewood.[22] She noted that she had interacted regularly with Brunings during this long-term project and that they were having "a continuing conversation about slavery," in which they could "agree to disagree," to which Brunings responded that there was "no disagreement." Butler continued that she believed that the United States as a country could not "go forward without learning its history" and that there had been "too much denial" thus far.

Following the presentations, there was a lively discussion between the speakers and some of the opera visitors that brought to the surface many of the unresolved tensions and controversial issues that the reclamation of the Margaret Garner story elicits. First, Gregg Baker stated that slavery involved a "denial of basic human principles," where the enslaved were "treated as subhuman," a practice that was more important to him than whether *Margaret Garner* was historically accurate. Baker also asserted that the issue of dehumanization endemic during slavery was crucial, indicating to Brunings, "You cannot understand." She then averred, "We can try." Baker responded that, no, she could "only empathize," and he believed there was "nothing noble" about the slave owners' actions, which contradicted the "Africans' majesty." Butler referred to the "indelible stamp of inferiority" inflicted upon those enslaved and the widespread misconceptions and rationalizations related to connections between Christianity and slavery. At this point, Richard Danielpour thanked everyone for speaking and shared his view, which Janelle Gelfand presents in the *Cincinnati Enquirer* article dated July 10, 2005:

> "This is the taboo within the taboo," Danielpour said. "The pattern was quite often that women were raped (and children were fathered). . . . Because of all that, we (with author Toni Morrison) realized that this is an opportunity for us. . . . We were suddenly conveying an essential issue that historians never really had talked about—or had been terrified of talking about," Danielpour said. "Not the slavery issue, but the issue of women who were raped and children who were born of that circumstance."[23]

Danielpour also stated that his and Morrison's intention did not lie in conveying a "factual," historical sensibility, but in "conveying the spirit" of Margaret Garner "in the largest sense possible," and that if we "really knew what had happened, it would be even more difficult to discuss." Brunings said that she could agree and accept that the opera went beyond the facts, but that the Gaines family would object if it were presented as fact and not fiction and that she and they had already been "offended by what's in print."

Anne Butler interjected that she saw Brunings's "issue" as not being with the opera but with Steven Weisenburger's *Modern Medea*, especially with respect to the question of Margaret's rape. Butler said that she personally respected Weisenburger's book and could recognize the "motives of the slave owners," as well as their "hypocrisy," particularly the inconsistencies demonstrated by practitioners of Christianity who supported slavery. She candidly stated that she believed Brunings did not like *Modern Medea*, to which Brunings confirmed that she objected to Weisenburger's book "because he defamed [her] ancestors" and that many of his "names and dates were inaccurate."[24] The final statement came from Danielpour, who said that these controversial issues were why Morrison wrote the libretto and he composed the opera, and that he hoped it captured "the heart of the law," even if it did not capture "the letter of the law."

Following the documentary filming, Ruth Brunings spoke to me directly about the spirited exchange that had taken place earlier in the day, explaining her position further and expressing her displeasure with the way it unfolded. She also notified me that the upcoming Toni Morrison Society participants' tour to Maplewood could only occur if both Steven Weisenburger, who was the invited keynote speaker for the Society's Authors' and Editors' Recognition Luncheon during the conference, and Delores Walters, who was on the conference schedule to present a paper, were excluded from the visit.

In the July 10, 2005, *Cincinnati Enquirer* article "Hot Debate over Escape from Slavery," Janelle Gelfand reported the June 27 visit of the *Margaret Garner* premiere cast, crew, and creative team to Maplewood, as well as the July 6 visit by Denyce Graves, Rod Gilfry, and other opera cast members. Gelfand writes that the second group also engaged in debate with the farm's docent, during which Graves was "shocked to hear Brunings describe slave owners as benevolent."[25]

As early as 1999, Ruth Brunings, in a public lecture for the Boone County Historical Society on "Slavery in Kentucky," had repeatedly used the term "benevolent slavery." In her presentation, the text of which is available online at the writing of this essay, Brunings makes an emphatic case that her ancestors, the Bedingers, who lived very close to the Gaineses' farm in Richwood, were an example of what she calls "benevolent slave-owners."[26] Here, Brunings praises Toni Morrison's *Beloved* for depicting both "kind" and "cruel" enslavers, while she castigates Steven Weisenburger's *Modern Medea* for writing "only with anger and negative assumptions about cruelty." She also alleges that his text includes multiple inaccuracies. But Brunings's primary mission in the 1999 talk seems to be to exonerate her ancestors because she regards their practice of slavery as being especially humane for the enslaved, asserting that "manumission, or gradual emancipation, was preferred by benevolent slave-owners as slaves could first be educated and trained so that they could become financially independent as free persons in a generally hostile society. Abolition of slavery by the government did not offer this preparation and protection to the individual." Furthermore, in her presentation, Brunings addresses questions of the morality of slavery, noting that her churchgoing ancestors were not liable for their practice of slavery: "The Presbyterian Church in Kentucky in 1797 determined that slavery was a moral evil but that all persons who owned slaves were not guilty of a moral evil." Therefore, she makes clear that while she personally disapproves of slavery as a practice, she maintains pride in her ancestors and sanctions their behavior.

Denyce Graves's response to Brunings's reiteration of this perspective during the July 2005 visit was passionate: "It's not okay to own another human being and to oppress them. . . . It made my blood boil."[27] Gelfand's July 10 article ends with a quotation from Anne Butler: "You can take a topic like slavery that's very threatening, and people go into immediate denial. . . . That's why opera . . . is so good; it treats topics that are difficult to talk about."[28]

## Toni Morrison and Sites of Memory: The Fourth Biennial Conference of the Toni Morrison Society

Planning for the Fourth Biennial Conference of the Toni Morrison Society, which took place from Thursday, July 14, to Sunday, July 17, 2005, at Northern Kentucky University and in Greater Cincinnati, involved setting up sites for its participants to present seventy-nine papers; arranging for the two keynote addresses—the first by Weisenburger at the luncheon and the second by Trudier Harris, J. Carlyle Sitterson Professor of English at the University of North Carolina at Chapel Hill, at the conference's banquet—and accommodating a music panel, featuring Bernice Johnson Reagon, renowned founder of the a cappella ensemble Sweet Honey in the Rock and formerly of American University. The conference codirectors—Carolyn Denard, Maryemma Graham, and I— also worked closely with staffers at Cincinnati Opera to coordinate conference and opera events, which included the Toni Morrison Society's 250 registered participants attending the *Margaret Garner* opera on its opening night, Thursday, July 14, at Cincinnati's Music Hall. The registered participants attended a pre-opera reception at the Hilton Cincinnati Netherland Plaza and the cast party after the performance, held at the National Underground Railroad Freedom Center. Toni Morrison Society directors and Cincinnati Opera staffers also worked together to offer a post-premiere discussion at Music Hall on Friday, July 15, entitled "Meet the Margaret Garner Creative Team: On Stage with Toni Morrison and Richard Danielpour," in which the opera's librettist and composer shared with those in attendance the evolution of their collaboration.

A large portion of planning time and energy, particularly in the final weeks leading up to the conference, went into arranging for all the participants to visit our target destinations—Maplewood Farm and Richwood Presbyterian Church in Richwood, Kentucky.[29] To transport us to these destinations, we hired four tour buses to carry the participants to Richwood, on Saturday afternoon, July 16.

Earlier, on May 11, 2005, just after Brunings had attended the *Margaret Garner* world premiere in Detroit, I received an e-mail from her, directing me that she would like the Toni Morrison Society conference participants to be given copies of her article entitled "Slavery and the Tragic Story of Two Families—Gaines and Garner," which had appeared in *Northern Kentucky Heritage* in 2004. In the essay, Brunings describes interaction between Margaret Garner and her enslaver, Archibald K. Gaines, as possibly "sexual abuse" or a "love relationship," and acknowledges that there is a great deal of "evidence that Archibald was the father of [Margaret Garner's] children." She also makes the case that Margaret Garner's joining Richwood Presbyterian Church in March 1855 could have resulted in "a moral conflict about a presumed adulterous relationship" with her slave master.[30] In addition to requesting distribution of her ten-page article to all conference participants, Brunings describes in the May 11 e-mail her reaction to the opera: she found the music to be "moving" and the story to be "compelling," but she regarded it all as "obviously fiction."[31]

But after Brunings, at the end of June, stipulated that Steven Weisenburger and Delores Walters had to be removed from the guests list for the Toni Morrison Society's visit to Maplewood, Carolyn Denard, Maryemma Graham, and I—along with my Northern Kentucky University colleagues Prince Brown Jr., Delores Walters, and Robert K. Wallace—decided that these exclusions were unacceptable. We believed that the very reason the public now knew about Maplewood's history was because of serious scholarship and imaginative literary art, to which Weisenburger and Walters had contributed substantially in the former category. We hoped to further uncover the previously forgotten historical past by allowing for an honest conversation among all people interested in confronting that history. So we elected in early July to cancel the Richwood trip, planning instead to drive by the sites in order that conference participants might see, if only from a distance, the farm and the church where Margaret Garner had worked and worshipped while enslaved.

A few days later, however, Walters and I decided to try another approach to gain full inclusion for the conference visit. We contacted George J. Budig, owner of Maplewood Farm, seeking his direct permission to visit the site without the exclusions of Weisenburger and Walters. In an e-mail to Budig that Walters and I sent on July 7, we wrote, "We encourage an open dialogue surrounding the Margaret Garner story as part of our upcoming and future visits to this historic site. We seek to include, rather than exclude, individuals with divergent viewpoints, which ultimately will lead to peacemaking on the issues of slavery and anti-slavery pertaining to the case."[32] Budig responded to us in a handwritten fax the next day that he approved of the visit, and he suggested we include Brunings in the program because, as he wrote, "she is most familiar [with] the history of the property."[33]

Simultaneously, Delores Walters requested that Anne Butler serve as intermediary for planning the Budig-sanctioned visit, which Butler did on July 7, spending a great deal of time talking with Brunings and finally negotiating an itinerary for the visit that both parties found acceptable. The plan called for participants on two of the four buses to go first to the Maplewood cookhouse where Margaret Garner performed domestic work and where Butler would speak about the archaeological research done there, with Walters in attendance. Meanwhile, the other two buses would carry the remaining participants to Richwood Presbyterian Church to hear Frable and Brunings. Once the two groups completed the first round of the visit, they would exchange venues, though Walters would remain at the cookhouse. Brunings made the request through Butler that she receive an official invitation to participate in the Richwood events. Butler suggested that the invitation come from me because of my role as local conference director. On the next day, Friday, July 8, Butler reported that Brunings had informed her that she had invited John Gaines and Philip Naff to attend the Toni Morrison Society Maplewood visit on July 16 and that they would in all likelihood participate in the conversation at the cookhouse. While this latest departure from the earlier agreed-upon plan required additional negotiation, the newspaper article that appeared over the weekend containing reports of the opera cast, crew, and creative team's visits to Richwood further altered the scheduled itinerary of the Toni Morrison Society conference visit.

On Sunday, July 10, Janelle Gelfand's article, "Hot Debate over Escape from Slavery," discussed above, appeared in the *Cincinnati Enquirer* on the day that I had chosen to call Brunings to extend the formal invitation she had requested. Brunings informed me in what was to be a lengthy conversation that she was quite upset about Gelfand's article, stating that it was inaccurate, as she had not referred to slave owners as "benevolent." Brunings also asked to be "warned" if Steven Weisenburger were to participate in the Toni Morrison Society conference visit to Maplewood, and she also stated that "saying Delores Walters was not welcome did not equal that she cannot be there." Despite her displeasure, she agreed to accommodate the schedule of events as Anne Butler had presented them to her.[34]

On Tuesday, July 12, an editorial appeared in the *Cincinnati Enquirer*, "Garner Story Has Much to Teach," which made many powerful and cogent points. While noting that the opera was premiering in just a few days, the editorial recapped Margaret Garner's local history and its implications for the United States Constitution and the Civil War. The editorial includes the following assessment of the Margaret Garner story:

> Seeing and discussing this story is an opportunity to educate ourselves about the horror of slavery and the role it played in our com-

munity. Garner killed her daughter when she and her family were caught in Cincinnati after having escaped from Maplewood Farm in Boone County.

Hers is not an easy story. It is horrific and tragic. It is indeed part of the underbelly of our community's history. We live with slavery's legacy today in many forms, though immense progress has been made since Garner's tragedy played out in 1856. Amazingly, as the *Enquirer* reported Sunday, stories are still told in Boone County that Garner's decision to flee the plantation was because of a moral conflict she had about a presumed adulterous relationship she had with the plantation owner, Archibald Gaines—rather than a desire to flee slavery. Such a notion ignores the reality of slavery. Enslaved women like Garner were the property of their masters and didn't have the power to say "no." They were rape victims.[35]

The unsigned editorial invites community members to learn more about Cincinnati's history of slavery and to put the opera's rendition of Margaret Garner's life into perspective rather than to focus on whether it was historically accurate.

On Wednesday, July 13, I received two extensive e-mail messages from Brunings, both requesting that I contact her, in which she raised a number of objections to the previously agreed-upon plans for the Toni Morrison Society's upcoming visits to Maplewood Farm and Richwood Presbyterian Church. First, regarding her 2004 article that she had earlier requested that all Maplewood visitors receive, she wrote that she no longer wished to have it—or another document she had recently given to Anne Butler—disseminated to participants: "I do not want them distributed after the *Enquirer* article and the perception that I am 'whitewashing' history."[36] Her comment alluded to the July 10 *Cincinnati Enquirer* article, in which Gelfand quotes Gregg Baker stating that the discussions at Maplewood constituted "the whitewashing of history."[37] Furthermore, in both e-mail messages that day, Brunings sought to redefine Delores Walters's involvement in the visit to Maplewood, stating that she had only consented to Walters serving "as a hostess on one of the buses but [she] has no other role during the visit to Maplewood. Please help her understand this."[38] Brunings also stated in both e-mail messages that the guidelines for future visits to Maplewood would be revised and clarified. I responded in an e-mail message, reiterating the already established plans for dividing up the group, thanking her, and telling her that the Toni Morrison Society looked forward to what it hoped would be "an excellent experience for the conference participants."[39]

The next day, Thursday, July 14, the Toni Morrison Society conference began with concurrent paper sessions at the conference hotel, the Hilton Cincinnati Netherland Plaza. After an opening reception at the hotel, that evening participants attended the opera premiere, which was sold out at Cincinnati's Music Hall, with Toni Morrison and Richard Danielpour in attendance. Afterward, the National Underground Railroad Freedom Center was the site for a lavish cast party, where attendees saluted not only the librettist and composer, but Denyce Graves, Rod Gilfry, and the other opera singers for their stellar performances.

Friday, July 15, found us spending the day at Northern Kentucky University, with an opening plenary session followed by concurrent paper sessions and the Authors' and Editors' Recognition Luncheon. Its keynoter Steven Weisenburger spoke about the historical context of Margaret Garner's life and her story's local and national significance. In an informal discussion after his talk, luncheon attendees raised questions about the local media's coverage of the controversial views in the community, particularly those that had appeared in the *Cincinnati Enquirer*, and Weisenburger asked me to comment on Ruth Brunings's role in the events. Following afternoon paper sessions, a return to Music Hall for the discussion "Meet the Margaret Garner Creative Team: On Stage with Toni Morrison and Richard Danielpour" highlighted the evening.

On Saturday morning, July 16, the presentation of concurrent paper sessions resumed at the Hilton Cincinnati Netherland Plaza, followed by a special session, "Music and the Echoes of Memory," held at the University of Cincinnati-College Conservatory of Music, featuring composer, singer, activist, and cultural historian Bernice Johnson Reagon. Morrison attended the special session along with the Toni Morrison Society participants. In the afternoon, the group visited Maplewood Farm and Richwood Presbyterian Church, following the plan that Anne Butler had negotiated, with the tour buses alternating between the cookhouse and the church. Both John Gaines and Philip Naff were present at the Maplewood cookhouse, and both Rev. Frable and Brunings spoke to the alternating groups.[40] Steven Weisenburger declined the Richwood visit.

While Saturday evening's banquet and Trudier Harris's keynote address entitled "Sites of Memory" (the conference's theme) and Sunday's concurrent paper sessions and a tour of the National Underground Railroad Freedom Center still loomed ahead, it was what happened on these rolling hills of Maplewood Farm more than 150 years ago that had brought all of us there together to interrogate why, and, if that proved too difficult, to question how. Afterward, the conference participants visited two sites in Covington, Kentucky, where the Garners crossed the frozen Ohio River into Cincinnati. First, they stopped briefly at the historic marker in downtown Covington, which documents the Garners' January 1856 flight to free soil. Next, the group visited the flood wall on the southern bank of the Ohio River where a mural entitled *The Flight of the Garner Family*, by Robert Dafford, depicts eight members of the Garner family walking across the frozen Ohio River to Cincinnati. Dafford's representation is part of a series of eighteen Roebling Murals, named after John Roebling, who is best known for designing the Brooklyn Bridge. His nearby suspension bridge, completed one year after the end of the Civil War, connects the north and south banks of the Ohio River, which had promised but failed to deliver liberation for the Garners ten years earlier.

## Afterword

In an interview with Celeste Headlee on National Public Radio's Weekend Edition Saturday, on May 7, 2005, the day of the world premiere of the *Margaret Garner* opera in Detroit, composer Richard Danielpour summed up his view of the project: "This is a subject that makes Afro-Americans uncomfortable, and it also makes white Americans uncomfortable—which is exactly why we should be doing it."[41]

In another interview that same week, Janelle Gelfand asked Toni Morrison whether here, in Cincinnati, "especially on the [historic] border between a free and a slave state, ... this opera [could] help this region confront its past." Morrison's response is compelling: "We've come a long way—there's no question about that. It's like we're just being covered by a veil that need not exist, which is the racial veil. And I would think that white people would love to be as free of the burden of it as black people. But I don't think any of that can happen until we actually look at what it was like before—if all of us, and particularly Cincinnati, understand the richness of that history."[42]

Clearly, all of these complex interactions demonstrate precisely the discomfort to which Danielpour alludes and that Morrison exposes. They also show that the growth of a healthy community can result from honest discussion, even one so long overdue. In part because of these public debates, *Margaret Garner* has provoked powerful community reactions about the true history of slavery, leading, we hope, to the birth pangs of understanding that just may, someday, dissolve that racial veil.

### NOTES

The epigraph quotation is from Robert B. Stepto, "'Intimate Things in Place': A Conversation with Toni Morrison," *Massachusetts Review* 18 (Autumn 1977): 475.

1. Toni Morrison, *Margaret Garner: Opera in Two Acts*, composed by Richard Danielpour, rev. ed. (New York: Associated Music, 2004). Cincinnati's population of 115,435 in 1850 ranked sixth in the United States, far ahead of St. Louis with 77,860 and Chicago at 29,963. Its cross-river neighbors of Covington and Newport, Kentucky, were home to 20,000 more residents.

2. John P. Parker, *His Promised Land: The Autobiography of John P. Parker, Former Slave and Conductor on the Underground Railroad*, ed. Stuart Seely Sprague (New York: W. W. Norton, 1996), 71. John Parker dictated this oral autobiography recorded in the 1880s—the precise year is unknown—and first published in 1996, to Frank Moody Gregg and Frank A. Stivers.

3. A National Park Service Map of the Underground Railroad Routes indicating the primary escape routes for runaways from slavery and showing great numbers going through Cincinnati can be accessed at www.nps.gov/history/nr/travel/underground/routes.htm.

4. Julius Yanuck, "The Garner Fugitive Slave Case," *Mississippi Valley Historical Review* 40.1 (1953): 47–66. Rpt. in Research Papers and Articles About Boone County History, BooneCountyHeritage.org.

5. Toni Morrison, *Beloved* (New York: Knopf, 1987).

6. On the February 2005 visit, Delores Walters told me that as unpleasant as the prohibition was, she found it instructive and eye-opening for her students.

7. Margaret Garner, also called Peggy, was born at Maplewood on June 4,

1834. Her mother was an enslaved woman named Priscilla, and her father is officially listed as an enslaved African American named Duke. However, Steven Weisenburger, in *Modern Medea: A Family Story of Slavery and Child-Murder from the Old South* (New York: Hill and Wang, 1998), theorizes that the biological father of Margaret may have been white. Weisenburger writes: "Priscilla, listed in the 1850 census as a black female, must have known the sexual subordination of slave women, as Peggy's mulatto status clearly indicates" (32).

8. In addition to his seminal work on the history of Margaret Garner, Weisenburger, shortly after *Modern Medea*'s publication, led a group of Northern Kentucky University faculty, myself included, to Richwood showing those in attendance Maplewood Farm, where Margaret lived in bondage under Archibald K. Gaines and where her husband, Robert Garner, worked as a slave on the neighboring Bedinger farm, under the ownership of James Marshall. Weisenburger also pointed out Richwood Presbyterian Church, where Margaret had been a member. During his guided tour of Richwood, he remarked that the prosperous landholdings still in evidence in that neighborhood continue as a contemporary manifestation of the enduring "legacy of slavery."

9. See Weisenburger, *Modern Medea*. Also see Ruth Brunings, "Slavery and the Tragic Story of Two Families—Gaines and Garner," *Northern Kentucky Heritage*, Fall–Winter 2004, 37–45, www.boonecountyheritage.org/content/History/Research.asp.

   Maplewood Farm's current size is unclear. In a facsimile message permitting our group to visit the farm, the portion Budig cites as Maplewood—which includes the cookhouse where Garner worked and is presently designated as 1154 Richwood Road—is now almost thirteen acres. However, the Budig family land holdings (nineteen contiguous parcels) are much more extensive, well over a thousand acres, and located on both sides of Richwood Road. Therefore, where Maplewood Farm presently begins and ends is difficult to decipher.

10. See "Historic Sites and Places," www.boonecountyheritage.org/content/explore/HistoricSites.asp#11, for details regarding the content of visits and contact information for Maplewood Farm.

11. See Brunings's "Slavery and the Tragic Story of Two Families—Gaines and Garner," 37–45, and "Slavery in Kentucky," Research Papers and Articles about Boone County History, www.boonecountyheritage.org/content/History/Research.asp.

12. *Cincinnati Opera 2005 Opera Raps* (Cincinnati: Cincinnati Opera, 2005).

13. As Steven Weisenburger explains, there is scant information detailing Robert Garner's military service. See *Modern Medea*, 283–84.

14. Delores Walters made a similar, sustained case in a letter to Toni Morrison in November 2004, in which she implored the librettist to consider changing Robert's fate in the opera to reflect history. Walters gave me a copy of her letter in 2004, and it says in part, "This work has the potential of validating the courage of a man whose identity is primarily associated with non-violence. Can we afford not to make such a statement?"

15. In addition to Tracie Luck, the "Introducing *Margaret Garner*" previews also included Michael Mayes (Edward Gaines, enslaver of Margaret), John Fulton (Robert Garner, Margaret's husband), Adrienne Danrich (Cilla, Robert's mother), and Mark T. Panuccio (Casey, the foreman).

16. Janelle Gelfand, "Sojourn of Sorrow," *Cincinnati Enquirer*, 27 Feb. 2005.

17. Ibid., 28.

18. Ibid.

19. Ibid.

20. I also attended the 27 June visit and took four pages of notes, which are the source for the following quotations, unless attributed elsewhere.

21. Alphonzo Wesson III and a team from the local ABC affiliate, Channel 9-WCPO, filmed interviews for *The Journey of Margaret Garner* with members of the cast who were present, as well as with Richard Danielpour and myself. The documentary aired locally on 12 July 2005 and includes interviews with Carl Westmoreland and Spencer Crew, of the National Underground Railroad Freedom Center; Patricia Beggs, of the Cincinnati Opera; as well as other members of the opera cast, including titular star Denyce Graves, which were taped later. Wesson, its producer and director, won a Remi award in 2006 for the documentary.

22. The Kentucky Archaeological Survey led the archaeological inquiry at Maplewood in 1998. Proceedings from a conference in 2000 in Bowling Green, Kentucky, provide a description of the research: Kim A. McBride and M. Jay Stottman, "In Search of Margaret Garner: Preliminary Archaeological Investigations at Maplewood, 15Be483, Boone County, Kentucky," *Current Archaeological Research in Kentucky*, http://heritage.ky.gov/kas/pubsvids/archpubs.htm.

23. Janelle Gelfand, "Hot Debate over Escape from Slavery," *Cincinnati Enquirer*, 10 July 2005, A1, A10.

24. I have in my files on Margaret Garner a nine-page, single-spaced, ten-

point font document given to me by Ruth Brunings in 2005. In it, Brunings enumerates the many "Mistakes, Errors, Assumptions & Speculations . . . highlighted in RED" that she alleges Steven Weisenburger makes in *Modern Medea.* In an apparent effort to discredit him, Brunings sent a similar document to Steven Weisenburger and to Dennis Foster, the English Department chair at Southern Methodist University, where Weisenburger is Jacob and Frances Mossiker Chair in Humanities and Professor of English.

25. Gelfand, "Hot Debate," A10.

26. Ruth Brunings, "Slavery in Kentucky." See www.boonecountyheritage. org/content/History/SlaveryKentucky.pdf for the full text of Brunings's 1999 presentation, which I attended and where she used the term *benevolent* in reference to slavery eight times—as well as her related article, "Slavery and the Tragic Story of Two Families—Gaines and Garner." In addition, the site also includes Julius Yanuck's 1953 article "The Garner Fugitive Slave Case," discussed above.

27. Gelfand, "Hot Debate," A10.

28. Ibid.

29. My records from this portion of the conference planning include extensive e-mail exchanges, letters, notes from phone calls, a fax, and written advice from colleagues on how to proceed with the trip, as I sought to accommodate both the requirements of Ruth Brunings and our needs and desires for the conference.

30. Brunings, "Slavery and the Tragic Story of Two Families—Gaines and Garner," 39.

31. Ruth Brunings, "Toni Morrison Society Visit to Maplewood," e-mail to the author, 11 May 2005.

32. Delores M. Walters and Kristine Yohe, "Visit to Maplewood by the Toni Morrison Society," e-mail to George Budig, 4 July 2005.

33. George Budig, fax message to the author and Delores Walters, 8 July 2005.

34. Ruth Brunings, phone conversation with the author, 10 July 2005.

35. "Garner Story Has Much to Teach," editorial, *Cincinnati Enquirer,* 12 July 2005.

36. Ruth Brunings, "Toni Morrison Society," e-mail to the author, 13 July 2005.

37. Gelfand, "Hot Debate," A1.

38. Ruth Brunings, "Phone call from George Budig," e-mail to the author, 13 July 2005.

39. The e-mail exchange of July 13 was the last contact I had with Ruth Brunings. After the conference was over, Northern Kentucky University colleagues and I worked with our president, James C. Votruba, who arranged for revised guidelines for visits to Maplewood Farm with the property owner, George Budig. No longer must we contact Brunings; instead, we call the farm's resident caretaker directly. I have since taken two Toni Morrison–focused classes to Maplewood, where I have led the discussions myself.

40. In an anonymous blog under the heading "The City. Toni Morrison," posted 17 July 2005, one conference participant, who pseudonymously calls herself Wanda Ball, notes this of the experience of listening to the speakers at Maplewood, making particular reference to John Gaines: "Never [before] have I witnessed such a spectacle of white guilt, evasion, denial, and shame, such a grave misjudgment of one's audience, such a surreal charade of sympathy." I wrote to "Wanda Ball" on the blog, requesting her real name for attribution, but I did not receive a response.

41. Quoted in Celeste Headlee, "Opera Tells Saga of *Margaret Garner*," *Weekend Edition Saturday*, National Public Radio, 7 May 2005, 1–6.

42. Janelle Gelfand, "Author Brings Focus to Boone Slave's Life: Nobel, Pulitzer Prize Winner Reflects on Opera's Premiere," *Cincinnati Enquirer*, 11 July 2005, A6.

# Haiti, the African-American Libretto Tradition, and *Margaret Garner*

＊ LA VINIA DELOIS JENNINGS ＊

The first African-American librettists chose as principal cultural sig-
nifiers of blackness the representations of traditional priest(esse)s, divinities, symbols, and practices that enslaved West and Central Africans
brought to the Western hemisphere between the seventeenth and nineteenth centuries and creolized into the Haitian religion of Voudoun.
Treatments of these features of Voudoun—the diasporic derivative of
Vodun, the faith of the Fon people of Dahomey (present-day Benin),
to which the BaKongo contributed its central symbol, a cross-within-
a-circle ancestral cosmogram—recur in the libretti that these literary
pioneers wrote for grand operas in the first half of the twentieth century.[1] Reprising the representation of African traditional beliefs[2] amalgamated in Haiti in *Margaret Garner: Opera in Two Acts* (2004), her only
libretto to date, Toni Morrison presses into literary service allusions to
the religion that assisted in the black nation's liberation.[3] An indicator
that Morrison had Haiti in mind as she drafted the libretto appears in
its penultimate scene during the early April 1861 Richwood, Kentucky,
trial of the enslaved Margaret charged with stealing and destroying her
master Edward Gaines's property: she kills her two children when a slave
posse approaches to apprehend her family in the free state of Ohio. During his testimony Gaines angrily argues, "She owns *nothing*." Caroline,
his daughter, respectfully responds that Margaret's children "are hers
until they come of age."[4] The Judges hearing the case "sarcastically"
question Caroline in unison:

> Where have you been, Madam?
> On an island in the sea?

You are speaking of a slave,
Not someone like you or me.

(ACT 2, SCENE 3)[5]

The Judges' (and Morrison's textual) allusion to the black-ruled island nation within days of the Confederates' April 12, 1861, bombardment of Fort Sumter is a coincidence that the librettist makes possible by reset-ting the February 1856 trial of the historical Margaret Garner five years later. In 1791 Haitians launched a military resistance to French enslave-ment that culminated in their liberation in 1804 on the island of His-paniola in the Caribbean Sea. Morrison's calling attention in her libret-to to the free, black nation on the eve of the Civil War underscores the racial and political tensions igniting the latter conflict and the plight of Margaret Garner and countless other persons of African descent held in bondage in the United States. The courtroom invocation of Haiti is not Morrison's first allusion to the island nation in her literary canon. The principal action of her fourth novel, *Tar Baby* (1981), takes place on two formerly French-colonized islands that she fabricates, Isle des Chevaliers and St. Dominique. The latter Caribbean island bears the pre-independence name for Haiti.

Traditional religious elements derived from Voudoun become visi-ble when one reads Morrison's libretto through an African-Caribbeanist lens. First, the titular character personifies Erzulie, the Voudoun *loa*—divinity—of love. A Haitian creation with many manifestations, Erzu-lie, as she relates to the representation of the libretto Margaret Garner, is the embodiment of maternal love and is associated with the Virgin Mary as the *Mater Dolorosa*—the suffering mother, the Immaculate Heart, and the fierce protector of newborns. Her iconographical depic-tion is typically the Virgin holding the Child protectively in her arms. Her symbol is the heart pierced with knives or swords, and her colors are red, blue, and white. Forever lamenting the inconstancy of love, she weeps profusely. Her *serviteurs* honor her with fine dresses, scarfs, ribbons, jewelry, perfume, liqueurs, and tantalizing desserts. Second, an African-Caribbeanist reading also brings into relief the Haitian re-ligion's preeminent, geometric cosmogram, the cross-within-a-circle, which Morrison, deploying an African aesthetic strategy that simultaneously conceals and reveals, partially obscures by accumulating—overlaying or clustering—two or more natural elements, events, and/or physical actions.[6]

*Beloved* (1987)—Morrison's first imaginative re-creation of the events surrounding the historical Margaret Garner, the enslaved Kentucky mother who killed her two-and-a-half-year-old daughter to prevent her return to chattel slavery—provides evidence for her intertextual transfer from the novel to the libretto of partially concealed esoteric features of the African creolized religion. According to Mary H. Nooter, the act of partially obscuring information to codify secret information—the method that Morrison deploys—has provenance in African art, past and present, and appears in "two-and three-dimensional objects—including masks, textiles, tablets, and figural sculptures." To mask information in their art, many cultural groups throughout Africa rely on a visual grammar strategically based on "abstraction, accumulation, obscurity, omission, and containment." These strategies, "through an aesthetic of partial revelation and partial concealment . . . all produce ambiguity of form and meaning" aimed at disclosing information to some while withholding it from others.[7] Nooter goes on to explain that "the arts associated with secrecy are often focal points of ritual and ceremony, cosmology, mythology and mystical belief, yet the aesthetics of secrecy operate at every level of human discourse and interaction."[8] Thus in *Margaret Garner,* Morrison reprises both an African-American libretto tradition celebrating an empowering African diaspora religion that played a crucial role in freeing its New World practitioners from European enslavement and an African art aesthetic that conceals and reveals. In doing so she grounds her literary work as identifiably black when read through the prism of an African aesthetic. To identify Morrison's partial concealing of African traditional religious elements in the libretto, I draw upon Nooter's designated categories from visual art to discuss Morrison's process in literary art of strategically abstracting, accumulating, and obscuring information.[9]

## The Inaugural African-American Librettists

During the inaugural years of the African-American operatic and libretto tradition, from the early 1890s to 1950, H(arry) Lawrence Freeman

(1869–1954), Scott Joplin (1867–1917), Shirley Graham (1896–1977), and Langston Hughes (1902–1967) included the representations of African traditional priest(esse)s, symbols, and practices in the lyrical narratives they wrote for grand operas.[10] The recurrences of these representations in the first African-American libretti did not evolve by happenstance or in artistic isolation. Freeman, who calls himself "the father of Negro grand opera" in his 376-page unpublished manuscript, "The Negro in Music and Drama," drafted in 1906 while residing in Cleveland, the city of his nativity, a one-act libretto and score for the story of a Voodoo queen embroiled in a love triangle that would become his most famous opera, Voodoo.[11] By 1914, and now living in Harlem, he had expanded it to three acts. New York's WGBS radio broadcast a scaled-back version on May 20, 1928, and Broadway's Winter Palm Garden Theatre staged a fully mounted production the following September.

The composer-librettist for more than twenty grand operas, Freeman discussed Treemonisha (1910) with Joplin in 1912 after the famous ragtime innovator sought his advice about revising the score and libretto for his second and only extant opera.[12] Both resided in Manhattan and then within blocks of each other in Harlem between 1910 and 1917 but may have met earlier at the Chicago World's Fair Columbian Exposition of 1893.[13] Joplin had given a piano concert of Treemonisha, the story of a foundling discovered under a tree who grows up to be the leader of her black community, in a rented hall in 1911,[14] but had failed to secure producers for its staging. In 1915 the Winter Palm Garden Theatre performed the opera's ballet, "The Frolic of the Bears,"—renamed "Dance of the Bears"—after the featured African-British composer Samuel Coleridge-Taylor's rhapsody Kubla Khan. Accompanied by a full orchestra, the ballet was the only professionally rendered selection from Treemonisha that Joplin, dying two years later, ever heard and the second and last public exposure the opera and its libretto received until its world premiere in Georgia by Morehouse College and the Atlanta Symphony Orchestra at the Memorial Arts Center in late January 1972.[15] Treemonisha made its debuts on Broadway, appearing at the Uris and Palace Theatres, in the fall and winter of 1975.

Shirley Graham consulted with Freeman on her highly successful Tom-Tom: An Opera in Three Acts, which chronicles the Africa-to-America journey of four archetypal characters: Voodoo Man, Mother, Girl, and Boy. First submitted to Cleveland's Karamu House Theatre directors, who recommended that she submit it to the Cleveland Opera, Graham's grand opera received two full performances at the Cleveland Stadium on June 30 and July 3, 1932, before audiences of ten and fifteen thousand. The lead singers for her only opera, Jules Bledsoe (Voodoo Man) and Charlotte Murray (Mother), had worked with Freeman in 1920 on a production of *Voodoo*.

Freeman also had professional ties with composer William Grant Still (1895–1978). In "The Negro in Music and Drama," Freeman writes that Still, who worked as an arranger for Handy Brothers, first called on him "in his New York studio in 1920."[16] In the fall of the following year Freeman solicited Still to orchestrate a production of *Voodoo*, but the younger composer responded that he "would not consider" undertaking the work "for less than $1,500," an exorbitant fee at that time that Freeman was unable to pay.[17] In the mid-1930s, Still commissioned Langston Hughes to write the three-act libretto, *Troubled Island* (1937), dramatizing the political rise and fall of Jean-Jacques Dessalines, a lieutenant in the Haitian Revolution who became the governor and first emperor of the independent republic.[18] Still's opera of the same name premiered at the New York City Opera in 1949.

Morrison's reprise in *Margaret Garner* of African traditional religious features via Haiti that hark back to Freeman's initial imaginative topical use of Voodoo is also not a serendipitous, isolated occurrence.[19] Morrison knew of his and these other African Americans' libretti long before penning her own work in the genre. Her formative introduction to African-American operatic composers and their texts came by way of her mother, Ella Ramah Wofford, and her coming of age in Lorain, Ohio, less than thirty miles from Cleveland, where African-American operatic performance germinated and flourished.

## The African-American Libretti, Cleveland, and Morrison

Toni Morrison's decade and place of birth, as well as the musical influence of her mother, played key roles in shaping her early familiarity with diasporic, African traditional beliefs and the pioneers of the African-American operatic and libretto tradition. Born Chloe Ardelia Wofford in 1931, while the Harlem Renaissance was still in vogue and the US occupation of Haiti from July 28, 1915, to August 1, 1934, kept the island nation ubiquitously in the news, Morrison began her life in an America whose popular imaginary had taken a keen interest in Africa and in African diasporic cultures and performance.

In the first two decades of her life an interrelated group of anthropologists, writers, and performance artists intensively researched the African and Haitian cultures that the Chicago Exposition's Dahomey Village and Haitian Pavilion in 1893 had first showcased to the world and that the United States' nineteen-year Haitian occupation continued to headline globally. Lippincott published Zora Neale Hurston's novel written during seven weeks in Haiti, *Their Eyes Were Watching God*, in 1937 and the anthropological research that took her to the black-ruled nation, *Tell My Horse: Voodoo and Life in Haiti and Jamaica*, in 1938. Dancer and friend to Shirley Graham, Katherine Dunham took many trips to Haiti starting in 1936 that influenced the dance performances that she popularized throughout her life and drew upon to choreograph the 1972 world premiere of *Treemonisha*. Both Hurston and Dunham worked with Melville J. Herskovits, whose *Life in a Haitian Valley*, published in 1937, traces Haiti's Voudoun to Dahomey's Vodun. By the time Morrison finished working on her master's degree at Cornell University in 1955, Maya Deren, who apprenticed under Dunham, had published her sensitively nuanced exegesis on the religion's philosophy and pantheon, *Divine Horsemen: The Voodoo Gods of Haiti*, two years earlier.

Morrison grew up not far from Cleveland, where Freeman had been born and reared and where several of the first African-American grand operas had been written, workshopped, and performed. By the time he was a teenager Freeman's Cleveland home at 686 Sterling Avenue had become an artistic salon and rest stop for the greatest prima donnas and poets of the day: "The home my grandfather had erected two decades prior to the Civil War ... in Cleveland, Ohio, as early as the late '80s, had become the focal point—the Half-Way-Rendezvous of the sepian artistic nomad; and they came from all parts of this country, Europe, Africa and the West Indies—in certain isolated instances as native inhabitants; in the majority of cases fresh from international triumphs."[20] A musical prodigy, young Freeman studied under Johann Heinrich Beck, conductor of the Cleveland Symphony, and pianists Edwin W. Schonert and Carlos Sobrino. His first grand opera, *The Martyr*—the story of Platonus, an Egyptian nobleman who chooses death over renouncing Jehovah and worshipping the Egyptian gods Isis and Osiris—premiered first in 1893 in Denver and at the Chicago World's Fair and two years later received a Cleveland staging.[21] *Valdo*, his second opera with a Mexican-themed libretto, also received a Cleveland debut in 1895. In the first decade of the new century, *Voodoo*, which Freeman numbers his eighth opera, set in Louisiana during Reconstruction, started to take shape. Its central character, Voodoo queen Lolo, is in love with Mando, but he is in love with Cleota. In act 3, Lolo, descending from a tree throne guarded by a snake god suggesting the Voudoun *loa* Damballah, uses mystical powers to combat her hated rival.[22] Acknowledging Freeman's ability to incorporate "jazz, ragtime, [and] vodun," in the grand opera European tradition, George Lewis asserts that the composer's "engagement with political, historical, and cultural issues in his work was strongly complemented by his deep recognition of how Africa and its diaspora were crucially informing a new American musical [and libretto] identity."[23] During Morrison's first decade, the northern industrial city on Lake Erie was also the site for the world premiere of Graham's *Tom-Tom* and the dramatic laboratory for Hughes's libretto *Troubled Island*.

Shirley Graham's three-act libretto for *Tom-Tom*, set first in an African jungle, next on an American slave plantation, and finally in a Harlem jazz club, centers on Voodoo Man. In its respective acts, the traditional priest warns neighboring African villages with tom-tom drums of approaching slave hunters; leads the escape of Mother, Girl, Boy, and other plantation slaves to a nearby swamp where he calls for a revolt; and starts a back-to-Africa movement that money-hungry Real Estate Man, and Boy—now a Harlem preacher—thwart. Notably, *Tom-Tom's* second act depicts Mother poised to stab Girl as slave catchers approach to apprehend them.[24]

Langston Hughes, who had planned to write as early as the top of 1928 a "singing play" with the working title of "Emperor of Haiti" centering on Dessalines, started work at the bottom of 1936 on *Troubled Island* in Cleveland.[25] Five years earlier he had travelled to Haiti, where his great uncle, John Mercer Langston, had twice served as the US minister. Mary Langston, his grandmother and aunt of Cleveland fiction writer Charles W. Chesnutt, "had been invited to Haiti" many years before and had reared a foster son named in honor of Dessalines.[26]

From 2256 East Eighty-Sixth Street in Cleveland, Hughes wrote to Verna Arvey, the second wife of William Grant Still, on October 7, 1936, that he had "a complete dramatic version of . . . the Haitian story from which [he] now intended to make a lyrical version for the opera." He had written "it in straight prose first so as to get the action and characterizations all set down before attempting the libretto."[27] On January 7, 1937, he wrote directly to Still: "A few days ago I mailed to you a copy of *Troubled Island*, the dramatic version of the Haitian story of which I'm now (believe it or not) working into a libretto. . . . The play as presented by the Gilpin Players here who tried it out for me, seemed to be quite well liked by its audience during its week's run."[28] The November 18, 1936, opening of the drama had been "the glittering highlight of the black Cleveland season," and "the production itself was something of a success."[29] Hughes suggested that Still, who had not been to Haiti, read *The Magic Island*, by William Seabrook, "and a more recent book called *Voodoo Fires in Haiti*," by Richard Loederer "for voodoo in a colorful but quite exaggerated fashion."[30] Hughes's libretto includes the characters Papaloi and Mamaloi, Voodoo priest and priestess, who petition Legba, Ogun, Shango, and Damballah, the "Gods of Congoland [and] Dahomey" for Dessalines's victory over their French enslavers.[31]

A gifted vocalist who loved opera and jazz, Ella Ramah Wofford introduced her four children to opera through the Lorain and Cleveland musical performance scenes. Morrison recalls in her youth her mother singing in a Cleveland opera: "If my ebullient and astute mother had had more choices, my guess is she would have established herself as a singer, as her voice resembled Ella Fitzgerald's. When I was a child, I remember, she'd had a taste of a public life and enjoyed it. Once, she performed in a production of the opera *Carmen* in Cleveland. And, regularly, she would sing for visiting politicians."[32] She also soloed in church performances locally in Lorain and throughout Cleveland. Years later, when Morrison, working as a project editor for Random House, assisted Middleton Harris in editing *The Black Book* (1974), both her mother and her father, George Carl Wofford, contributed "stories, pictures, recollections, and general aid" in its scrapbooking of important black events spanning three centuries. Their names are credited in the acknowledgments and their photographs appear on the cover's photomontage. Following information on Joplin and *Treemonisha*, *The Black Book* references Freeman and his son Valdo (1900–1972):

Once in New York City, an elderly man with failing eyesight sat and hoped that delayed lightning would strike again so that some of his composer-father's operettas would be played for appreciative audiences. The man was Valdo Freeman and his father was H. Lawrence Freeman, who was a native of Cleveland, Ohio, and a thoroughly trained composer and conductor. In Cleveland, where he had the honor of conducting the city symphony at the turn of the century, Harry Freeman was referred to in awe as "the black [*sic*: colored] Wagner."[33]

*The Black Book* is a veritable African-American cultural and historical treasure trove that Morrison mined for her fiction. It contains a reprint of an 1856 jail-cell interview with Margaret Garner and an extensive section on Voodoo featuring a drawing of the knife-pierced heart symbol for Erzulie.[34] Its entries on Joplin and Freeman indicate that both Morrison and her mother had knowledge of these inaugural African-American librettists through her Random House editorship in the early seventies and that the latter may have supplied the information. Ella Ramah Wofford's earlier operatic aspirations in Lorain, Ohio, within close proximity of Cleveland's bustling dynamic black operatic culture in the first half of the twentieth century, also suggests that Morrison had knowledge of the early composers and librettist long before the 1970s.[35]

## The Historical and Libretto Margaret Garners

The historical details of Margaret Garner's escaping to Ohio and killing her daughter are the stuff of which great operas are made. The fact that she was pregnant with her fifth child at the time of her filicide added to the sensationalism of the court case that ensued. The act would earn her the title "The Modern Medea." But unlike Euripides's mythological Medea, who commits vengeful filicide because of marital betrayal, a profound maternal love and the horrors of chattel slavery incited Margaret Garner to deadly action.

On January 28, 1856, the morning after the Garners had fled enslavement in Kentucky, Gaines and a US Marshals posse surrounded her uncle Joseph Kite's Cincinnati, Ohio, cabin where they had been given refuge. Spurred on by the inevitable certainty that her children would be remanded to slavery on Maplewood, Gaines's farm, Margaret Garner seized a butcher knife and slit the throat of her daughter Mary, a toddler.

Before the posse could apprehend them, she moved quickly, as Steven Weisenburger's historical account reports, "to put as many of her children as possible in a place where slave catchers could never reach them." She failed, only wounding her remaining three offspring.[36]

Morrison's *Beloved* depicts the fugitive slave Sethe, the Margaret Garner equivalent, cutting the throat of one child and seriously wounding two others in the way station outside Cincinnati where they reside when her second Sweet Home plantation slave master, called schoolteacher, and a Kentucky posse arrive. Schoolteacher, concluding that the wild Sethe and mutilated children are not worth reclaiming, leaves them in Ohio. Conversely, the two-act, seven-scene libretto narrates Garner's killing two children and being sentenced to death by hanging for stealing and destroying Gaines's property. It does not contain a Beloved parallel, the revenant of the child that Sethe kills, who returns from the afterworld.

*Beloved* relies on authorial description, nuance, and background to construct the persona of Beloved, who displays traits readable as Erzulie's—such as her craving for sweets and exhibiting excessive love—through red and heart imagery. The libretto, a genre that requires a scaled-back authorial commentary, however, relies on the monologues and dialogues (arias, duets, ensembles, and choruses) of its characters to imbue Garner with the qualities of the love divinity. Throughout the libretto, characters allude to red and sweet food (strawberries and syrup); flowers and plants with red and "sweet" varieties and names (sweet william, columbine, roses, rosemary, and clover); and red and "sweet" trees (maple, birch, pine, mimosa, and elm).

The comments of characters also reference natural elements that accumulate to form the cross-within-a-circle cosmogram, also called the Yowa or "the four moments of the sun." Signifying renaissance, remembrance, and mediation of spiritual power, the cosmogram emblematizes—in contradistinction to Western thought—the backward or counterclockwise spatialization of time as governed by nature. The counterclockwise, east-west rise and descent of the sun reinforce the flow of time from generation to generation, each spiraling backward into an infinite past. The right, east, or "sunrise" of the cross's horizontal axis indicates birth; its left, west or "sunset" point indicates approaching death. The "midday" or vertical summit marks the strongest moment of one's earthly existence. And the southern or "midnight" point, below the east-west axis, designates one's crossing the river into the afterworld. The intersection of the cross marks the crossroads: the intersection of spirit and flesh, where the former vivifies the latter. It marks the point where the *loa* "mount" (possess) *serviteurs*. During a Voudoun ceremony, a circle of *serviteurs* move counterclockwise around a sacred tree or *poteau mitan* (center post) to symbolize the cross-within-a-circle formation. They encircle its base with lighted candles and draw *vevers*, lacy patterns made with flour or ashes, to honor the divinities. Sterling Stuckey traces the performance of the cosmogram to the ring shout, a shuffling counterclockwise religious dance performed in the black Atlantic.[37] The symbol codifies the traditional African's belief in the spiritual transcendence of death.

The libretto's first scene of act 1 opens in the town square of Richwood Station, Kentucky, in April 1856. Edward Gaines, a widower with one daughter, returns after a twenty-year absence to claim Maplewood, his deceased brother's slave plantation. Margaret Garner, part of Gaines's newly claimed property, accidentally drops a red scarf, which he picks up and puts in his pocket. Although he left Richwood Station because of sexual misconduct involving a young girl, it troubles Gaines that its residents, as well as its trees, do not remember him:

> Maple, birch and the odor of pine.
> I remember every tree
> But none of them remembers me.
>
> (ACT 1, SCENE 1)

Six months later in the Garners' cabin, Margaret, her husband Robert, and his mother Cilla discuss Gaines's heartlessness and Margaret's excessive love for her only child. Casey, Maplewood's foreman, enters, informing Robert that Gaines has rented him to another plantation owner. He then presents Margaret with a red, "stylish housedress," announcing her work reassignment from the fields to Gaines's house. Robert and Margaret "exchange troubled glances" but reassure each other that "love is the only master / The heart obeys" (act 1, scene 2).

In early summer of 1858, Gaines hosts a lavish Maplewood wedding reception for his daughter Caroline and new son-in-law, George Hancock, who debates with him the nature and language of love. Caroline asks Margaret to give her perspective on love. She initially declines but then thoughtfully states her opinion:

> Words of love are moths;
> Easy food for flame.
> Actions alone
> Say what love may be.
>
> (ACT 1, SCENE 3)

Shocked that Caroline has asked a slave for an opinion and, more egregiously, one concerning human feeling, the guests depart abruptly. The newlyweds leave for their honeymoon. While Margaret cleans the parlor and sings about a "quality love," Gaines, who has lingered unseen, "looks her over with unmistakable intent." Revealing his presence, he asserts that he has "remedies" for her "fine sentiments," which are "too fine . . . /For a slave." He pulls her red scarf from his pocket and slowly ties it around her neck. She replies that his remedies "can not touch/The secret soul." Sardonically informing Margaret that her "soul" is not on his mind, Gaines *"overpowers her, and drags her forcibly out of the parlor"* to rape her (act 1, scene 3).[38]

The first scene of act 2 resumes the narrative four and a half years later on Sunday, February 24, 1861, in Cilla's cabin. In the interim Margaret has given birth to a second child. Robert announces his plan for the family's escape to Ohio. Margaret, overwhelmed by the love she feels for her husband, breaks down in tears. Robert sings an arietta, instructing her to "Go Cry, Girl." Cilla, pleading age, informs them that she will remain behind. Casey unexpectedly enters, deduces their escape plan, and threatens them with his pistol. A struggle ensues between the two men, ending with Casey's strangulation. Hastening his departure, Robert instructs Margaret to bring the children to "the bottom . . . /By the mimosa. / . . . /When the moon hits/The top of the pines," where he will be waiting with a wagon (act 2, scene 1).

Three weeks later, in late March 1861, between Abraham Lincoln's first inauguration and the start of the Civil War, the Garners, after crossing the Ohio River, take shelter in an underground shed. Standing underneath a huge protecting elm tree, Robert reports that "this new president/Doesn't hiss like a snake" (act 2, scene 2). Margaret anticipates war and advises him to make his spirit ready. Following slave catchers carrying torches, Gaines enters their camp. He removes Margaret's red scarf from his pocket.[39] She snatches red-hot coals from a smoldering fire in an attempt to burn him after he alludes to her warming his bed sexually. Placing a noose strung from the elm around Robert's neck, the slave catchers "plant their torches in the ground," circling the tree and "the condemned man with fire" (act 2, scene 2). Witnessing Robert's lynching and instant death, Margaret grabs a knife, shouting, "Never to be born again into slavery!" as she slits the throat of her daughter and stabs the younger child (act 2, scene 2).

In the intermezzo Margaret emerges from total darkness in a moment "out of time." She sings of "a river rushing/From the grip of its banks."

Her trial in a Richwood Station courtroom in early April follows. Three presiding judges sentence Margaret "to be executed/By sunrise" for theft and destruction of Gaines's property (act 2, scene 3). Caroline, however, begs her father to seek clemency for Margaret.

The concluding scene of the libretto returns to its opening setting: the Richwood Station town square. It is dawn of the next morning. Hoping to secure the love and respect of his daughter, Gaines rushes in waving clemency papers. Margaret, standing on the square's gallows with a noose encircling her neck, declares to a crowd gathered, "Death is dead"; she "will live/ . . . /Ringed by a harvest of love" (act 2, scene 4). While the crowd is distracted, she deliberately trips the gallows lever, choosing death over a last-minute clemency that will not invalidate her enslavement. Caroline notices the red scarf in her father's coat pocket, removes it, ascends the scaffold, and ties it around the hanged woman's waist.

## The Haitian Loa Erzulie

Prior to the book-length studies of Therese Higgins (2001), La Vinia Delois Jennings (2008), and K. Zauditu-Sellasie (2009) and the book chapter by Justine Tally (2009) centering on Africanist readings of Morrison's fiction, articles by Vashti Crutcher Lewis (1987) and Holly

Fils-Aimé (1995) identify respectively Morrison's title character of *Sula* (1973) as a West African priestess and Pilate in *Song of Solomon* (1977) as the Voudoun *loa* Legba.[40] However, St. Thomas native Barbara Christian (1993), the first to detect an ambiguity in Beloved's infantile representation, interprets her newborn traits as those specific to the Voudoun *loa* Erzulie:

> Practices derived from African religions . . . still persist in the culture from which I come. . . . I was . . . struck by the way the character Beloved needs constantly to be fed, especially sweet things, the food that ancestors, even voduns like Erzulie, the Haitian vodun of love, relish. Like bodies, the ancestral spirits in my Caribbean context who come back to visit us eat and drink and are carnal. Yet they differ from the living in that while they do appear as bodies, their eyes and skin, like Beloved's, are those of newborn babes.[41]

Beloved's uncontrollable temper; excessive jealousy, love, and need to be loved; unrestrained carnality; and insatiable craving for sweet food and drink and beautiful clothing and jewelry suspend her personality between two Erzuliean identities: Erzulie Ge-Rouge (Red Eyed) and Erzulie Freida/Maîtresse. Both identities have red iconography associated with them, as do both postmortem manifestations of the crawling-already? girl whom Sethe kills. As disembodied spirit, the crawling-already? girl makes her initial return as "a pool of red and undulating light." As spiritually reembodied flesh, Beloved receives the referent "red heart" from Paul D—a former Kentucky, Sweet Home plantation slave—who reunites with Sethe and becomes her lover in Ohio.[42]

Erzulie Ge-Rouge is a Haitian-originated *loa* created exclusively for and in the Americas. According to Maya Deren, Voudoun practitioners created the New World divinity not from evil motives but from rage at the displacement they suffered when European enslavers separated their family members at will.[43] *Serviteurs* and artists depict Erzulie Ge-Rouge as a baby in the fetal position "with her knees drawn up, the fists clenched, the jaw rigid and tears streaming from her tight-shut eyes, she is the cosmic tantrum . . . [who] cannot understand—and *will* not understand— why accidents should ever befall what is cherished, or why death should ever come to the beloved."[44] Beloved, like Erzulie Ge-Rouge, is inconsolable. She cannot comprehend Sethe's motive for ending her life.

Erzulie Freida/Maîtresse is the *loa* of intense love, which historians trace to Dahomey's Vodun.[45] A jealous female spirit who destroys romantic relationships, she has "love [that] is so strong and binding that it cannot tolerate a rival."[46] She suffers no compunction when she calls a *serviteur* away from his mortal lover—just as Beloved feels no remorse when she "moves" Paul D, her love rival, out of Sethe's bed. His shouting "Red heart"[47] while having sexual intercourse with Beloved in the way station's cold house outside Cincinnati is an obscured homage to her figuring as Erzulie Freida/Maîtresse. In Haitian worship, *serviteurs* appropriate the iconic red heart commemorating the Catholic Saint Valentine to represent Erzulie. They draw a valentine *vever* to honor and invoke her ceremonially.[48]

In the absence of a Beloved figure in the libretto, Morrison transfers red/heart imagery and the infantile, excessive love traits of the revenant that the novel renders via authorial commentary to Margaret Garner, by way of her own and other characters' comments. In the libretto, however, the manifestation of Erzulie is the embodiment of maternal love. In their cabin, Margaret, Robert, and Cilla exchange a round of jokes about Edward Gaines's heartlessness before Margaret's husband and mother-in-law chide her about the excessive love that she displays for her infant daughter. Margaret first expresses pleasure that they have "milk and strawberries" for their supper (act 1, scene 2), food that is both red and sweet, the type that Erzulie relishes. She then speaks metaphorically of her baby as the sweet food that she craves for her heart. She cannot eat for plying Cilla with questions about her sleeping daughter:

> How's my baby?
> Not crying for me?
> How's my sweetness?
> Not missing me?
>
> . . .
>
> She is my supper,
> The food of my heart.
>
> (ACT 1, SCENE 2)

Robert teases his wife about her inversion of the maternal and filial roles, suggesting that she is now the infant:

Did you ever see a mother like that?
The child supposed to need the mother;
Now here the mother needs the child more.

(ACT 1, SCENE 2)

Cilla cautions Margaret concerning her unbridled love, stating:

It's dangerous, daughter,
To love too much.

. . .

Come to your supper before you wake her.

(ACT 1, SCENE 2)

But Cilla relents, telling her daughter-in-law, "Go get your heart / before you break mine" (act 1, scene 2). The scene ends with Robert and Margaret reassuring one another that "love is the only master / The heart obeys" (act 1, scene 2), after Casey, informing them that Margaret will now work in Gaines's house, presents her with the red stylish housedress.

Margaret's figuring as the *loa* of intense love continues throughout the libretto. Caroline's turning to her as an authority on love at her wedding reception and Margaret's assertion when she believes that she is alone after it that "only unharnessed hearts / Can survive a locked-down life" set her apart as an expert on the profound human feeling. The response she gives concerning "words of love" turns on red, "flame" imagery (act 1, scene 3). After Margaret takes her own life, Cilla alludes to a postmortem reunion with her: "Soon, soon my bold-hearted girl / I'll be there. I'll be there" (act 2, scene 4).

Edward Gaines's repeated caressing of the red scarf belonging to Margaret and requiring her to wear a fancy red dress in his house suggest that he has a psychic connection with her other than the infusion of power and sexual lust that a conventional reading of his actions and these objects might reveal. Erzulie particularly likes beautiful clothing and jewelry, and *serviteurs* honor her by keeping an altar in their homes bearing the finery that will please her and a bed lavishly made for her. Gaines first picks up her scarf and mindlessly puts it in his pocket as he reminisces about a youthful indiscretion. In his obsessive, sexual pursuit of Margaret, he displays her red scarf as if it is a fetish at each of their encounters—including at the underground shed where he alludes to her warming his bed. His daughter, the recipient of the enslaved woman's maternal love after she arrives at Maplewood with Gaines, also salutes Margaret in *serviteur* fashion by returning the scarf to her lifeless body after she removes it from his pocket.

## The Cross-within-a-Circle Cosmogram

A closer inspection of the neo-slave narrative *Beloved* as an intertexual precursor to *Margaret Garner* reveals that Morrison ambiguously associates the ancestral cosmogram of spiritual remembrance and continuance after death typically with those who are African born or not far removed from the continent generationally. Sethe's mother, Ma'am, who survived a slave ship passage from Africa, to the Caribbean, and later to the North American mainland, has a cross-within-a-circle mark under her breast. Readers typically interpret it as a slave master's brand. Yet its precise geometricity calls attention to its ambiguity, since body tattooing or cicatricing of the cosmogram is a religious practice traceable to peoples of the Kongo.[49] Ma'am's instruction to Sethe that the mark will serve as the way that she will "know" her after death has an alternate meaning.[50] Sethe understands that it will assist in identifying her mother's dead body. Yet "Ma'am," a polite address for a woman, is also an abbreviation for "Mamam," a respectful title given to a Voudoun priestess. The symbol, therefore, also codifies the way by which Sethe and her mother will continue to remain spiritually connected with—or "know"—each other after her death. In another example from *Beloved*, Morrison overlays a natural element and a physical action that align the cosmogram's meaning with Sixo, an enslaved African at Sweet Home. Under a tree bearing the personified, familial title of Brother, he digs a hole at midday, the moment of the sun symbolizing the highest point of his earthly life. He later sacrifices his life to slave catchers to ensure both the survival of his progeny, Seven-O, and his own spiritual remembrance and continuation by the next generation of his lineage. Sethe's mother-in-law, Baby Suggs, who is steeped in religious ambiguity, provides a third example. Her role as an "unchurched" leader for a congregation of black people in a clearing encircled by trees near the way station situates her squarely as a caller of the ring shout.

In *Margaret Garner*, the accumulation of two natural elements synchronized by a temporal event conceals and reveals the cross within a circle, while the actions that follow it by slave catchers under a tree ambiguously underscore spiritual renaissance. After Robert strangles Casey and determines that he must run for freedom ahead of his family, the couple quickly devises a plan to meet at a wooded location via African time, time quantified by a natural event or phenomenon, in opposition to the measured calibration of Western time.[51] Robert instructs Margaret to meet him "When the moon hits / The tops of the pines" (act 2, scene 1); thus the moon, a circle, intersects with a pine, a symbolic cross. Later, the posse that encircles the tree used to lynch him ritualistically rings its trunk "one by one" with torches (act 2, scene 2) similarly to the way that *serviteurs* place lighted candles around the base of a sacred tree during a Voudoun ceremony. Margaret's shouting "Never to be born again into slavery!" at Robert's death and the killing of her children highlighted by the cross-and-circle formation affirms the intersection, coming together and breaking apart, of spirit and flesh, her traditional ontological belief with regard to spiritual rebirth (act 2, scene 2).[52]

While the moon and pine overlay is subtle, others equally obscured appear in *Beloved*. After Paul D learns of Sethe's filicide from Stamp Paid, an Underground Railroad conductor, he secludes himself in a building with a cross atop it that used to be a church. Authorial commentary during his residency there centers on blacks', Sixo's, and his own genealogies. It informs the reader of Paul D's willingness in Alfred, Georgia, where he served on a chain gang after Sweet Home, "to stay alive in a place where a moon he had no right to was nevertheless there" and of "his little love" for "an aspen that confirmed" life.[53] During a visit by Stamp Paid at the former church, a mounted rider, looking for a slaughterhouse—a house of death—on Plank Road, a straight axis, stops to ask for directions. As he rides off, Stamp Paid makes "small circles in the palm of his left hand with two fingers of his right."[54] The "unchurched" Baby Suggs referenced above and a building displaying a cross that used to be a church complicate an exclusively Western, Christian reading in these descriptions.[55]

## Why Voodoo?

In *American Opera*, Elise K. Kirk notes that a number of early twentieth-century American librettists and dramatists, especially between the interwar years, "turned to themes of voodooism" and interrogates "why the obsession with the . . . ritual of voodoo?"[56] Sensationalism largely spearheaded the works of European Americans,[57] while the African-derived religion's mythical allure fueled the recurring treatments by African-American literary artists of the era: "The cult had become a kind of African American mythology that played a role in twentieth-century black theatre history, as Greek mythology did in seventeenth- and eighteenth-century Western opera and drama. Voodooism, as woven into the action, placed characters within intense dramatic postures of love, conflict, and heroism, always with a certain mythic presence."[58] In the final decade of the nineteenth century, the Chicago World's Fair contributed to Americans' myth building and imaginative regard of Haiti and its beliefs. The Dahomey Village and the Haitian Pavilion on the fairground's midway drew streams of American and international visitors and continual media attention. Americans' scrutiny of the Fon people of Dahomey, whose contributions to Haiti's Voudoun exceeded those of other African and indigenous cultures, led to the imaginative treatment and serious study of the Fon in their African and New World spaces.[59]

More than a century later, Morrison, too, draws on African traditional religious elements via Haiti to make her imaginative work's identifiable blackness resonate with a West and Central African mythic presence. She states:

> I remember hearing people screaming, back in the sixties, that we need our own myth, we have to make our own myths. . . . Well, I think that indeed some of us have done that, but I didn't make any, I just tried to see what was already there, and to use that as a kind of well-spring for my own work. Instead of inventing myths . . . I was just interested in finding what myths already existed. . . . I used it as a springboard out of which to say something which I thought had contemporary implications.[60]

To understand her turning to what was already there and using it as a springboard for her work, one has to have a keen insight into the historical moment out of which the first African-American librettists' sociopolitical sensibility and literary imaginary sprung.

Attending the Columbian Exposition twenty-eight years after the ratification of the Thirteenth Amendment that abolished slavery and involuntary servitude except as a punishment for a crime, African Americans who had not known slavery and older ones who had known it all too well claimed the early nineteenth-century victory of the African-descended peoples over the French in Saint Domingue as if it were their own.[61] The black republic that emerged with the reinstated Taino Indian name of Haiti had achieved in 1804 what the United States proudly declared in 1776, and later in 1783 at the signing of the Treaty of Paris, as its exceptional accomplishment: self-liberation through revolution from the oppressive stronghold of a European power. The Haitian Revolution, however, has been excluded from many accounts of the revolutionary period that shaped Western modernity despite it being on a par with the American Revolution (1765–1783) and temporally overlapping with the French Revolution (1789–1799). In the final decade of the nineteenth century, African Americans, particularly of the political and artistic intelligentsia, were unwilling to ignore or disavow the only revolution that had centered on the issue of race and ended in a successful slave rebellion. Christopher Robert Reed explains: "The Haytian Pavilion proudly stood in the northwest section of the fairgrounds. . . . It was one place, above all, where recognizable pride in color of skin existed for the mass of African Americans. . . . And although not completely under the influence of the Fon of Dahomey, whose numbers had filled the revolutionary ranks of the peasant army that won liberation, Hayti still knew Dahomey intimately."[62] By the second quarter of the twentieth century, African-American writers and artists, incensed by the US occupation, "used Haiti and its history as proxies for their own heritage and as a rallying cry for civil rights in the Unites States."[63]

Inversely, the fairground's Dahomey Village for African Americans represented Africa under European siege. The Berlin and Brussels conferences, respectively in 1884–85 and 1889, foretold that Europe's "scramble for Africa" was a clear and present colonial threat. From the morning of August 14 to the evening of August 21, 1893, continental and diaspora Africa, "along with Caucasians from Europe, Africa, and America," met at the exposition's Congress on Africa, which became the unexpected precursor to the first Pan-African Congress in 1900.[64] One European threat to Africa became a reality in the year following the exposition; the French successfully removed King Behanzia from the Dahomean throne.

Kirk's assertion that Voodooism "for black composers . . . was a symbolic voice from the past—a symbol of ignorance and bondage from which blacks such as Treemonisha longed to break free" is shortsighted.[65] It fails to acknowledge the respect and reverence that the religion has received and continues to garner from millions in its diaspora as a world religion and as a spiritual and political liberatory force in Haiti's revolution. African-American visual, literary, musical, and performance artists, after enslavement and in the first half of the twentieth century, depicted features of it as an objective correlative for blackness commensurate with the drum and the African mask.[66] These features in their art often go unseen critically or are dismissed summarily. Scott Joplin's libretto is a case in point.

Literary and opera scholars have not given *Treemonisha* a substantive, Africanist religious reading. Joplin biographer Edward A. Berlin, for example, observes the work lacks Christian references and "religious songs," explaining away their omissions as the composer/librettist's rejection of "organized religion" and "Joplin's ambivalence about the church." He questions why "the tree under which Treemonisha was found [as a newborn after a violent storm in an all-black Texarkana, Arkansas, 1884 plantation community encircled by trees not far from the Red River] is referred to as 'The Sacred Tree' . . . but the sacredness of the tree plays no function in the story."[67]

Joplin sets *Treemonisha* where he grew up, in Texarkana, which is called the "crossroads of the Southwest." The town's main street, State Line Avenue, a straight vertical axis and state border, divides Texarkana, Texas, which is predominantly white, and Texarkana, Arkansas, which is predominantly black. Placing a sacred tree and a title character with "Tree" grafted onto her name in an all-black crossroads community encircled with trees with a river that runs east-west through it are central to Joplin's accumulation of cross and circle elements in his libretto devoid of Christian references. Treemonisha's first directive to her community is to have a ring play, a circular dance akin to the ring shout. Her last is to lead a "'Real Slow Drag,' an ancient African form of procession."[68] Berlin states that Joplin told the *New York Age* that the opera was "strictly Negro,"[69] his way, perhaps, of classifying it as "identifiably black."

Morrison calls for her works to be "dismissed or embraced on the success of their accomplishment within the culture out of which [she] writes"; a culture that is both African and American. Pursuing what she calls the "elusive but identifiable style" of black literature[70] has resulted in her returning to an African-American libretto tradition that features New World, amalgamated, African traditional beliefs and mythologies and to an African art aesthetic of secrecy that conceals and reveals that she first strategically implemented in her novel writing. Morrison's obscured representations of Margaret Garner as a manifestation of Erzulie, the New World–originated divinity that Haitians created out of rage at enslavers' destruction of their families, and of the Voudoun cosmogram make her imaginative ambiguities at once identifiably black and a distinct creation of the Americas. Just as the libretto's narrative agitates for the humanity of all African-descended peoples, Morrison's obscuring of an identifiably black religion agitates to restore Africa's traditional beliefs to rightful remembrance and interpretation and to validate the black subject's humanity and reality in American and global post-enslavement and postcolonial life and literatures.

## NOTES

I wish to thank Marjorie Bradley Kellogg; Kenny Leon; Helena Woodard; Barry Hoberman; William Edward Willard; Jennifer B. Lee, Curator for the Performing Arts at Columbia University's Rare Book and Manuscript Library; and Amelia Peck and the Antonio Ratti Textile Center at the Metropolitan Museum of Art for their assistance with this text.

1. The libretto of a grand opera typically centers on or around a mythical or historical event. Performers sing all of its lyrics. A large-scale cast, orchestra, and lavish stage designs and effects characterize its operatic staging.

2. African traditional religions are the indigenous religious beliefs and practices of African peoples that have been passed down orally from one generation to the next. While generalizations are difficult due to the di-

versity of African cultures, most African traditional religions advocate harmonizing nature with the supernatural. They share in common the belief in a supreme being and in spirits and other divinities that function in many respects like saints and in the veneration of ancestors. Candomblé, Umbanda, and Quimbanda in Brazil; Santeria in Cuba and the United States; Lucumi in the Caribbean; and Voudoun in Haiti and the United States are among the major traditional religions that blacks in the diaspora practice. See John S. Mbiti, *African Religions and Philosophy* (New York: Doubleday, 1970); E. Geoffrey Parrinder, *African Traditional Religion* (London: Sheldon, 1974); and Kofi Asare Opoku, "African Traditional Religion: An Enduring Heritage," in *Religious Plurality in Africa: Essays in Honour of John S. Mbiti*, ed. Jacob K. Olupona and Sulayman S. Nyang (New York: Mouton de Gruyter, 1993), 67–82.

3. For discussions on the role Voudoun played in the Haitian Revolution, see Joan Dayan, *Haiti, History and the Gods* (Berkeley: U of California P, 1995); Carolyn E. Fick, *The Making of Haiti: The Saint Domingue Revolution from Below* (Knoxville: U of Tennessee P, 2000); and Kate Ramsey, *The Spirits and the Law: Vodou and Power in Haiti* (Chicago: U of Chicago P, 2011).

4. Toni Morrison, *Margaret Garner: Opera in Two Acts*, composed by Richard Danielpour, rev. ed. (New York: Associated Music, 2004), act 2, scene 3. All references to the libretto in the text are to this edition.

5. In an earlier version of the libretto, dated 10 June 2004, that was distributed to scholars and consultants who attended the August 2004 Detroit rehearsal performance and workshop, the Judges, substituting "sir" for "madam," repeat the allusion to Haiti to Caroline's husband, George Hancock, when he questions, "How can you condemn her / And not the crime that belittles her crime?" In *Their Eyes Were Watching God* (Philadelphia: Lippincott, 1937), Zora Neale Hurston similarly alludes to Haiti, where she wrote her most famous novel. Nanny, the grandmother of its protagonist Janie Mae Crawford, states, "Honey, de white man is de ruler of everything as fur as Ah been able tuh find out. Maybe it's some place way off in de ocean where de black man is in power, but we don't know nothin' but what we see" (29). Hurston also obliquely figures Janie as an Erzulie figure. For collected readings of Janie as Erzulie, see La Vinia Delois Jennings, *Zora Neale Hurston, Haiti, and "Their Eyes Were Watching God"* (Evanston: Northwestern UP, 2013).

6. Marjorie Bradley Kellogg, scenic designer for *Margaret Garner*'s Detroit premiere in 2005, also added, unknowingly, layered ambiguities to the

staged opera. First, she selected the pattern from a Star of Bethlehem quilt—sewn between 1837 and 1850 by two sisters, Ellen and Margaret Morton, who were enslaved on the Marmaduke Beckwith Morton plantation in Russellville, Logan County, Kentucky—for the opera's backdrop and surround. While documented, historical evidence is unavailable, the eight-point quilt pattern, a variation of the crossroads and the compass points between formed by a + and x overlay, may contain an African message of spiritual renaissance. Second, she used an eight-point overlay or star inside a circle that was architecturally in vogue in the United States from the 1830s until after the Civil War to adorn the triangular, Greek Revival pediment suspended over the courtroom's set. The star's design replicates the stars used in Haitian *vevers* and on banners honoring the *loa*. Following Robert's lynching and her commission of filicide, Margaret Garner sits mute at her trial under and surrounded by the crossroads and points between symbols. Kellogg "selected [the latter pediment feature] for its [architectural] historical accuracy. It was an intuitive thing that just happened. It didn't have an intellectual motive" (Telephone interview with Marjorie Bradley Kellogg, 4 Apr. 2008). For more on the Morton quilt and its enslaved, Kentucky quilters, see Claire Somersille Nolan, "The Star of Bethlehem Variation Quilt at the Metropolitan Museum of Art," *Uncoverings 2005* 26 (9–7 Oct. 2005): 93–119.

7. Mary H. Nooter, ed., "The Aesthetics and Politics of Things Unseen," Introduction, *Secrecy: African Art That Conceals and Reveals* (New York: Museum for African Art, 1993), 25. T. O. Beidelman, in "Secrecy and Society: The Paradox of Knowing and the Knowing of Paradox," states that the "complexities of . . . secrecy permeates all [African] societies" and "range from the Igbo and Ebira of Nigeria, the Nuer and other Nilotes and the Azande of southern Sudan, the Kongo of Zaire, the Ndembu of Zambia, the Lugbara of Uganda, the Kaguru of Tanzania, and Swazi and Sotho of southern Africa" among others (43). Suzanne Preston Blier, in "Art and Secret Agency: Concealment and Revelation in Artistic Expression," places the "accumulations of diverse materials . . . used for aggressive and protective ends" in "the Fon tradition of *bocio* carvings" and "deity shrines" (186, 187). Both essays appear in Nooter.

8. Nooter, "The Aesthetics and Politics of Things Unseen," 33.

9. Nooter, "The Visual Language of Secrecy," in *Secrecy: African Art That Conceals and Reveals*, 49–63.

10. For contributions to opera and the operetta before 1893 by African

Americans—John Thomas Douglass (1847–1886) and Louisa Melvin De-
los Mars (dates unknown)—see Elise K. Kirk, *American Opera* (Urbana: U
of Illinois P, 2001). African Americans did not write the libretti for the
grand operas of New Orleans-born and free persons of color Edmond
Dédé (1827–1903) and Charles-Lucien Lambert (1826–1896).

11. H. Lawrence Freeman, *Voodoo: A Grand Opera in Three Acts* (New York: Negro Opera Company, 1926). Also see his "The Negro in Music and Drama."
N.d. MS. H. Lawrence Freeman Papers. Columbia University Rare Book
and Manuscript Library, New York. 276, 75.

12. Valdo Freeman confirmed his father and Joplin's discussion of *Treemoni-
sha* in a letter dated 19 Oct. 1971 to Addison W. Reed. See Addison W. Reed.
"Scott Joplin, Pioneer," in *Ragtime: Its History, Composers, and Music,* ed.
John Edward Hasse (New York: Schirmer, 1985), 132, 135. Joplin's first
grand opera score and libretto, *A Guest of Honor* (1903), has been lost. See
Edward A. Berlin, *King of Ragtime: Scott Joplin and His Era* (Oxford: Oxford
UP, 1994).

13. Freeman moved from Cleveland to Harlem around 1910. He and his family lived on the famous Strivers' Row at 239 West 139th Street. They later
moved to 214 West 127th Street. The 1910 Census lists Joplin residing at 128
West Twenty-Ninth Street, New York, New York. In 1914, Joplin moved
uptown from 252 West Forty-Seventh Street to 133 West 138th Street. See
Berlin, *King of Ragtime,* 222–23, 234. In 1893 Freeman attended the Chicago
World's Fair to oversee the staging of *The Martyr.* Joplin played his syncopated piano rags outside the fairgrounds along Dearborn Street, which
was lined with integrated cafés and saloons. See Christopher Robert
Reed, *"All the World Is Here!": The Black at White City* (Bloomington: Indi-
ana UP, 2000); and Celia Elizabeth Davidson, "Operas by Afro-American
Composers: A Critical Survey and Analysis of Selected Works," PhD
diss., Catholic University of America, Washington, DC. 1980.

14. See Berlin, *King of Ragtime,* 214–15.

15. Ibid., 235.

16. Freeman, "The Negro in Music and Drama," 82.

17. The return address of Still's 15 Nov. 1921 letter to Freeman listed the
younger composer's address as 1381 Leland Ave, Bronx, New York.

18. John Frederick Matheus's libretto for Clarence Cameron White's *Ouanga!*
(1932; Creole for "spell"), a grand opera that falls within this tradition,
also treats Dessalines's reign and features of Voudoun.

19. The spelling "Voodoo" indicates the US derivative of Dahomean Vodun.

20. Freeman, "The Negro in Music and Drama," 4–5.

21. H. Lawrence Freeman, "The Martyr," 1893, MS. H. Lawrence Freeman Papers, Columbia University Rare Book and Manuscript Library, New York. In "The Negro in Music and Drama" Freeman does not list *Epthelia* (1891), an operetta that he wrote before *The Martyr*, among his later works perhaps because it was a first attempt that did not measure up to his personal standards and because it did not meet the criteria for a grand opera. His final public operatic appearance would take place in 1947 when he conducted a production of *The Martyr* at Carnegie Hall.

22. On 26 and 27 June 2015, Annie Holt, who had cataloged Freeman's papers as a graduate student for Columbia University's Rare Book and Manuscript Library, produced a concert performance of Freeman's *Voodoo* at Columbia University's Miller Theatre. Soprano Janinah Burnett sang the role of Lolo. Alberta Zuber, a relative of Freeman's by marriage, who had performed a small role in *The Martyr* at Carnegie Hall in 1947 was present at the premiere performance of the revival.

23. "Columbia's Rare Book and Manuscript Library Acquires Papers of H. Lawrence Freeman, Musician and Composer," *Columbia U Libraries News*, 5 Feb. 2008.

24. Shirley Graham, *Tom-Tom*, in *The Roots of African-American Drama: An Anthology of Early Plays,* ed. Leo Hamalian and James V. Hatch (Detroit: Wayne State UP, 1991), 238–86. Graham's one-act play *It's Morning* (1940) also depicts a slave mother's filicide.

25. Arnold Rampersad, *The Life of Langston Hughes, vol. 1: 1902–1941* (Oxford: Oxford UP, 2002), 330.

26. Ibid., 7, 19. Chesnutt published *The Conjure Woman* in 1899, seven short stories that drawn upon Voodoo myths and practices and profiles black resistance to enslavement and white culture.

27. Langston Hughes, letter to Verna Arvey, 7 Oct. 1936, MS. William Grant Still Papers, Special Collections, U of Arkansas Fayetteville Libraries.

28. Langston Hughes, letter to William Grant Still, 7 Jan. 1937, MS. William Grant Still Papers, Special Collections. U of Arkansas Fayetteville Libraries.

29. Rampersad, *The Life of Langston Hughes,* 330–31.

30. Langston Hughes, letter to William Grant Still, 7 Jan. 1937.

31. Hughes, *Troubled Island: An Opera in Three Acts,* composed by William Grant Still (New York: Leeds, 1949), act 1, scene 1.

32. Toni Morrison, "Pride and Joy," *Time,* 5 Apr. 2004.

33. Middleton Harris, ed., *The Black Book* (New York: Random, 1974), 41.

34. P. S. Bassett, "From the American Baptist: A Visit to the Slave Mother Who Killed Her Child," *National Anti-Slavery Standard*, 15 Mar. 1856. Rpt. in Harris, *The Black Book*, 10. Harris, *The Black Book*, 133–48.

35. *Beloved* (New York: Plume, 1987), contains an extended passage comparing Ohio's seasons to an opera (116).

36. Steven Weisenburger, *Modern Medea: A Family Story of Slavery and Child-Murder from the Old South* (New York: Hill and Wang, 1998), 279.

37. Sterling Stuckey, *Slave Culture: Nationalist Theory and the Foundations of Black America* (Oxford: Oxford UP, 1987), 11–12. See Robert Farris Thompson and Joseph Cornet, *The Four Moments of the Sun: Kongo Art in Two Worlds* (Washington, DC: National Gallery of Art, 1981).

38. In the tri-city performances Margaret wears a fancy, red dress in Gaines's house. The red scarf receives expanded authorial treatment in the libretto draft distributed for the 2004 Detroit rehearsal performance and workshop. In act 1, scene 2, Casey, after delivering the fancy dress to Margaret, meets with Gaines, who sits in his parlor stroking her red scarf as he sings about it. Casey and Robert's parlor meeting was excised from the published libretto.

39. While Gaines's display of the red scarf here is not indicated in the libretto, it was enacted onstage during the premiere performances. Morrison's approval was needed for any libretto changes.

40. See Theresa Higgins, *Religiosity, Cosmology, and Folklore: The African Influence in the Novels of Toni Morrison* (New York: Routledge, 2001); La Vinia Delois Jennings, *Toni Morrison and the Idea of Africa* (Cambridge: Cambridge UP, 2008); K. Zauditu-Sellasie, *African Spiritual Traditions in the Novels of Toni Morrison* (Gainesville: UP of Florida, 2009); Justine Tally, *Toni Morrison's "Beloved": Origins* (New York: Routledge, 2009); Vashti Crutcher Lewis, "African Tradition in Toni Morrison's *Sula*," *Phylon* 48.1 (1987): 91–97; and Holly Fils-Aimé, "The Living Dead Learn to Fly: Themes of Spiritual Death, Initiation and Empowerment in *A Praisesong for the Widow* and *Song of Solomon*," *Mid-Atlantic Writers Association Review* 10.1 (June 1995): 3–12.

41. Barbara Christian, "Fixing Methodologies, *Beloved*," *Cultural Critique* 24 (Spring 1993): 9–10.

42. Morrison, *Beloved*, 8, 117.

43. Maya Deren, *Divine Horsemen: The Voodoo Gods of Haiti* (1953; London: Thames and Hudson, 1970), 62.

44. Ibid., 143.

45. Ibid., 61–71.

46. Zora Neale Hurston, *Tell My Horse: Voodoo and Life in Haiti and Jamaica* (Philadelphia: Lippincott, 1938), 144.

47. Morrison, *Beloved*, 114–17.

48. Deren, *Divine Horsemen*, 26. Iconography depicts Erzulie Dantor, another emanation of the divinity of love, as a black woman holding a child protectively in her arms. Her *serviteurs* represent her with the image of Poland's Black Madonna of Czestochowa.

49. Wilfrid D. Hambly, *The Ovimbundu of Angola*. Anthropological Series 21.2 (Chicago: Field Museum of Natural History, 1934), n.p.; Maureen Warner-Lewis, *Central Africa in the Caribbean: Transcending Time, Transforming Cultures* (Kingston: U of West Indies P, 2003), 75.

50. Morrison, *Beloved*, 6.

51. John S. Mbiti, *African Religions and Philosophy* (New York: Doubleday, 1970), 21, 23.

52. The pine and moon accumulation, however, bears a closer resemblance to the sun rising behind "the outline of a huge cross . . . where there used to be a Jesus" (12) in the Convent during the opening scene of Morrison's novel *Paradise* (New York: Knopf, 1998). Once a residence for Catholic nuns, the Convent has become a refuge for outcast women whose Brazilian-born leader practices a fusion of Catholicism and Candomblé. In act 2, scene 3 of the 2004 Detroit rehearsal performance libretto, "Margaret and Robert dance a teasing, 'catch me' dance around the tree. Margaret picks a leaf from the tree and caresses Robert's face with it." Robert, "suddenly coming to his senses . . . gently plac[es] the leaf in Margaret's hair." Their circular dance around a tree and the temporary displacement of Robert's senses support an abstracting or obscuring of images/events designed to conceal and reveal an invocation of African traditional elements. The dance was excised from the published libretto.

53. Morrison, *Beloved*, 221.

54. Ibid., 231.

55. See Jennings, *Toni Morrison and the Idea of Africa*, 166–77.

56. Kirk, *American Opera*, 195.

57. Two examples are Laurence Stallings's voodoo-themed libretto set in 1834 New Orleans for W. Franke Harling's opera *Deep River* (1926), and John Houseman's production of *Macbeth* (1936), known as "the Voodoo Macbeth," directed by Orson Welles.

58. Kirk, *American Opera*, 195–96.

59. Not all imaginative treatments were serious. Composer Will Marion Cook and lyricist Paul Laurence Dunbar, meeting at the exposition, collaborated on the successful Broadway musical comedy with a high operetta finale, *In Dahomey* (1903), based on the book of the same name by Jesse A. Shipp.

60. Cecil Brown, "Interview with Toni Morrison," in *Toni Morrison: Conversations*, ed. Carolyn C. Denard (Jackson: UP of Mississippi, 2008), 114.

61. Similarly, an African-American celebration of Ethiopia (Abyssinia) increased after Italy failed to colonize the east African nation in 1896.

62. Reed, *"All the World Is Here!,"* 173.

63. Karen M. Bryan, "Clarence Cameron White's *Ouanga!* in the World of the Harlem Renaissance," in *Blackness in Opera*, ed. Naomi André et al. (Urbana: U of Illinois P, 2012), 117.

64. Reed, *"All the World Is Here!,"* 189.

65. Kirk, *American Opera*, 194.

66. Alain Locke illustrated *The New Negro* (1925) with African masks prints, while Eugene O'Neill in *The Emperor Jones* (1920) relied on the drum to evoke blackness. O'Neill's play inspired Kathleen de Jaffa's libretto for Louis Gruenberg's 1933 opera of the same name.

67. Berlin, *King of Ragtime*, 206, 203.

68. Scott Joplin, *Treemonisha. Opera in Three Acts* (New York: Published by the composer, 1911). Klaus-Dieter Gross, "The Politics of Scott Joplin's *Treemonisha*," *Amerikastudien* 45.3 (2000): 391. Notably, scenic designer Franco Colavecchia displays the ancestral cosmogram in the Houston Grand Opera's 1982 video recording of *Treemonisha*.

69. Berlin, *King of Ragtime*, 202.

70. Toni Morrison, "Rootedness: The Ancestor as Foundation," in *Black Women Writers (1950–1980): A Critical Evaluation*, ed. Mari Evans (New York: Doubleday, 1984), 342.

# Imagining Margaret Garner

*Classical and Contemporary Texts and Intertexts*

* AIMABLE TWAGILIMANA *

From the time the press broke the story of the Garners in Cincinnati, Ohio, in January 1856, Margaret Garner inspired political and literary reactions across the nation until the 1870s, and then her story faded from the national consciousness. Toni Morrison's novel *Beloved* (1987) resurrected it to the latter, twentieth-century, American historical and literary landscape. An iconic figure of antebellum America whose infanticide and trial in the free state of Ohio propelled her to national legend, mostly through ventriloquisms—others speaking for and through her[1]—Margaret Garner seemed relegated to oblivion after Reconstruction. Morrison, however, read about the enslaved, Kentucky woman in a nineteenth-century newspaper story when she served as the project editor for *The Black Book* (1974), an overview of black American history, at Random House and decided to write a novel about the tragic saga. The Cincinnati newspapers gave more or less the following account. On January 27, 1856, Margaret Garner, her husband Robert, and other family members clandestinely left Richwood, Kentucky, crossed the frozen Ohio River, and reached Cincinnati, Ohio, where slavery was illegal. Before they could be taken to a secure location, the owner of Margaret Garner and her children, Archibald K. Gaines, a posse of slave catchers, and US Marshals surrounded the cabin of Joe and Elijah Kite where she and her family had sought temporary refuge. James Marshall, who owned Robert, was not a member of the posse. His son, however, was among the group to represent his interests. From here journalistic reports and their ventriloquisms inserted themselves. Reportedly reacting on instinct, Margaret Garner killed Mary, her two-and-a-half-year-old daughter, with a knife, and only managed to wound her three other children. Her intention was to kill all four children and herself rather than have them returned to a life of enslavement. Arrested and put on trial in a Cincinnati court, she was eventually released to Gaines, her Kentucky slave master, and returned to slavery, an institution she abhorred. This is the abbreviated, real-life story that many who were engrossed in the political and ideological debates surrounding slavery that preceded and accompanied the American Civil War immediately repeated or appropriated. Journalists reported accounts of it in national newspapers. Politicians debated it in the Ohio legislature. Religious leaders used it as a text for their sermons and speeches. Since she was not at liberty to represent herself to all these groups, the popular imagination constructed Margaret Garner in various ways that, paradoxically, created a mythic image of her that also reflected her ventriloquists' anxieties about the self, the other, and the nation.

Once Margaret Garner's child murder became a national fixation and a cause célèbre, her story's narrativizing issued an invitation for the appropriating of similarly plotted classical stories and contemporary popular narratives as intertexts. Thus preexisting narratives available to those who followed the reports of her story influenced their reading of the Kentucky slave mother who had committed infanticide. In the contemporary category, the slave narrative[2] and the sentimental narrative, with its panoply of themes including motherhood, the Cult of True Womanhood, and sympathy—popularized by Harriet Beecher Stowe's *Uncle Tom's Cabin* (1851)[3]—fueled the ongoing political debates surrounding slavery, especially following the passage of the Fugitive Slave Law in 1850.

A critical investigation of classical texts that contemporary commentators invoked as earlier paradigms for Margaret Garner's real-life infanticide, particularly *Virginius, Medea,* and the reworking of these tragedies over the years, reveals a nineteenth-century narrative wearing its storiness on its sleeve, so to speak. From literary and visual artists' reactions to it in the years before and after the Civil War, to Toni Morrison's resurrection of Garner's story in her 1987 Pulitzer Prize–winning novel *Beloved* and in her 2004 libretto *Margaret Garner,* the task of establishing Garner's motive lingers. When she committed infanticide, her contemporaries, faced with the extreme violence of the act and the epistemological challenges that came with it, turned to familiar references to explain the seemingly inexplicable phenomenon of a mother killing her own child. Roman and Greek mythologies and their incarnations in

Western literatures emerged as the most fitting intertexts to understand the impulses of a murderous mother.

Julia Kristeva's concept of "intertextuality" refers to the literary reality that texts refer to and enrich other texts, among other things, and thus have the potential to create communities of texts and readers. Like writers, readers associate their analytical perspectives with authoritative texts as a way of appropriating an authority that confers upon them membership in a select, interpretive community. Texts are available on the world scene; anyone can claim them, adapt them, and make their canonical authority carry the burden of a textually compatible story. By invoking authoritative texts and ideas, readers of the historical Margaret Garner's story bestowed authority on her as a text by invoking intellectual tools that gave them access to her experience and allowed them to make bold connections between her and the state of the nation.[4]

Like the protagonists in ancient Greek tragedy, Margaret Garner became a corporeal text on which her contemporaries inscribed both the anxiety of a nation in thrall to an unjust and inhumane institution and the locus of political, cultural, and gender issues that went to the heart of where the nation stood on the argument concerning legalized chattel slavery. To process the cruel realities of American slavery, however, they needed to turn her into a metaphor that allowed them to interpret in her a wide range of private and public issues and motives. Connecting her to Livy's Virginius, to Medea through Euripides's, Seneca's, and Pierre Corneille's tragedies, and to François-Benoît Hoffmann's libretto for Luigi Cherubini's 1797 opera *Médée*, I read Margaret Garner, following the scholarship of I. A. Richards, as the "vehicle" of a textual metaphor whose "tenor" encompasses the various issues that her infanticide allowed her contemporaries to debate. Those issues included the state of the nation regarding slavery in the years leading up to the Civil War; the commodification of enslaved persons in antebellum America; women's identity in general and the peculiar plight of women of African descent in particular in nineteenth-century America; the betrayal of American ideals; and the heroic (if extreme) sacrifice a mother was capable of in the name of freedom and love.[5] Depictions of Margaret Garner's story ranged from those of abolitionists such as John Jolliffe, Levi Coffin, and Lucy Stone imagining her as a female Virginius to other commentators, in newspapers editorials in Cincinnati and around the nation, drawing similar classical parallels. For example, a writer for the *New York*

*Daily Tribune* of 1856 compared her to "the Greek hero Mithridates, who sacrifices his wife and sister rather than surrender them to a life of concubinage."[6] Frances Ellen Watkins Harper, in the 1859 poem "The Slave Mother: A Tale of Ohio," commemorates Margaret Garner's killing of her daughter rather than returning her to slavery. Thomas Satterwhite Noble in the 1867 painting *The Modern Medea*, following the narrative of the painting's titular subject, deposits two male children dead at Garner's feet rather than a single daughter. Each of these works assisted in transforming Margaret Garner into a myth that Toni Morrison amplifies in her novel and libretto as does the abundant literary criticism that followed these two, latter-day adaptations of Garner's story. With the help of these various intertexts, Margaret Garner has come to represent the consequences of extreme injustice trampling on the ideals of a nation and thus making her story not just an individual tragedy but a national tragedy that unfolded on the public stage before the entire country just as the aforementioned tragedies unfolded on the dramatic stage in ancient Rome and Greece.

Following Margaret Garner's infanticide, abolitionists, especially those directly involved in her defense in Cincinnati, compared her action to the Roman legend of the centurion Lucius Virginius. According to Roman historian Livy, Virginius killed his daughter Virginia in order to place her beyond the reach of the tyrant Appius Claudius, who was intent on manipulating the law in order to commit her to a life of sexual slavery.[7] As the story goes, Appius Claudius, known for his brutality and his lust, desired Virginia and used legal maneuvering to argue that she was his slave and not Virginius's daughter. In the courtroom Virginius calmly proceeded to stab his daughter with a knife to free her from Appius Claudius's plot of sexual enslavement.

Following a conversation that she had with Margaret Garner in her jail cell, Lucy Stone, who was also a women's rights activist, was granted an audience in the courtroom on the last day of the trial after a special marshal had taken out the Garners and Commissioner John L. Pendery, whose job it was to decide the legal fate of the Garners in their Cincinnati trial, had left the scene. Stone alluded to the "faded faces"—light skin complexions—of Margaret Garner's children telling to "what degradation female slaves submit" as Garner's infanticide motive.[8] Thus Stone argued that Garner's action aimed to protect her children from experiencing a similar dehumanization, humiliation, and sexual exploitation.

Nineteenth-century Americans were familiar with the story of Virginius as told by Roman historian Livy (Titus Livius) and popularized by the Irish dramatist James Sheridan Knowles's 1820 tragedy *Virginius: A Tragedy in Five Acts*, which was first performed in Covent Garden. Knowles published his rendering in America in 1826, and according to a February 8, 1856, editorial in the *New York Daily Tribune*, it was subsequently performed on American stages as "one of the most touching and effective of recent tragedies."[9] Thomas Babington Macaulay's *Lays of Ancient Rome*, published in the United States three years before Margaret Garner's run for freedom, also popularized Virginius's story.[10]

Lucius Virginius's killing of his daughter led the Roman citizenry to overthrow the tyrant Appius Claudius, forcing a return to a just republic. As literary critic Mark Reinhardt argues, "The advantages of identifying Margaret's virtues with those of this classical hero are obvious. In understanding that there are things worse than death, things worth the deliberate sacrifice of human life, Virginius is the quintessential man of honor; that is why he deserves the freedom that is restored to him when the people join him in defeating tyranny."[11] So the invocation of Virginius in the Margaret Garner story is a locutionary act that stages several illocutionary acts. First, it proclaims Margaret Garner's action a heroic one in the name of a higher ideal—freedom—worth dying for. Second, it condemns slavery and its attendant laws, for example, the 1850 Fugitive Slave Act, as worse than death. Third, it functions as an indirect warning to the court to give Margaret Garner her freedom lest it should be seen as condoning servitude. Fourth, it spearheads a national conversation about the sexual exploitation of enslaved women and elicits sympathy for them in a democratic society that treasures sexual purity, one of the defining cardinal virtues of the Cult of True Womanhood.[12]

The invocation of Virginius in the heat of the Margaret Garner trial provided her supporters with a public stage to talk about her love of freedom for herself, for her family, and for her fellow African Americans in bondage, as well as to address her willingness to make the ultimate sacrifice for the national ideal of freedom. The *New York Daily Tribune*'s invocation of Virginius's heroism conferred the same heroism on Margaret Garner, thus equating slavery and the Fugitive Slave Law with the moral corruption of Appius Claudius in the pursuit of Virginia. Just as Appius Claudius was a corrupt leader, slavery and the laws that sustained its institutionalization had long corrupted American democratic ideals and threatened the integrity and founding ethos of the nation.

Honor, control, and deliberation, as Virginius demonstrated in calmly taking his daughter's life, were the defining attributes of a stalwart, public Roman figure, yet Margaret Garner's action of killing her daughter in the real-life story and in the plot of Morrison's libretto was the spontaneous result of a justified delirium—"justified" for someone like Garner, who had intimately experienced slavery, and for those who have studied it and know of its dehumanizing power. As Reinhardt remarks, "The adjectives [that reporters] used to characterize her state of mind [at the moment of the crime]—used repeatedly, with remarkable lack of variation—were 'frantic' and 'frenzied,' as in the 'instinct of the frantic mother was truer than reason' and 'perhaps . . . a jury of freemen would have found a mitigation of crime in the sudden frenzy of the mother.'"[13] In other words, Margaret Garner's action of attempting to stab her children and successfully slashing the throat of one of them when she saw the slave catchers approaching stands in sharp relief to the calm stoicism that Virginius displays in the courtroom when he stabs his daughter Virginia to thwart Appius Claudius's plot to possess her sexually. But the "frantic" and "frenzied" descriptions may have been simply a deliberate, rhetorical strategy to rationalize her repulsive act.

The reference to Lucius Virginius in the *New York Daily Tribune* on February 8, 1856, may have, with a deranged twist, served to amplify Margaret Garner's tragedy and to explain her unspeakable action even to those who were sympathetic with her formidable plight yet unable to grasp fully its horror. The Virginius allusion was a direct and unequivocal indictment of an unjust institution that made her infanticide possible, and it was also a call to action. As Reinhardt argues, "The use of Virginius is a reminder, too, of the ultimate hope of those who sought to use the Garner case to inspire antislavery action; the result of this violence is a political rebellion that reestablishes freedom."[14]

Similarly, Margaret Garner's story became the subject of intense debates in the courthouse and streets of Cincinnati as well as in the national media concerning its impact on constitutional law.[15] Her infanticide spearheaded arguments about one of the cruelest aspects of bondage—chattel slavery—the commodification of human beings who were not recognized as being human. Would Garner be tried as a human being—her personhood validated—and thus be charged with the murder of her daughter? With a charge of murder, which abolitionists involved in the case on the side of the defense wanted, the Ohio State Court would validate her legal personhood. Or would the court regard her as a nonperson who had destroyed her master's property and, therefore, as property herself under the federal Fugitive Slave Law? The latter, not surprisingly, was the position of Gaines, Marshall, and the prosecution that upheld the Southern ideology that enslaved persons were the property of their slave masters. Jolliffe and Stone argued for state laws to prevail, as Margaret Garner had crossed the Ohio River and resided, albeit briefly, in the free state of Ohio. She, therefore, was free under the jurisprudence established by freedom suits, whereby free states held that slaves were wrongfully enslaved if their owners traveled or resided with them in these states. Even though one such case, *Dred Scott v. Sandford,* reached the US Supreme Court and was finally adjudicated in an 1857 landmark decision that declared slaves private properties that therefore could not be taken away from their owners without due process, numerous other freedom suits were successful in the 1840s and 1850s. Jolliffe also made another argument based on the First Amendment of the US Constitution. The Fugitive Slave Law, he asserted, violated religious freedom by forcing citizens, against their faiths, to return fugitive slaves once they had entered free states. His argument was more an emotional appeal to the public than an argument of jurisprudence that he hoped would carry weight with Commissioner Pendery.

Unlike other cases involving enslaved persons that had been quickly tried and a ruling rendered in less than a day, the Garner case, *Archibald K. Gaines, Claimant, v. Margaret Garner and Her Three Children,* took four weeks. What is significant about its protracted adjudication is that it became a public spectacle with tragic connotations. Not only was it "the longest-running and most expensive fugitive slave trial in American history,"[16] but it also attracted large crowds both inside and outside the courthouse. Thousands of people converged on Cincinnati to witness the event. More than four hundred people were hired to keep order. Those who gathered to witness the two weeks of arguments inside the courtroom and outside it on the streets mirrored an Athenian audience flocking to a play by Aeschylus, Euripides, and Sophocles. After the closing arguments of Jolliffe and of Colonel Francis Chambers, the Cincinnati attorney who led the team representing Gaines's and Marshall's claims to the Garner fugitives, Pendery deliberated two weeks before ruling in favor of the prosecution and the slaveholders. Gaines then took Margaret Garner and her family back to Kentucky, back to the throes of slavery, back to the inhumanity that she had feared for herself and for her children.

The contemporary appropriating of another classical tragedy, the story of Medea in Greek mythology, which Thomas Satterwhite Noble's painting invoked eleven years later, stands out as a posttrial, intertextual, classical narrative that visually contributes to preserving the Garner story for posterity. Not only the mythological origin of the Medea story but its numerous reiterations, first in drama and opera and later in cinema and television, have secured it a fixed place in the popular American imaginary. In the classical versions, Medea kills her two children accidentally, the Corinthians murder them, or, as Euripides's version depicts, she deliberately kills them to spite her husband, Jason, for abandoning her for another woman. Although the mythical plot was not immediately invoked during the Margaret Garner case, Americans at that time were familiar with Medea's story through Giovanni Mayr's *Medea in Corinth* (1813) and Ernest Legouvé's *Medea, a Tragedy in Three Acts* (1856). Productions of both had toured in the United States.[17]

While the juxtaposition of Medea and Margaret Garner might seem unjustified because of the incongruities between Medea's and Garner's motives for infanticide, a careful study of play scripts and libretti devoted to their representations readily points to far-reaching ideological affiliations that justify the references to Margaret Garner as the "Modern Medea," as Noble's 1867 painting depicts her and as Steven Weisenburger's historiographical investigation of Garner echoes in its title more than a century later. Both mothers' displays of unrestrained, extreme emotions untempered by the control of reason and behavioral moderation, in fact, underscore the enduring connection between the individual and national concerns, one of the topical staples of classical tragedy. The demise of a noble citizen—a plot convention that befalls the hero/ine of a tragedy—often has major sociopolitical implications for the nation as a whole.

While Medea has many traits of nobility, Margaret Garner does not, at least not any supportable by the paucity of particulars known about her life before the Cincinnati trial. Medea is the granddaughter of the sun god, who sends a chariot for her at the end of Euripides's tragedy. She is the daughter of a king, thus a princess, albeit from a barbarian land. She is also the former wife of Jason, a hero, and indeed she possesses magical powers that she often uses for deadly schemes. Ultimately, her familial background, marital status, and fantastical capabilities are inconsequential once she comes to represent issues larger than herself, notably the abject social plight of women in ancient Greece and the Mediterranean region. Conversely, the historical and libretto Margaret Garner, an American slave, has no claim to nobility. In fact, slavery has dehumanized and denationalized her, that is, reduced her, her family, and others in her Richwood, Kentucky, slave community to mere "Zoë" (Greek for "naked life"), to use Giorgio Agamben's term.[18] Still, the discourses that her infanticide generated propelled the historical Garner to a level that transcended her individuality and allowed her to embody the anxieties of an entire nation on the eve of and during the Civil War. Granted, infanticide in both cases is morally reprehensible, but Medea's and Garner's actions, or rather reactions, are symptomatic of larger human, racial, and gender issues that go beyond individual preoccupations and affect ways of understanding democratic values in both ancient Greece and antebellum America. If Greek tragedy were a venue for experimentation in democracy, one might ask whether a woman has any inalienable rights in a male-dominated society in which her respect, dignity, and personhood come from and through the father or husband who, in a sense, is her owner. One might also question the inalienable rights of a woman who subordinates herself to and for her husband or to patriarchy in general, as conveyed through the extreme ways by which Medea empowers and submits herself to Jason, who then, in turn, has the right to cast her off arbitrarily.

The historical and libretto Margaret Garner's extreme action matches mid-nineteenth-century America's extreme racial injustice to its African-American population in general and to women of African descent in particular. Thus critics making this nexus might construe her commission of infanticide as a metaphor for the extreme dehumanization, denationalization, and humiliation of those enslaved, especially women, in a male-dominated society. The tragedy of Margaret Garner, an enslaved mother, was in that sense a national tragedy, an interpretation that Toni Morrison's libretto underscores by placing the infanticide and the trial within the timeline of the onset of the Civil War, several years removed from the dates of the original story, and framing it in the classical format of a tragedy—act 1 of the libretto takes places in 1856 and 1858, while act 2 is set in February, March, and April of 1861.

Thomas Satterwhite Noble was the first formal visual artist to connect classically the ancient Medea and the modern Garner, representing the latter in portraiture as heroic. Steven Weisenburger drew upon the classical allusion, titling his 1998 book on Garner *Modern Medea: A Family History of Slavery and Child-Murder from the Old South*, but without any direct attempt to prove that Margaret Garner met the paradigms of a modern Medea, except through the subtitle's allusion to infanticide. Toni Morrison herself has on more than one occasion resisted the comparison, stating, for example, that Margaret Garner "is not Medea who kills her children because she's mad at some dude, and she's going to get back at him. Here is something that is huge and very intimate."[19] Yet, in her libretto, she clearly brings Garner closer to the ancient Medea by presenting her in the format of a tragedy and having her kill two children, as does Euripides in his dramatization of Medea. Morrison's connecting Margaret Garner to Medea in this detail further increases the critical likelihood of committing Garner to posterity through yet another revivification of classical intertextuality. In addition, the invocation of Medea as an intertext in the discourse surrounding the infanticide speaks directly to two ideas associated with intertextuality, alienation and knowledge, and the retrospective and introspective relationship between them.

Both Medea and Margaret Garner are products of severe alienation from every meaningful relationship. Falling in love with Jason when he arrives in her homeland, Colchis, to recover the golden fleece that has been taken from his homeland, Iolcus, Medea flees with Jason after using her magical arts against her own family to assist him with its retrieval. Therefore, she cannot return to Colchis, having duped her father and murdered her brother. In Iolcus Medea and Jason find refuge, until she tricks the daughters of its king, Pelias, into killing their father, Jason's usurper uncle. King Pelias had given Jason the seemingly impossible task of recovering the fleece to keep him indefinitely preoccupied outside the country and therefore incapable of succeeding to the throne that he promises to abdicate when his nephew returns with the purloined wool. Medea can no longer reside in Colchis or Iolcus.

Set in Corinth, where both Jason and Medea are exiles, Euripides's play begins with the couple established in the city that has welcomed them as citizens. They have been there for several years and have two sons. But following Jason's marriage to the Corinthian king Creon's daughter, Glauce, Jason banishes Medea, who again becomes the quint-essential exile and wanderer—an abandoned and homeless wife, with-out a patriarchal identity. Medea's passion for Jason objectifies her, and thus undermines her identity as a human being. Spurred on by a less than human identity that recalls Margaret Garner's ontological status as subhuman based on the lawful dictates of the day, a deliberate, calcu-lated, cold rage guides Medea, permitting her to rationalize that if she does not kill her sons, then Creon, who sanctions Jason's marriage to Glauce and banishes her from Corinth, will ultimately kill them. Simi-larly Margaret takes her children's lives with her own hands rather than allow Gaines and the horrors of slavery ultimately to "murder" them "by piece-meal" in mind and body,[20] for slavery is a fate worse than death. In Toni Morrison's libretto, Margaret Garner stabs her two children while uttering "Never to be born again into slavery!" (act 2, scene 2).[21] From the outset, Euripides presents Medea as an abandoned and helpless wife who cannot psychically reconcile her husband's marital betrayal. Ini-tially, Euripides has her speak from offstage so that the spectator/reader can focus on the depth of Medea's despair while he or she sees and hears the Nurse and the Chorus. Medea's absence onstage conveys that she has been emptied of her wifely identity—the only identity in her society that gives her value and personhood. She invested all her powers in becom-ing and being Jason's wife, and now that he has abandoned her, she has nothing left. "The man was everything to me" (l.260),[22] she laments and then asks what is a woman who has sacrificed everything only to be left by her husband to do. In response to her self-interrogation, she opts for vengeance against Jason by killing their two sons.

In the libretto, Margaret Garner's alienation from personhood and from every meaningful relationship stems from her condition of en-slavement. Its plot opens with a political statement, "No more," a rejec-tion of slavery, accented with the African-American call-and-response antiphony. The Slaves' (Black Chorus's) "No more" alternates with the central character Margaret Garner's graphic cataloging of cruel acts and images associated with slavery: "Ankles circled with a chain," "Skin broken by a cane," "Bloody pillows under my head;/Wishing, praying I was dead" (act 1, scene 1). The opening frames the libretto's theme: the quest for freedom from enslavement that has engendered an impatient outcry against human injustices that have been enacted for far too long. Unfortunately, a sharp contrast follows, as the spectator/reader witnesses an auction scene that is familiar to readers of African-American literature and history. Family members anticipate being sold individually; the Townspeople (White Chorus) bid for the "picknies and mammies and breeders and bucks" (act 1, scene 1); and slave traders assert self-righteously that chattel property is a burden to their white owners who have to feed, clothe, and teach them. All these elements combine to convey the dehumanization of the enslaved. Directly following the Slaves' clamor for liberty, the Townspeople of *Margaret Garner* basically reiterate the same refrain, thus rejecting the clamor for freedom by the Slaves. They hold fast to the South's justification for the commodification of people of African descent. The Townspeople affirm that slavery is beneficial to the Slaves; it provides them food, shelter, and civilization. By juxtaposing the two choruses at the outset, the libretto foregrounds the corruption of the American ideal articulated in the Declaration of Independence and the US Constitution. A nation that lives contrary to its own founding principles is an American tragedy that plays out in Morrison's plotting of the libretto. In 1858, Abraham Lincoln famously conveyed this sentiment in a speech to the nation: "A house divided against itself cannot stand. I believe this government cannot endure, permanently, half slave and half free."[23]

Toni Morrison adroitly weaves the Civil War political drama into the libretto by changing the dates of the Margaret Garner story, situating them after the real-life story dates. While the historical Garners escaped in January 1856, the Garners' escape in the libretto's timeline occurs after the election of Lincoln in January 1861 and the secession of some Southern states but before his first inauguration on March 4, 1861. Margaret Garner and her family live free until late March, before a slave posse discovers their hideout and apprehends them. During the three-week interval, Robert Garner, Margaret's husband, repeats Lincoln's pronouncement—"That a house divided / Cannot stand. / And that the Union is sacred" (act 2, scene 2)—and reports rumors of an impending civil war. During this time Robert and Margaret dream of a normal life as husband and wife, a future in which Robert will be paid for his labor and the children will be educated and have leisure time to play instead of being forced to work for white landowners. The sudden appearance of Edward Gaines, Margaret's owner, and the posse of slave catchers shatters the family's hope for a free, autonomous future. Morrison's changing of dates for the Margaret Garner infanticide and trial situates the story squarely in the center of the national politics of the day, merging the individual, regional tragedy of Margaret Garner with the collective, national tragedy of innumerable persons of African descent. The merging of these two tragedies highlights Margaret Garner and all enslaved peoples' alienation from humanity. Commodified as were all slaves of her day, she is a consumable object at the service of her owner with no claim to the unalienable rights promised by the founding documents of the American republic.

Furthermore, because of her condition of servitude, the fictional Margaret Garner is alienated from every meaningful relationship. Early in the libretto (act 1, scene 2), there is a semblance of normal family life around supper time, when she is with Robert, her mother-in-law Cilla, and her baby, to whom she sings a lullaby. The appearance of Casey, the foreman of Gaines's Maplewood plantation, shatters the moment of familial bliss. He announces that Gaines has rented Robert to another plantation and assigned Margaret to his plantation house, a move that foreshadows Gaines's sexual exploitation of Margaret and her alienation from a normal marital relationship with her husband, since their separation will reduce them to seeing each other infrequently and clandestinely. Robert and Margaret's anticipation of a free and fulfilling family life after they escape to Cincinnati is thwarted. The slave posse's lynching of Robert signals an end to their freedom quest, and Margaret Garner's double infanticide puts an end to the pursuit of a liberated family altogether. Cilla, declining the run for freedom, has stayed behind at Maplewood. The intermezzo, placed between scenes 2 and 3 of act 2, punctuates Margaret Garner's total dejection, even though she embraces her "out of time" and "lonely" situation.

The outcome of Margaret Garner's trial in the libretto upholds her status as the property of her slave master, a utilitarian commodity that can be sold in slave markets throughout the American South. It empties her of humanity and underscores a slaveholder's power to subjugate her, and all those held in bondage, to ontological dehumanization. Being tried not as a person but as property reaffirms her lack of personhood. The Judges describe her running for freedom with the children as theft, her infanticide as destruction of property, and reference her deceased children as "stolen goods" (act 2, scene 3). The Judges' ruling nullifies her motherhood, one of the pillars of female personhood in nineteenth-century America.

Even though contemporary newspaper accounts largely described Margaret Garner's act of killing her daughter as "frantic" and "frenzied," and the result of a sudden delirium, it seems misguided to endorse their reductive reports, since these assessments forward the assumption that she was not conscious of her alienation as an individual within slavery. Enslaved individuals, who had both the daring and intellectual savvy to plan and execute their escape from slavery, also knew the consequences of a failed escape. One would imagine that a life spent enslaved is a life also spent asking oneself, "Who am I?"; "Why am I treated like a brute?" Frederick Douglass's *Narrative* (1845) provides insight into the psychic interiority of the slave as he ponders his own existential plight. The first chapter of Douglass's narrative is replete with his delineation of the unknown details of his early life that reflect the ontological annihilation wrought by his enslavement. He does not know his birth date, his age, who his father and mother are—personal data that typically play a central role in defining one's identity of self. Later in the narrative, as he stands on the shore of the Chesapeake Bay watching ships sail from the harbor, Douglass plunges into an existential debate on life versus death in slavery that is not unlike Hamlet's "To be, or not to be" soliloquy in Shakespeare's *Tragedy of Hamlet: Prince of Denmark*.[24] At the end of his deliberation he resolves to flee from slavery at any cost—even if the price is death. If contemporary readers of Margaret Garner's story—and many of them were familiar with the fictional Kentucky house slave Eliza's dramatic crossing of the frozen Ohio River to prevent her son from being sold from his family in Stowe's *Uncle Tom's Cabin*—believed that she loved her children and did not want them to live an enslaved life, then latter-day readers must also consider the possibility that she was psychologically prepared to secure their liberty by any means necessary. Awareness of one's alienation is a propaedeutic to action. Denying her awareness and preparedness also denies the motive—love for her children and herself—that propels her to kill them and herself if necessary in order to prevent their return to slavery. It also denies the reality that, after all, enslaved individuals evaluated their plight and resisted it, as exemplified by those who disobeyed the unjust system that denied them literacy, which was also a gateway to freedom, by learning to read and write. Others were ready to pay the high price of long self-alienation for freedom, including Harriet A. Jacobs, who self-published her story of enslavement in *Incidents in the Life of a Slave Girl* (1861) five years after

Margaret Garner's run for freedom. Jacobs sequestered herself seven years in a cramped, stifling, garret cell measuring approximately three by seven by nine feet waiting for a propitious time to escape from Edenton, North Carolina, to New York. She did so "in preference to her master's bed."[25] Jacobs's seven-years' delay in fleeing enslavement primarily hinged on her reluctance to leave behind her two small children, Benny and Ellen. Her grandmother's counsel that "nobody respects a mother who forsakes her children" compounded her reluctance.[26] Nevertheless, she went to the North without them.

Accepting the possibility that Margaret Garner had a contingent plan of action if she and her family were captured does not necessarily invalidate her "delirium" at the moment of infanticide that, in fact, humanizes her action. Moreover, the reports that characterized her as "frantic" and "frenzied" may actually have been the imaginative impositions of writers wanting to sensationalize Garner's case. A jail cell interview of Margaret Garner conducted by the Reverend P. S. Bassett, which Toni Morrison offers as her initial source on the case, supports the latter possibility:

> I found an article in a magazine of the period, and there was this young woman [Margaret Garner] in her 20's, being interviewed—oh, a lot of people interviewed her, mostly preachers and journalists, and she was very calm, she was very serene. They kept remarking on the fact that she was not frothing at the mouth, she was not a madwoman, and she kept saying, "No, they're not going to live like that. They will not live the way I have lived."[27]

Bassett's Sunday, February 10, 1856, interview contains the following narration in which Garner reports that she was "cool" during the assaults on her children:

> She said that when the officers and slave-hunters came to the house in which they were concealed, she caught a shovel and struck two of her children on the head, and then took a knife and cut the throat of the third, and tried to kill the other—that if they had given her time, she would have killed them all—that with regard to herself she cared but little; but she was unwilling to have her children suffer as she had done.

I inquired if she were not excited almost to madness when she committed the act. No, she replied, I was as cool as I now am; and would much rather kill them at once, and thus end their sufferings, than have then taken back to slavery and be murdered by piece-meal.[28]

The interview delineates Margaret Garner in her full humanity, calmly focused on the American ideal—freedom.

As is the case with Euripides's Medea, extreme emotion, no longer checked by conventional reason and socially sanctioned control, characterizes Morrison's Margaret Garner. The Chorus is generally sympathetic to Medea's plight, but it refuses to condone infanticide because it violates a sacred law of human life—she does not have the right to kill her children.[29] Her doing so to spite Jason is the central moral debate in Euripides's play; it was the central moral question that Euripides posed for an Athenian audience in 431 BCE that perhaps saw in Medea's barbarous actions evidence of the superiority of Greek civilization, just as the slaveholders of the South and their supporters saw in the historical Margaret Garner's infanticide proof of her savagery and insanity and, therefore, justification for slavery as beneficial to those they enslaved. Medea is, after all, from Colchis, an island in the Black Sea, a place that Greeks of the day believed barbarians inhabited. Moreover, she is a sorceress who uses supernatural powers to bring about death and destruction, which was an additional marker of barbarism for a contemporary Greek audience, especially when a woman possessed those exceptional powers. Although there is a level of pathos for Medea's abandonment and alienation in Euripides's play, her seeming failure to consider the consequences of her action or to restrain her passion condemns her. For the American South, Margaret Garner's action justified subjugating people of African descent to the "civilizing" control of the European, male-dominated society, and it repudiated the abolitionist agenda as dangerous agitation.

Margaret Garner's story assisted in illuminating the treacherous exploitation of black women in American chattel slavery that opponents of the institution wanted to see abolished. The gender exploitation of her story is reminiscent of Pierre Corneille's treatment of the Medea story, which foregrounds Jason's perfidy with women. Corneille's 1635 debut tragedy *Médée* mediates her representations by Euripides and Seneca the Younger. Euripides's Medea foregrounds a betrayed, forsaken, and dejected wife, who is still capable of intelligence, courage, and dignity, as indicative of her first speech onstage after she emerges from offstage. Her argument about the appalling social plight of women is compelling and in no way pales when compared with twentieth- and twenty-first-century feminist discourse. Seneca's version, which scholars believe he wrote in the first century CE during the second half of his life, delves directly into the theme of vengeance as if to condemn outrightly its unbridled nature. At the outset, Medea implores the gods to aid her in her plot. For Seneca, not using reason and control is utterly criminal, her rage unconscionable. Thus Medea violates logical, rational law, but her lawlessness and excessive emotion do not mean that her motive lacks justification. As she laments Jason's rejection, Creon also banishes her, highlighting her total social and national estrangement.

Corneille presents Medea as deprived of her homeland, Colchis; her family; her royal status, albeit in a barbarian land; her rightful husband, Jason, since she is convinced that the gods sanction marital vows; her newly adopted country, Corinth, where she has been accepted; and her children, the product of her god-sanctioned union with Jason. As is the case in the other Medea tragedies, she does not have an autonomous identity; only her status as Jason's wife defines her, and once it is gone, she is left empty, helpless, and a homeless exile.

While Seneca's tragedy centers on the criminal nature of extreme emotions such as rage and jealousy, Corneille's version underscores Jason's betrayal of Medea, who has given up her homeland and family for him. The spectator/reader first hears from Jason boasting that she is not the first woman he has abandoned. Like his previous wife Hypsipyle, whom he discarded after exploiting for his own interests, he confides in Pollux, an Argonautic compatriot, that Medea will resist but she will eventually reconcile herself to her cast-off status. Jason then reveals his true exploitive nature by saying, "J'accommode ma flamme au sein de mes affaires" (I adapt my love life to my business interests).[30] He then confesses that his policy extends to Medea's replacement, Creusa.[31]

Similarly, Corneille presents Medea as a woman who treasures herself to the utmost. His play dwells principally on her choosing between vengeance or motherly love, relegating only eight lines to the criminality of her infanticide. He grounds her story in the existentialist dilemma that recalls Hamlet's questioning "To be, or not to be" when living or dying is equally painful. She preserves her humanity in dealing with this dilemma. Although abandoned, she is still a loving mother. At the end, she takes her offspring's lives so as not to lose her dignity and "her self."[32] When she perpetrates the crime, the spectator/reader observes an inhuman act that Corneille's text conveys humanely with a sense of heroism and dignity in the act of vengeance. Medea has taken time to reason with Jason, taken time to deliberate, without losing sight of justice.

Corneille refuses to condemn Medea, just as many contemporary commentators of Margaret Garner praised her heroism and love of freedom. For example Frederick Douglass, in a speech delivered on August 3, 1857, asserts that "every mother who, like Margaret Garner, plunges a knife into the bosom of her infant to save it from the hell of our Christian Slavery, should be held and honored as a benefactress."[33] Those who opposed slavery commended Garner for her dignified comportment during the trial, arguing that indeed she understood the price of freedom if she was ready to sacrifice what was most dear to her: her children and herself. Before killing her two children, the fictional Margaret Garner clearly indicts human bondage—"Never to be born again into slavery" (act 2, scene 2)—underscoring the perfidy of chattel slavery. She is conscious of her action. She collapses after it, and Morrison depicts her shrouded in darkness and isolation in the intermezzo, after which, in scenes 3 and 4 of act 2, she calmly embraces her plight. At her execution she defiantly claims her identity and her dignity by deliberately tripping the lever that sets in motion her own hanging, thus blatantly rejecting Gaines's and the court's last-minute granting of clemency that would have remanded her to slavery for the balance of her life.

Comparable to Margaret Garner's justification for her excessive love and act, François-Benoît Hoffmann's libretto *Médée* for Cherubini's opera (1797) presents a Medea who reasons that if there is no limit to her love for Jason, then there should be no limit to her hatred. Morrison's Margaret Garner holds boundless hatred for slavery and puts no limits on her resistance to it because of both her maternal love and her self-love. Hoffmann's libretto opens with Medea's replacement in Jason's affections, Dirce, along with the Chorus, foregrounding her fear that if Jason could leave his previous wife, he may also leave her. She fears that Medea will come to reclaim her husband. In spite of Jason's reassurance that Medea is powerless and probably dead, and Creon's counsel to leave the future to the gods, Dirce's fear persists. After Creon and his entourage bless Jason and Dirce's imminent nuptials, Medea arrives veiled and in the company of one servant. She instills fear in the assembly because her reputation for being adept in the magical arts precedes her, and she announces to Corinth that her objective is to avenge herself and reclaim her unfaithful husband. She threatens disaster if Creon allows the marriage to proceed.

As in Pierre Corneille's tragedy, Hoffmann's Medea apparently opposes killing her children despite her assertion, "O mon cœur! Mettrais-tu des bornes à ta haine? Tu n'en mis point à ton amour" (act 1, scene 5; Oh my heart! Would you put limits to your hatred? You didn't put any to your love).[34] In a calculated change of mood, however, she feigns acceptance of her cast-off status and asks Jason to allow her to take their sons, but he declines her request, since he does not want them banished with her. She then laments his denial of granting her parental custody and the reality that she will never see them again. Jason states that she will be granted one last opportunity to spend time with them before her banishment, and it is at this moment that she severs her emotional tie with her sons after he has stripped her of maternal authority and possession: "Je les hais, je ne suis plus leur mère" (I hate them; I am not their mother anymore).[35] Since the children are no longer psychically hers and physically in her possession, the maternal dilemma concerning the killing of them in her vengeful scheme does not approach the one we see in Corneille's depiction of Medea. The remainder of the libretto shows Medea enacting her earlier vow of vengeance.

In contrast to the limitless spousal love of Hoffmann's Medea, limitless maternal love solely inspires Morrison's Margaret Garner; her children are hers. In Cleveland, Ohio, in May 1856, the Reverend H. Bushnell gave a sermon that recounted the visit of an unidentified preacher with Margaret Garner in jail. When asked about the killing of her daughter, she reportedly replied, "It was my own . . . given me of God to do the best a mother could in its behalf. *I have done the best I could!*"[36] Medea divests herself of maternal ownership when maternal custody is denied her. Even though the Judges, Edward Gaines, his daughter Caroline, his son-in-law George Hancock, and the Townspeople debate ownership of Garner's children, Margaret herself reaffirms her maternal ownership of them by killing them and explaining later that it was the best choice she could make for them under the circumstances of slavery.

As literary artists have done with the Medea story and its theme of maternal infanticide over three millennia, Toni Morrison first tackled the theme in *Beloved*, trying to make sense of the impetus behind yet another mother who commits the same "deed of horror," only this time in antebellum America.[37] In contrast to Medea's story, Margaret Garner's story responds to the "necessity for remembering the horror" that spurs her on, but Morrison also uses it as a public platform to talk about the psychological impact of slavery that, in this case, is "something . . . undigestible and unabsorbable, completely . . . something that has no precedent in the history of the world, in terms of length of time and the nature and specificity of its devastation."[38] Written as a memorial for the "sixty million and more" who perished as a result of the transatlantic Middle Passage and the enslavement of persons of African descent in the Americas, *Beloved* captures with poetic and painful intensity what the author terms "anaconda love," an extreme, captive love that leads those who harbor it to self-destruction or, in its worst form, to the destruction of the beloved. In the case of Margaret Garner's real experience and those of her fictional avatars, that extreme, captive love comes in the form of a mother killing her child(ren) instead of surrendering them or herself to a lifetime of slavery, a fate worse than death. Toni Morrison's imagination in both the novel and the libretto acquires a life of its own, just as the original stories of Virginius and Medea were reimagined by latter-day visual and literary artists.

A critical intersection of texts that were invoked to interpret the story of one individual slave woman who was intent on killing her children and herself rather than returning to a life of slavery opened up intertextual linkages that allowed those prosecuting and defending her, as well as the Cincinnati and the national audience that followed the case, to grapple with the pressing national issues surrounding human bondage, morality, and law. Perceived as benign by those who benefited from it and as evil by those who opposed and were oppressed by it, slavery and the right of states to practice it were at the center of the national divide. As the story of Margaret Garner unfolded in 1856, the United States was still a fledgling democracy whose revolution was incomplete as long as the peculiar institution of slavery was part and parcel of its social, economic, and political fabric. The invocation of Virginius's sacrifice by execution of his daughter to free her from sexual exploitation helped to center and validate extreme personal sacrifice as an often necessary requisite for (re)securing a just republic. Nodding to the myth of Medea and its various adaptations in literature and the arts also allowed Morrison, and others before her, to portray Margaret Garner beyond her individuality. Margaret Garner's complex character unfolds as reminiscent of Medea's ability to carry "within herself mutually contradictory traits [as] an ideal vehicle through whom authors and artists could explore what modern scholarship has called the problem of 'self' and 'other'" and Seneca's intimation that "it is the one who really loves properly and loyally who will be the most upset by a loss of love and thus most liable to wreak havoc."[39] Medea's and Margaret Garner's profundity of love and its attendant passions propel both to posterity as texts and intertexts that convey the national, calamitous plights of women with respect to motherhood, marriage, family, and social conventions. Like the narratives with which they connect, the historical Margaret Garner and her libretto counterpart have been transformed into texts within a network of other texts, repeatable stories that can be passed on in classical, artistic, and literary variations.

## NOTES

1. See Mark Reinhardt, "Who Speaks for Margaret Garner? Slavery, Silence, and the Politics of Ventriloquism," *Critical Inquiry* 29.1 (Fall 2002): 81–119; and "An Extraordinary Case?," introduction to *Who Speaks for Margaret Garner? The True Story That Inspired Toni Morrison's "Beloved"* (Minneapolis: U of Minnesota P, 2010), 1–45. Reinhardt's book contains reprints of speeches, sermons, and editorials on Margaret Garner that appeared in the *New York Daily Tribune* and other popular print media of the day.

2. See Frederick Douglass, *Narrative of the Life of Frederick Douglass, an American Slave, Written by Himself*, ed. David W. Blight (1845; Boston: Bedford, 1993); and Harriet A. Jacobs, *Incidents in the Life of a Slave Girl, Written by Herself* (1861; Cambridge, MA: Harvard UP, 1987).

3. See Harriet Beecher Stowe, *Uncle Tom's Cabin* (1852; New York: Barnes and Noble, 2003). Stowe first serialized *Uncle Tom's Cabin* in 1851 over a forty-week period. At the end of its first year of publication as a book in 1852, Americans had purchased 300,000 copies, while 1.5 million copies had been sold in Great Britain. Countless copies were pirated. The years before the Garners' escape, *Uncle Tom's Cabin* was the most popular book of its day, and it went on to become the best-selling novel of the nineteenth century. Its sales were second only to the Bible. As Reinhardt notes in

*Who Speaks for Margaret Garner?*, "Stowe's characters were ubiquitous: available for purchase on cups and lamps, forks and spoons, as figurines, in card games, and in many other incarnations, [and] they were emblematic commodities of the nation's incipient mass culture" (244). The house slave Eliza's dramatic escape across the frozen Ohio River as well as the depiction of Topsy, a young, ragamuffin slave girl, helped the American public to frame imaginatively Margaret Garner's flight and infanticide. For critical readings of this period, see Mary Ryan, *The Empire of the Mother: American Writing about Domesticity, 1830–1860* (New York: Routledge, 1985); Ann Douglass, *The Feminization of American Culture* (New York: Knopf, 1977); and Shirley Samuels, ed., *The Culture of Sentiment: Race, Gender, and Sentimentality in Nineteenth-Century America* (New York: Oxford UP, 1992).

4. Julia Kristeva, "Word, Dialogue and the Novel," in *Desire and Language: A Semiotic Approach to Literature and Art*, ed. Leon S. Roudiez, trans. Alice Jardine et al. (New York: Columbia UP, 1980), 64–91.

5. In I. A. Richards's *The Philosophy of Rhetoric* a metaphor consists of the vehicle and the tenor. The vehicle is the element used for comparison, while the tenor encompasses all the attributes associated with the vehicle. For example, in "Caesar is a lion," "lion" serves as the vehicle and allows us to talk about Caesar's fierceness, fear instilled in subjects, strength, leadership, and possibly more attributes depending on the interpreter of the metaphor. Thus metaphorization expands and elevates meaning.

6. See Steven Weisenburger, *Modern Medea: A Family Story of Slavery and Child-Murder from the Old South* (New York: Hill and Wang, 1998), 202.

7. Ibid., 86–89.

8. Ibid., 173.

9. "The Slave Mother," *New York Daily Tribune*, 8 Feb. 1856. Rpt. in Mark Reinhardt, *Who Speaks for Margaret Garner? The True Story That Inspired Toni Morrison's "Beloved"* (Minneapolis: U of Minnesota P, 2010), 166. See James Sheridan Knowles, *The Modern Standard Drama: Virginius: A Tragedy in Five Acts* (New York: John Douglas, 1848).

10. Weisenburger, *Modern Medea*, 88.

11. Reinhardt, "An Extraordinary Case?," 35.

12. The Cult of True Womanhood imagined a true woman as characterized by purity (i.e., sexual purity), piety, submissiveness, and domesticity, among other qualities. As Harriet A. Jacobs's *Incidents in the Life of a Slave Girl* explicitly states, slave women also aspired to these values, but sex-

ual exploitation within the institution of slavery prevented them from achieving purity. See Jacobs, *Incidents;* Ryan, *The Empire of the Mother;* Barbara Welter, *Dimity Convictions: The American Woman in the Nineteenth-Century* (Columbus: Ohio State UP, 1985); and "The Cult of True Womanhood: 1820–1860," *American Quarterly* 18.2, part 1 (Summer 1966): 151–74.

13. Reinhardt, "An Extraordinary Case?," 36.

14. Ibid., 37.

15. For a detailed discussion of these arguments, see ibid., 33–38; and Weisenburger, *Modern Medea*, 62–176.

16. Weisenburger, *Modern Medea*, 192.

17. Ibid., 228.

18. See Giorgio Agamben, *Homo Sacer: Sovereign Power and Bare Life*, trans. Daniel Heller-Roazen (Stanford, CA: Stanford UP, 1998). The figure of "homo sacer" (the "sacred man" in ancient Roman law) finds its manifestation in the exile and the refugee in the contemporary world, figures without any rights, figures with mere, naked life. Based on Agamben's definition, the American slave can also be considered an extreme incarnation of the "homo sacer," as he or she has no political rights and can be killed but not sacrificed. The bare, naked life (the Zoë) is the product of biopolitics, the domain of the sovereign, who can use his juridico-constitutional power to establish a state of exception that suspends all laws and renders killing possible. American slavery functioned in a similar fluid, arbitrary manner.

19. Amanda Smith, "Toni Morrison," *Publishers Weekly*, 21 Aug. 1987, 51.

20. P. S. Bassett, "From the American Baptist: A Visit To the Slave Mother Who Killed Her Child," *National Anti-Slavery Standard*, 15 Mar. 1856. Rpt. in Middleton Harris, *The Black Book* (New York: Random House, 1974), 10. Also see Bassett. Rpt. in Reinhardt, *Who Speaks for Margaret Garner?*, 215.

21. Toni Morrison, *Margaret Garner: Opera in Two Acts*, composed by Richard Danielpour, rev. ed. (New York: Associated Music, 2004). All references to the libretto are to this edition.

22. Euripides, *Medea*, trans. Ian Johnston, http://records.viu.ca/~johnstoi/euripides/medea.htm. All other references to Euripides's *Medea* are to this translation.

23. Abraham Lincoln, "A House Divided: Speech Delivered at Springfield, Illinois, at the Close of the Republican State Convention, June 16, 1858." Rpt. in *Norton Anthology of American Literature*, 5th ed., vol. 1, ed. Nina Baym (New York: W. W. Norton, 1998), 1582–88.

24. Douglass, *Narrative*, 74–75.

25. Jean Fagan Yellin, ed., introduction to *Incidents in the Life of a Slave Girl, Written by Herself*, by Harriet A. Jacobs (Cambridge, MA: Harvard UP, 1987), xxxi.

26. Jacobs, *Incidents in the Life of a Slave Girl*, 91.

27. Mervyn Rohtstein, "Toni Morrison, in Her New Novel, Defends Women," *New York Times*, 26 Aug. 1987, late ed., C17.

28. Bassett, "From the American Baptist: A Visit to the Slave Mother Who Killed Her Child," 215.

29. Rothstein, "Toni Morrison, in Her New Novel, Defends Women," C17.

30. Pierre Corneille, *Médée*, http://fr.wikisource.org/wiki M%C3%A9d%C3% A9e_(Corneille); my translation. All other references to Corneille's *Médée* are to this text.

31. Latin texts use the name Creusa for Glauce.

32. Responding to her servant who asks what is left to her after she has lost her country and her husband, Medea replies, "Moi, / Moi, dis-je, et c'est assez" (Me, me, I say, and that's sufficient). Act 1, scene 5; my translation.

33. Frederick Douglass, "Speech on West Indian Emancipation," *Two Speeches*. Rpt. in Mark Reinhardt, *Who Speaks for Margaret Garner? The True Story That Inspired Toni Morrison's "Beloved"* (Minneapolis: U of Minnesota P, 2010), 227.

34. François-Benoît Hoffmann, *Médée*, composed by Luigi Cherubini, www. geocities.com/Vienna/Strasse/1523/libretto.htm#Ouverture. My translation. All other references to Hoffmann's *Médée* are to this text.

35. Act 2, scene 6; my translation.

36. Reverend H. Bushnell, "The Case of the Slave Mother, Margaret, at Cincinnati," *Liberator*, 16 May 1856. Rpt. in Mark Reinhardt, *Who Speaks for Margaret Garner? The True Story That Inspired Toni Morrison's "Beloved"* (Minneapolis: U of Minnesota P, 2010), 218. Emphasis in original.

37. Weisenburger, *Modern Medea*, 86.

38. Marsha Darling, "In the Realm of Responsibility: A Conversation with Toni Morrison," *Conversations with Toni Morrison*, ed. Danielle Taylor-Guthrie (Jackson: UP of Mississippi, 1994), 247; and Elsie B. Washington, "Talk with Toni Morrison," *Conversations with Toni Morrison*, ed. Danielle Taylor-Guthrie (Jackson: UP of Mississippi, 1994), 235.

39. For a detailed discussion of these ideas, see Clauss and Johnston, introduction to *Medea: Essays on Medea in Myth, Literature, Philosophy, and Art* (Princeton, NJ: Princeton UP, 1997), 3–17.

# Margaret Garner and Appomattox

## Performing Slavery/Rewriting Opera

✳ HELENA WOODARD ✳

At the world premiere of *Margaret Garner: A New American Opera* (Richard Danielpour, composer; Toni Morrison, librettist) in Detroit on May 7, 2005, the curtain rose to members of a black slave chorus at auction, clothed in grayish hues as they sang a solemn prayer: "No more, please God, no more" (act 1, scene 1).[1] Words and music combined to communicate an aura of sorrow and foreboding that engulfed the stage. In San Francisco on October 5, 2007, at the world premiere of *Appomattox, The Opera* (Philip Glass, composer; Christopher Hampton, librettist), Civil War widows cloaked in black chanted, "This is the last time / Let it be the last time," as they placed downstage photographs of their husbands killed in battle (prologue).[2] Produced in an art form long associated with whiteness, elitism, and the Italian language but only recently topically delineating race in the context of African enslavement, the *Margaret Garner* and *Appomattox* premieres signal that irresolution about American slavery and the Civil War has moved from popular historical reenactments and endless debate to the modern-day operatic stage.

But can opera best make sense of a fractured American past so entrenched in the complexities of race, slavery, and nation? Is it the final frontier that boldly goes where the classical dramatic genre has not gone before? While no creative art form can singularly resolve a nation's racial woes, *Margaret Garner* and *Appomattox* unite dramatic poetic expression with a performance aesthetic that anchors historical memory as a distinct contribution to modern opera. An assortment of historical fiction written in English in the nineteenth and twentieth centuries—ranging from Sir Walter Scott's traditional models, to Charles Johnson's and Octavia Butler's postmodern speculative novels, as well as other experimental forms such as Connie Willis's *Doomsday Book*, which pairs the fourteenth-century Black Death with a near-future of constant pandemics—similarly alters or binds incidents from disparate eras. A highly visual, dramatic, and expressive art form such as opera offers numerous possibilities for the imaginative reconstruction of historical memory by permitting selected events to be made contiguous with others from different times. A musical assemblage of movable people, places, and objects as occurs onstage can provide a template upon which the librettist and composer can inscribe the full measure of memory work. Shadowing the sesquicentennial of both the Civil War (1861–1865) and Lincoln's assassination (April 15, 1865) in a twenty-first-century climate dubiously dubbed "post racial," *Margaret Garner: A New American Opera* and *Appomattox, The Opera* stand as signature productions among a small but impressive slate of modern American operas that (re)constitute sites of memory around still trammeled aspects of race and slavery.[3]

The centrality of music as a cultural survival form of expression, particularly for African Americans from slavery to the present, has been long recognized. But scholars and critics have been remiss in examining opera's role as a black, expressive, cultural outlet. Their oversight is particularly true for works by early African-American opera composers Harry Lawrence Freeman, *The Martyr, Opera in Two Acts* (1893), and Scott Joplin, *Treemonisha* (1910), who wrote their own libretti, and composer William Grant Still who collaborated with librettists Harold Bruce Forsythe to create *Blue Steel* (1934) and Langston Hughes to produce *Troubled Island* (1937, 1949).[4]

Although they have not reached the prominence or circulation of *Margaret Garner* and *Appomattox* in the repertory, operas that thematize American slavery and the plight of the enslaved have increased in recent years. One contemporary opera that depicts the enslaved subject is *York: The Voice of Freedom* (2002), Bruce Trinkley, composer; Jason Charnesky, librettist, which premiered at Penn State's Opera Theater in November 2002 as part of an international conference and as a prelude to commemorating the Lewis and Clark Bicentennial. Enslaved to William Clark, York was the only African American to accompany Meriwether Lewis and his slave master on their historical, transcontinental expedition between July 1803 and September 1806. Less than a year after *York's* premiere, T. J. Anderson, composer, and Pulitzer Prize–winning poet Yusef Komunyakaa, librettist, unveiled *Slipknot* in a workshop production at Northwestern University on April 26, 2003. Based on the true story of an eighteenth-century black man, Arthur, who was enslaved near Worcester, Massachusetts, the opera treats his execution in 1768 at the age of twenty-one for the rape of a white woman who never charged him with the crime. Within the next half decade Cincinnati Opera commissioned *Rise for Freedom: The John P. Parker Story*, Adolphus Hailstork, composer, David Gonzalez, librettist, which was performed October 13–21, 2007, at the Aronoff Center's Jarson-Kaplan Theater. Born into slavery, Parker purchased his own freedom and later served as a conductor on the Underground Railroad, helping hundreds of fugitive slaves to escape to the North. Additional contemporary operas, *Amistad* (1997; 2008), Anthony Davis, composer, Thulani Davis, librettist; and the Mass Mutual and Old Deerfield Productions' *TRUTH, A New Folk Opera about the Life of Sojourner Truth* (2012), Paula M. Kimper, composer, Talaya Delaney, librettist, historicize a noted slave rebellion and a famed African-American abolitionist, respectively. The former opera received impressive reviews as part of Charleston, South Carolina's Spoleto Festival in 2008, while the latter appeared at the Academy of Music Theatre, Northampton, Massachusetts, February 16–18, 2012.

Juxtaposing slavery with the onset of the Civil War and the final days of the Civil War with the post-1950s civil rights movement, respectively, *Margaret Garner* and *Appomattox* demonstrate opera's ability to locate critical, defining moments in the nation's vexed racial past and to call attention to social issues in the present that grew out of that tempestuous, racialized past. In an ambitious collaboration, David DiChiera, founder of Michigan Opera Theatre, and other organizers invited Cincinnati's and Philadelphia's opera theaters to join Detroit in a tri-city sponsorship of *Margaret Garner* to shore up cultural and economic support for the northern cities still ravaged by racially informed discrimination, poverty, and violence. DiChiera and his team understood what Waldo E. Martin Jr. later asserts in "Beyond Appomattox: The Bitter Fruits of Freedom," an essay printed in *Appomattox*'s playbill, that the opera house, in equal measure with the school, the university, the courtroom, the boardroom, and the floor of the legislature, is a fitting venue in which to embrace the ideals of equality expressed in the Declaration of Independence.[5] Also included in the playbill, an interview by Thomas May, "Crossing Boundaries: *Appomattox*'s Creative Team on the Collaborative Process," features an open-casket photograph of the slain African-American civil rights activist Jimmie Lee Jackson. A white state trooper murdered Jackson during a riot that erupted in the midst of a voting rights march in Marion, Alabama, almost one hundred years after Robert E. Lee's surrender at Appomattox Court House, Virginia. In the interview, Philip Glass and Christopher Hampton discuss their rationale for incorporating Jackson's death into the opera in order to show that unresolved racial conflicts from the Civil War led to tragic consequences for blacks a century later during the civil rights movement.[6] By reconstructing historical memory in an unlikely forum, *Margaret Garner* and *Appomattox* gamely assert opera's preeminence as a prescient model to reset the nation's racial barometer.

*Margaret Garner* dramatizes the tragic, true story of an enslaved Kentucky African-American woman who, after a failed escape attempt, killed her infant daughter rather than have her returned to slavery. But in the reordering of her trial that took place in Cincinnati, Ohio, in February 1856, Morrison's libretto sets Garner's trial in early April 1861, near the official start of the Civil War. Thus the altered timeline of the opera's libretto contains a reference to Lincoln's presidency as the Garners run for freedom. Robert Garner (Gregg Baker, baritone) tells his wife, Margaret (Denyce Graves, mezzo-soprano), that the nation's new leader stands for a house united.

Conflating these historical events in *Margaret Garner* invites a call-and-response dialogue with *Appomattox*, whose 1865 to 1965 reach from civil war to civil rights sears slavery's raw wounds into the national consciousness. In the prologue to *Appomattox*, the wives of Lincoln, Grant, and Lee, joined by Civil War widows, lament the tragic consequences of war. In its first act Lincoln meets with Grant aboard the President's headquarters on the Potomac River, the Union steamer *River Queen*, to discuss the terms of surrender to offer Lee, known as the River Queen Doctrine. While a chorus of Civil War refugees flees Richmond, newly manumitted slaves sing a praise hymn to Lincoln. From Lee's surrender to Grant at Appomattox Court House, Virginia, in act 2, the opera flashes forward to the Colfax massacre of 1873 and later to the civil rights march in 1965 from Selma to Montgomery, Alabama. The opera not only blurs the temporal space between these past and recent events, but it also dissolves the remoteness of the past by projecting unresolved racial conflicts from the Civil War onto their inevitable consequences in the civil rights era a century later. Utilizing the plaintive lyrics of arias, dramatic intrigue, and compelling performances, coupled with the immediacy of action that the stage provides, *Margaret Garner* and *Appomattox* portray these historical conflicts in epic proportions.

Garner's destruction of property charge seems to anticipate the dispensation of property that Civil War titans Generals Robert E. Lee (Dwayne Croft, baritone) and Ulysses S. Grant (Andrew Shore, baritone) arrange in *Appomattox* early in act 2. In a scene of almost pristine civility that unfolds mostly as recitative, the opera dramatizes Lee's surrender to Grant at Appomattox Court House. Grant accedes to Lee's wishes that Confederate soldiers be permitted to keep their horses and return home to work their farms. Admonished to suppress boisterous celebration, Union soldiers salute the defeated army as it passes, homeward bound. But the reconciliation forged between the two generals is noticeably devoid of any provisions for or references to formerly enslaved persons of African descent. That single, grave omission marks the failure of postwar healing and, in its willful neglect, sets the tone for volatile race relations that take place over the next one hundred years. Regarded as disposable property and muted at her own trial by a pro-slavery legal process, Margaret Garner all but vanishes as an archival presence for approximately the same one-hundred-year time span—until revitalized by Morrison's seminal neo-slave narrative *Beloved* (1987), which spawned *Modern Medea: A Family Story of Slavery and Child-Murder from the Old South* (1998), Steven Weisenburger's biographical study of Garner.

Upon *Margaret Garner*'s appearance as an opera in 2005, Richard Danielpour articulated its mission "to show what can happen when we forget that we are part of the same human family."[7] Both Danielpour and Glass, as well as librettists Morrison and Hampton, cite a collective healing as a primary objective for their respective operas. Ironically, Danielpour's words evoke Grant's prophetic declaration spoken in *Appomattox*: "How we end the war today will still be felt a hundred years from now" (act 1, scene 1). Both comments magnify the century-long chasm between civil war and civil rights—the covenant that ended the former and the subsequent amnesia that ensued over the latter. A further illustration of that point appears in *Appomattox* when Hampton stages a chorus of black Union soldiers who, along with an integrated quartet of civil rights protesters as they march from Selma to Montgomery, sings "The Ballad of Jimmie Lee Jackson," a song about the murder of the civil rights worker. Jackson's shooting death by an Alabama state trooper inspired the 1965 march that drew 25,000 participants after an earlier march, also inspired by his death, ended in violence. Alabama state troopers and members of the sheriff's department attacked and beat protesters after they crossed Selma's Edmund Pettus Bridge.[8] The dramatic pairing of seemingly disparate historical events, performed to a spirited civil rights ballad, spotlights still unsettled issues of injustice and inequality in the 1950s and '60s.

Like the covenant between North and South at Appomattox Court House that failed to provide for ex-slaves, Margaret Garner's virtual erasure from archival dialogue about slavery is also symptomatic of a collective amnesia that erupted in the national imaginary. Both *Margaret Garner* and *Appomattox* aver that slavery's raw physical and psychological wounds can only be sutured through historical intervention or counter narratives that account for blacks' absence in the covenant, as well as their displacement in post–Civil War ideology. Historian David Blight suggests that race was so endemic to the Civil War's "causes and consequences" and so divisive in America's social psyche "that it served as the antithesis of a culture of reconciliation." *Appomattox* locates those strategies in white Southern Lost Cause narratives spun from psychic Civil War wounds that concomitantly purged slavery from the historical record or reinvented it as benign and civilizing. As Blight writes, "In its earliest manifestation the Lost Cause was born out of grief, but just as importantly, it formed in the desire to contend for control of the nation's memory."[9] In scenes sequenced during the surrender, *Appomattox* juxtaposes the private, insular space that the two generals shared with the public, chaotic world that unfolds over the next one hundred years. In subsequent scenes, the narrative "flashes forward" from the Civil War's conclusion in the mid-nineteenth century to the civil rights conflicts in the mid-twentieth century to dramatize the terrorism unleashed on blacks in the South by the Ku Klux Klan and other hate groups. Here, the opera's creative team juggles the expressive components of opera with what should have been unforgettable, representative events from history.

In act 1, black journalist T. Morris Chester (Noah Stewart, tenor), son of a former slave, triumphantly reports Union victories for the *Philadelphia Press* from the Speaker's chair at the Confederate Congress. But he returns later in act 2, in Colfax, Louisiana, where, traumatized, he reports the infamous Colfax massacre (1873), in which the Ku Klux Klan and the White League ruthlessly murdered one hundred black militiamen. In a horrifying dispatch about the senseless slaughter of the black infantry, Chester laments, "How misplaced was my optimism." That optimism is further undercut by an emergent neo-slavery that rears its head in the South between the Civil War and World War II. Douglas A. Blackmon writes in *Slavery by Another Name: The Re-Enslavement of Black Americans from the Civil War to World War II* that an estimated 100,000 to 200,000 black men in the South during this period were pressed into quasi slavery when trumped-up vagrancy charges and peonage led to false imprisonment and forced convict labor.[10]

*Appomattox* flashes forward to Jackson's murder by the Alabama state trooper and to civil rights activists James Chaney's, Andrew Goodman's, and Michael Schwerner's murders by a Mississippi Ku Klux Klan member and Baptist minister. Both took place roughly a century after the treaty signing at Appomattox. Both cases also resulted in convictions for the perpetrators more than four decades after their commissions of the crimes. The State of Alabama charged James Bonard Fowler on May 10, 2007, with first-degree and second-degree murder for shooting an unarmed Jackson at point-blank range forty-two years earlier. Fowler's indictment came five months before *Appomattox*'s premiere. He later pleaded guilty to one count of second-degree manslaughter and, on November 15, 2010, received a six-month prison sentence. In the latter case a Mississippi state court found Edgar Ray Killen guilty of three counts of manslaughter on June 21, 2005. He was sentenced to three consecutive twenty-year prison terms. Killen's conviction came on the day of the forty-first anniversary of the crime and less than seven weeks after the *Margaret Garner* world premiere.[11] He appealed the jury's verdict, but the Mississippi Supreme Court on January 12, 2007, upheld the lower court's ruling. Ironically, his first trial, in 1967, had ended in a mistrial when one juror refused to convict a preacher for murder. In 2007 at *Appomattox*'s premiere, Philip Skinner, bass baritone, gave a haunting portrayal of Killen at the opera's conclusion.

In a nostalgic aria sung in a commanding voice, Edward Gaines (Rod Gilfry, baritone) reminisces in *Margaret Garner* about a charmed life spent on a Richwood Station, Kentucky, plantation before a youthful indiscretion with a young girl forced him to leave town in disgrace: "I remember the curve of every hill / The swans in the pond; / I remember them still" (act 1, scene 1). Having returned as a widowed adult to acquire his deceased brother's slaves and other property, Gaines is miffed to discover that the Townspeople do not remember him, and he vows never to be forgotten again. In light of decorum as observed in Southern aristocracy, the community's dismissal of Gaines's importance is palpable. Thus, as Barbie Zelizer writes, forgetting can be "as strategic and central a practice as remembering itself [because] forgetting reflects a choice to put aside, for whatever reason, what [or whom] no longer matters."[12]

Efforts to regard slavery as a nostalgic remembrance for Southern planters militate against their slaves' remembrance of a horrid place that they would much rather forget. After Gaines concludes his performance, the Black Chorus sings in equally forceful but crisp staccato bursts. The chorus pleads NOT to be abandoned in a pseudo-utopian land: "O Mother, O Father / Don't abandon me / While my tears muddy the rich brown soil / Of dear old Kentucky" (act 1, scene 2). The Black Chorus thus transforms a mythical emblem of Southern historical tradition into an agonizing counter memory for enslaved people routinely separated from their families. In the prelude to a scene of sexual violence, Robert Garner, Margaret Garner, and her mother-in-law Cilla (Angela M. Brown, soprano), along with the Black Chorus, further illustrate this when they sing derisively of "dear old Kentucky" as a place where blood of the enslaved "floods the velvet dirt" (act 1, scene 2).

Unlike in *Margaret Garner*, where planters like Gaines apply selective memory in order to escape their own culpability, in *Appomattox*, members of the Confederacy naively express a nostalgic remembrance for an Old South plantocracy that they hope will be embraced by those that have been most socially crippled by it. For example, in act 1, scene 4, of *Appomattox*, the wife of Robert E. Lee, Mary Custis Lee (Elza Van den Heever, soprano), sings a self-protective, nostalgic aria that illustrates a willful forgetfulness in which she imagines that the enslaved would someday look back to the antebellum Southern era "as a golden age." Her delusional thinking greatly contrasts with the contemporary and future reality and contextualizes why the son of a former slave in act 1, T. Morris Chester, reports with jubilation Union victories, but expresses in act 2 his "misplaced optimism" with respect to the Ku Klux Klan massacre of one hundred black militiamen in Colfax, Louisiana.

In *Against Amnesia: Contemporary Women Writers and the Crises of Historical Memory*, Nancy J. Peterson convincingly argues that like selective remembrance, the archival exclusion or discarding of some ethnic minorities' past historical contributions to nation building has been a deliberate undertaking. She reveals, for instance, that contributions by

Chinese Americans to nation building via the transcontinental railroad were literally blotted from newspaper accounts and archival records.[13] Morrison puts it succinctly in the seminal article, "Unspeakable Things Unspoken: The Afro-American Presence in American Literature," when she expresses the need to examine the "willful oblivion" or the "strategies of escape *from* knowledge" that have resulted in the erasure of blacks "from a society seething with [their] presence."[14] To transform history into memory for spectators who never experienced slavery or the Civil War, both operas make distinct use of language through deploying the libretto quite literally in written form, along with the requisite components of performance aesthetics: dramaturgy, the recitative, and tonality or tessitura. Furthermore, both operas' simultaneous presentation of disparate historical moments imposes an immediacy and dramatic intensity onto an eclectic blend of musical compositions. To explore further the various ways the operas reconstruct historical memory in a dramatic, expressive form that the spectator can then take away from the experience, one must turn to the age-old debate about the preeminence of language—the libretto—versus music. This debate has gained momentum, appearing as the cover story, "The Unequal Marriage of Words and Music," for *Opera News* in August 2008.

Perhaps claims can be made that a greater emphasis on language has held sway, arguably typifying American operas—at least since Richard Wagner's domineering orchestral sounds from the nineteenth through early twentieth centuries superseded opera scholar-composer Christoph Gluck's highly favored equilibrium between words and music. Language empowers the libretto as poetry and unites with musical lyricism and dramatic performance. For example, in the case of American composer John Adams's *Nixon in China* (1987), which has achieved longevity in the repertory, poet Alice Goodman wrote the highly artistic libretto in rhymed couplets reminiscent of a heroic epic. For Philip Glass's *Satyagraha, An Opera in Three Acts* (1979), Constance DeJong and Glass penned the libretto, an adaptation of the Sanskrit *Bhagavad-Gita*.

Toni Morrison's libretto for *Margaret Garner* features highly poetic and meaningful language, which raises the stakes for the "literariness" of opera as counter memory. But the libretto vies with the music for equal recognition, leading to opposing views about whether the lyrics' need to dominate hijacks the music. For example, music critic Bernard Holland in the *New York Times* grouses that the lyrics should have been excised more sharply for an opera that is "too long for what it has to say." Most reviewers, however, concur with Lawrence B. Johnson, who refers to Morrison's libretto and Danielpour's musical compositions as "a hand-in-glove masterpiece of words fitted to music."[15] But immediacy and dramatic intensity, bolstered by vocal range and choral presentation, attend *Margaret Garner*'s and *Appomattox*'s simultaneous presentations of disparate historical moments.

Perhaps because of the prevalence of diphthongs in spoken English as opposed to the "pure" vowels of Italian, the English language can impair the singability of an aria. Addressing the complexity of using English in operatic song, Philip Glass writes that word clarity is difficult to understand when singing goes above the spoken voice. Therefore, opera singers often utilize vocal range or tessitura and enunciation with emphasis on the final consonant to aid clarity and comprehension. Furthermore, supertitles can be disadvantageous and distracting to the aural process. Glass also explains that in *Appomattox* vernacular elements and the vocal writing merge.[16] In this fashion, the mezzo-soprano voice of Denyce Graves and the baritone of Gregg Baker and Rod Gilfry in *Margaret Garner* and Dwayne Croft (Lee) and Andrew Shore (Grant) in *Appomattox* occupy the middle-voice range.

In addition to the dramatic and vocal intensity of language, both operas rely on material objects or seminal artifacts as memory sites. These artifacts can help illustrate a willful forgetfulness or self-protective nostalgia. On the other hand, material artifacts strategically positioned onstage may imply or assume the audience possesses a general knowledge of the historical events treated in the opera's narrative. The audience may also come, not so much as blank slates, but with confused fragments of culturally mediated information that these visual artifacts may resolve or assist in reclaiming the past. For example, Marjorie Bradley Kellogg, the set designer for *Margaret Garner*, selected a quilt pattern for the stage surround based on those sewn by enslaved women. This strategically placed material artifact reinforces that even commonplace or seemingly incidental items displayed on the opera stage may contain memories about the slave past.

The cumulative effect of visceral, unobtrusive material objects, such as photographs, severed human limbs, and animal carcasses onstage sequenced throughout *Appomattox* sustain memory as "a perpetually actual phenomenon" rather than as "a representation of the past."[17] For example, in the prologue, Civil War widows place photographs of deceased Union and Confederate soldiers at the stage front where they remain as a powerful visual presence until the opera's epilogue. Soldiers later remove amputated limbs from the stage in wheelbarrows to discard them. Perhaps most unforgettable are the carcasses of horses suspended from the interior space of the stage ceiling as if on a battlefield that match the steel-gray vault color of the set design. These images join with the dark, solemn ariosos and produce a somber tone for the opera.

Artistic anamnesis or recollection has the power to cause consternation in individuals emotionally or personally impacted by historical opera, and this is true for some cast members in the *Margaret Garner* opera and for others connected with the story of Margaret Garner. For example, Toni Morrison has famously said of Garner's infanticide, "It was absolutely the right thing to do, but she had no right to do it."[18] Rod Gilfry, who is reportedly a descendant of Colonel George Armstrong Custer and who perhaps closely identifies with carrying the weight of historical memory in his own family, expressed empathy for the Gaines descendants who were apparently discomfited by the opera's portrayal of their ancestor. In the documentary, *The Journey of Margaret Garner,* he opposes the use of the family surname "Gaines" in the operatic portrayal of the slave master, and suggests that the name choice violates the descendants' privacy. Gilfry speculates that Gaines's first name, however, was changed to "Edward" because "'Archibald' does not sing well in opera."[19] Morrison corroborated his speculation during the "Meet the Margaret Garner Creative Team: On Stage with Toni Morrison and Richard Danielpour" discussion the evening after the Cincinnati premiere. Offered a ticket presumably by an organizer for *Margaret Garner* to see the opera in Cincinnati, John Gaines—a direct descendant of John Pollard Gaines who originally enslaved Margaret Garner before selling her to his younger brother, Archibald—declined to attend for reasons he deemed "personal."[20] In an interview with National Public Radio on May 7, 2005, Gaines states that his thrice-great-uncle Archibald K. Gaines was not a moral monster and that slavery was a fact of life much like driving on the right side of the road.[21]

Before the debut of *Margaret Garner,* a brouhaha erupted during a visit by cast members to Maplewood Farm where Archibald K. Gaines enslaved Margaret Garner. Tour guide Ruth Brunings, who descends from the neighbors of the Gaines family, stated that the Gaineses were upset over their forebearer's portrayal in the opera. Denyce Graves and Gregg Baker took offense at the disclosure. Graves and Baker asserted that the tragedy surrounding the Garner family's enslavement took precedence over the Gaineses' hurt feelings. Richard Danielpour, who made no subsequent changes to the opera to assuage the Gaineses, said that the discomfort generated between blacks and whites "is exactly why we should be doing" this opera.[22]

Danielpour's imperative to make the opera relevant and accessible to a broader audience has clashed with purists who favor classical opera grandeur. And yet, the creative ideas of a gifted author straining against the instinctive compunctions of a revered composer inevitably proves challenging for the overly long opera fraught with pretty words. Danielpour's eclectic compositions merging folk songs, spirituals, and ballads with classical, traditional cadences also chafed at least one critic who found the music "derivative." Robert Fallon likened the music in *Margaret Garner* to Broadway show tunes rather than traditional opera: "I hear Danielpour imitating not black music, but rather white imitations of black music. The jazz riffs that characterize Edward Gaines sound closer to [those of Leonard] Bernstein, than [those of Charlie] Bird [Parker] . . . and the theme of the opera's intermezzo recalls Porgy's theme from Gershwin's *Porgy and Bess*."[23] But Morrison, given to casting aspersions on the inexact speech patterns that Gershwin scripted for black characters in *Porgy and Bess*, simply would not have sanctioned any inauthentic idioms in the opera that she found offensive. Composers like William Bolcom, on the other hand, saw a merging of musical theater tradition with opera as a uniquely American art form, and the *Cleveland Plain Dealer* pronounced Danielpour's music "a skillful stew of American idioms and influences, ranging from spirituals, folk and jazz."[24]

In act 1, scene 1, the Black Chorus sings the spiritually laced "No More," which begs its members' deliverance from the prospect of being sold at auction and separated from their families. It later follows "No More" with the decidedly gospel- and blues-inflected "A Little More Time," overjoyed at being spared the auction block—a fate altered by a single "master" stroke of the enslaver's pen. But the enslaved credit their measured fortune to a higher power: "We feel the mercy of our Lord God / With the grace of a little more time" (act 1, scene 1). Bernard Holland praises compositions like these as a "soothing eclecticism" and "a melting pot in tones."[25]

In his 1845 slave narrative, Frederick Douglass comments on the plaintive lyrics slaves sing that express sorrow and despair, and in his 1903 book of essays and sketches *The Souls of Black Folks* W. E. B. Du Bois recognizes spirituals or sorrow songs in that same vein. Houston Baker theorizes the effectivity of the blues as an expressive cultural form in his seminal study, *Blues, Ideology, and Afro-American Literature: A Vernacular Theory*. Black Atlantic scholar Paul Gilroy indicates that music replaced or dominated other cultural survival forms on slave plantations: "Music becomes vital at the point at which linguistic and semantic indeter-minacy/polyphony arise amidst the protracted battle between masters, mistresses, and slaves."[26]

In a similar regard for merging musical forms in *Appomattox*, Philip Glass writes: "I looked into the songs that were sung at the time of the Civil War and did what I could to make it sound like the time. For example, we're told one of the Psalms, 'Clap your hands all ye people,' was the hymn that was sung by the freed slaves when Abraham Lincoln came into Richmond."[27] Choosing among a variety of contemporary selections or folk music reminiscent of African-American culture, Glass composed his own music for the lyrics to "Song of the First of Arkansas" (1864), the marching song for the all-black First Arkansas Volunteer Infantry that fought for the Union. The composition contrasts with Mary Custis Lee's nostalgic aria of the Old South. Another mid-nineteenth-century song that Glass incorporated into the opera is Walter Kittredge's "Tenting On the Old Camp Ground" (1863). The Union and Confederate armies, in act 1, scene 1, sing the camp song as Grant and Lee watch the sunset from their respective headquarters.

In the prologue of *Appomattox*, set near the close of the Civil War, three Civil War wives, Julia Dent Grant (Rhoslyn Jones, soprano), Mary Custis Lee, and Mary Todd Lincoln (Heidi Melton, soprano), along with Mary Custis Lee's daughter Agnes (Ji Young Yang, soprano) and Mary Todd Lincoln's black seamstress and former slave, Elizabeth Keckley (Kendall Gladen, mezzo-soprano), in turn express their individual anxieties about the outcome of the war. The wives then jointly voice their foreboding about the injuries and death that are imminent. Julia Dent Grant fears for her husband. Mary Custis Lee and Agnes Lee worry that their Southern way of life will be destroyed and hope the war will end soon. Mary Todd Lincoln joins Elizabeth Keckley onstage and asks her to interpret a nightmare in which President Lincoln sees himself as a corpse. All sing of the sorrows of war and the hope that the war presently raging will be the last. A chorus of widows joins them. Dressed in dark clothing the widows move slowly to the front of the stage where they place photographs of deceased loved ones. But in the epilogue, Julia Dent Grant, who has referred to her husband as "the architect of war," sorrowfully realizes that the war is not the last as she had hoped. She leads the Widows' Chorus in a wordless lament to the sorrow of war. But the refrain turns on a hapless note that closes the opera: "And this is not the last time / What has occurred must ever recur / This will not be the last time. / This will not be the last time" (epilogue).

Women's prominence in both operas affirms rather than deviates from classical opera tradition. *Margaret Garner,* in particular, invites parallels with tragic heroines more reminiscent of the title characters of Georges Bizet's *Carmen* (1875) and Giacomo Puccini's *Madama Butterfly* (1904) than Giuseppe Verdi's *Aida* (1871). In Bizet's and Puccini's operas ethnic women encounter major conflicts with male antagonists who associate women of color with hypersexuality and racial taboos. Encountering conflicts with an Egyptian princess who enslaves her in the palace at Memphis, Verdi's Aida, an Ethiopian princess, is torn between love for her father, her country, and the Egyptian warrior, Radames. Carmen withholds love and grants it to whom she pleases. She, therefore, resists the advances of Don Jose, an obsessive suitor. But Carmen's flirtatious manner drives him to distraction and to murder at the opera's end. Cio-cio San, a geisha wife in *Madama Butterfly,* falls prey to the self-proclaimed, pleasure seeker American Navy Lieutenant, B. F. Pinkerton, who is stationed in Japan in the early 1900s. He "marries" Cio-cio San by entering into a 999-year contract that renews month-to-month and permits him to divorce her at any time. Eventually he returns to the United States. Three years pass, and he returns to Japan, but not for Cio-cio San, who waits for him, but with the American wife he has married in the interim. Discovering that Cio-cio San has borne him a son as a result of the earlier marriage, Pinkerton does not meet with her directly; his American wife does, offering to raise the child in the United States. Pinkerton's betrayal leads to Madame Butterfly's, Cio-cio San's, commission of suicide. Like Margaret Garner, Carmen and Cio-cio San experience sexual exploitation with male antagonists in demeaning relationships that lead to their tragic deaths.

*Margaret Garner* and *Appomattox* both close on indelible scenes in landmark cases in the US legal system that mock democratic ideals and dramatize a litany of injustices for persons of African descent. Consequently, the operas invite a call-and-response dialogue about racial conflicts and slavery's continued impact as the discussion above notes. The racial inequities of law govern nineteenth-century slave society in *Margaret Garner*. Troubled by charges of theft rather than murder against Margaret, Edward Gaines's daughter Caroline states that those charges should reflect "Our crime as well as hers." But the three white male judges appointed to hear the case retort,

> The law is clear
> In the Bible and here.
>
> We do not make laws
> Or forsake laws,
> We follow them precisely.
>
> (ACT 2, SCENE 3)

Margaret Garner's designation as property at the trial excludes her from equal protection under the law, while the willful neglect of former slaves in the Civil War covenant in *Appomattox* leads to inequities and injustices for blacks throughout the twentieth century. Denied personhood without any rights that the court must accord or respect, the operatic Margaret Garner, in the penultimate scene of the final act, sits mute leading up to the Judges' delivery of the verdict to execute her.

On the other hand, at the end of the final act of *Appomattox*, bass baritone Philip Skinner, appearing alone on a darkened stage as an aged, gnarled, and wheelchair-bound Edgar Ray Killen, delivers the pinnacle of a performance in a haunting scene in which he spews racist comments about blacks. Referring to civil rights workers as "scums of the earth," the operatic Killen commands a powerful, riveting presence and speaks words that the librettist lifted directly from the real-life court testimony of the Ku Klux Klansman. The members of the audience bear witness as jurors to the trial.

Skinner peers menacingly into the audience in the final scene of act 2 of *Appomattox* and emphatically states: "Um a good preacher. I do what I'm told. I'm proud of what I done. I'd love to shake [James Earl Ray's] hand. We have to keep on fighting the fight. Every movement has its martyrs. Am I right?"[28] At his 1967 trial in Mississippi, the real-life Killen had addressed an all-white jury. But Skinner's onstage performance of his statements in a very public space before a racially diverse audience shatters the intimacy of a courtroom and creates an aura of discomfited silence. The curtain closes on the venomous but vacuous testimony of the racist who in real life drew a lengthy prison sentence, albeit it forty-three years after his commission of triple murder.

Referencing the Killen case in "The History Boys," Philip Glass cites racism as "the greatest evil in human history, past, present, [and] future, and a threat to human survival and well-being."[29] By forcing a past-to-present confrontation with that "greatest evil," *Margaret Garner* and *Appomattox*, as well as *York, Slipknot, Rise for Freedom, Amistad, TRUTH*, and other contemporary operas about race and slavery move the genre into tepid territory in a manner seldom seen in traditional, classical operas. Most pertinently, through the imaginative reconstruction of historical memory, performance aesthetics, and eclectic musical forms, *Margaret Garner* and *Appomattox* warrant a renewed glance at opera's capacity to broaden its appeal in the mass culture arena.

## NOTES

1. Toni Morrison, *Margaret Garner: Opera in Two Acts*, composed by Richard Danielpour, rev. ed. (New York: Associated Music, 2004). All other references to the libretto are to this edition. The author of this article attended the 7 May world premiere performance in Detroit, the 14 July 14 2005 premiere in Cincinnati, and a late-February 2006 performance in Philadelphia.

2. Christopher Hampton, *Appomattox, The Opera, Libretto Synopsis*, composed by Philip Glass, *San Francisco Opera Magazine* 85.2 (Oct. 2007): 28. All other references to the libretto are to this source. San Francisco Opera premiered *Appomattox, The Opera* at the War Memorial Opera House. The author attended the performance on 20 Oct. 2007. Classical radio 102.1 KDFC FM, in cooperation with the San Francisco Opera, served as a media partner for community events during the company's 2007–2008 season. The radio station simulcasted the opera live on October 5, 2007. The Leeds Youth Opera performed *Appomattox*'s international premiere

in the United Kingdom on 8 July 2009. Washington National Opera presented a revised version of Glass and Hampton's *Appomattox* at the John F. Kennedy Center for the Performing Arts in Washington, DC, 14–22 Nov. 2015.

3. See Patrick H. Hutton, "Collective Memory and Collective Mentalities: The Halbwachs-Aries Connection," *Historical Reflections* 15.2 (Summer 1988): 314. In a reading of Halbwachs, Hutton regards memory work as obliging the past "to conform to present configurations." See also Patrick H. Hutton, *History As an Art of Memory* (Hanover: U of Vermont P, 1993).

4. While a nineteenth-century opera, Giacomo Meyerbeer's *L'Africaine* (The African Woman) with a French libretto by Eugène Scribe, seemingly treats the enslavement of an African woman, it does not. The opera centers on a fictional representation of the Portuguese explorer Vasco da Gama and a Madagascan or Indian slave, Sélika. Mezzo-soprano Jessye Norman has sung arias from the opera set in Lisbon and India, but it docs not feature an African woman. The Paris Opéra first premiered *L'Africaine* at the Salle Le Peletier on 28 Apr. 1865. It debuted at London's Covent Garden on 22 July 1865 and at New York's Academy of Music on 1 Dec. 1865.

5. Waldo E. Martin Jr., "Beyond Appomattox: The Bitter Fruits of Freedom," *San Francisco Opera Magazine* 85.2 (Oct. 2007): 37–39. See also Waldo E. Martin Jr., *No Coward Soldiers: Black Cultural Politics in Postwar America* (Cambridge, MA: Harvard UP, 2005), 282.

6. Thomas May, "Crossing Boundaries: *Appomattox*'s Creative Team on the Collaborative Process," *San Francisco Opera Magazine* 85.2 (Oct. 2007): 32.

7. Celeste Headlee, "Opera Tells Saga of *Margaret Garner*," *Weekend Edition Saturday*, National Public Radio, 7 May 2005.

8. See William R. Braun, "The History Boys," *Opera News* 72.3 (Sept. 2007): 47. Both Union soldiers and civil rights activists sing, "One hundred years and we ain't free, we're marching to Montgomery." Christopher Hampton notes the irony that the Alabama state trooper who shot Jackson forty-two years earlier was indicted for the crime during the making of the opera: "We happened to pick that case at random, and suddenly it's reactivated" (4).

9. David Blight, *Race and Reunion: The Civil War in American Memory* (Cambridge, MA: Belknap-Harvard UP, 2001), 261. Blight notes that in publications like Edward A. Pollard's *The Lost Cause* (1866), *Southern Review Magazine* (1867), and D. H. Hill's *The Land We Love* (1866–69), "the Lost Cause

may have originated out of mourning, but it soon found its premier objective in vying for control of the nation's memory," and "became an integral part of national reconciliation by dint of sheer sentimentalism, by political argument, and by recurrent celebrations and rituals" (260, 266). He adds that Lost Cause advocates used historical memory as a weapon "to engage in the struggle over political policy and as a means to sustain the social and racial order" (282).

10. Douglas A. Blackmon, *Slavery by Another Name: The Re-Enslavement of Black Americans from the Civil War to World War II* (New York: Doubleday, 2008). Blackmon writes, "It also became apparent how inextricably this quasi-slavery of the twentieth century was rooted in the nascent industrial slavery that had begun to flourish in the last years before the Civil War" (8).

11. See Shaila Dewan, "Former Klansman Guilty of Manslaughter in 1964 Deaths," *New York Times*, 22 June 2005, 1–2.

12. Barbie Zelizer, "Reading the Past Against the Grain: The Shape of Memory Studies," *Critical Studies in Mass Communication* 12 (1995): 220.

13. Nancy J. Peterson, *Against Amnesia: Contemporary Women Writers and the Crises of Historical Memory* (Pennsylvania: U of Pennsylvania P, 2001), 2.

14. Toni Morrison, "Unspeakable Things Unspoken: The Afro-American Presence in American Literature," *Michigan Quarterly Review* 28.1 (Winter 1989): 12; emphasis original.

15. Bernard Holland, "Giving New Voice to Former Slave's Tale of Sacrifice," *New York Times*, 9 May 2005, 2. Lawrence B. Johnson, "The Majestic 'Margaret' Sets Spirits Soaring: "Morrison's Libretto, Emotive Performances Infuse Opera with Power and Eloquence," *Detroit News*, 9 May 2005.

16. Braun, "The History Boys," 46.

17. Pierre Nora, "Between Memory and History: Les Lieux de Mémoire," trans. Mark Roudebus, *Representations* 26.1 (Spring 1989): 7–24. Those who experienced slavery's brutalities often preferred to forget them while their descendants, who never experienced slavery's brutalities, seem compelled to remember them. In "'You who never was there': Slavery and the New Historicism, Deconstruction and the Holocaust," *Narrative* 4.1 (Jan. 1996), Walter Benn Michaels sorts through this conundrum: "Without the idea of a history that is remembered or forgotten (not merely learned or unlearned), the events of the past can have only a limited relevance to the present, providing us at most with causal accounts of how things have come to be the way they are" (7). Michaels contends that the

past becomes an essential aspect of our identity when we fashion it as part of our own life experience. But traces of past events like slavery remain evident, quite literally as modern-day human trafficking, but also when reconstituted in less recognizable forms.

18. Mervyn Rothstein, "Toni Morrison, in Her New Novel, Defends Women," *New York Times*, 26 Aug. 1987, C17. Morrison also comments in an interview that Garner's act of infanticide shows what can happen "when one human being subjugates another." See Headlee, "Opera Tells Saga of *Margaret Garner*."

19. *The Journey of Margaret Garner*, dir. Alphonzo Wesson III (Cincinnati: Corbett Opera Center, 2005), DVD.

20. Gaines made this comment before members of the Toni Morrison Society during a 16 July 2005, tour of Maplewood Farm in Richwood, Kentucky.

21. Headlee, "Opera Tells Saga of *Margaret Garner*," 4.

22. See *Margaret Garner*, dir. Mustapha Hasnaoui (LuFilms, 2007. DVD. Headlee, "Opera Tells Saga of *Margaret Garner*," 3.

23. Robert Fallon, "Music and the Allegory of Memory in *Margaret Garner*," *Modern Fiction Studies* 52.2 (Summer 2006): 530.

24. See William Bolcom, quoted by Anne Midgette, "In Search of the Next Great American Opera," *New York Times*, 19 Mar. 2006, 4. Bolcom argues for "a special [American] art form" that merges opera with musical theater tradition. See also Donald Rosenberg, "Honorable Effort Lacks Contrast, Drama, Pace," *Cleveland Plain Dealer*, 9 May 2005, D1.

25. Holland, "Giving New Voice to Former Slave's Tale of Sacrifice," 2.

26. Paul Gilroy, *The Black Atlantic: Modernity and Double Consciousness* (Cambridge, MA: Harvard UP, 1993), 74.

27. May, "Crossing Boundaries: *Appomattox*'s Creative Team on the Collaborative Process," 30–34.

28. Hampton, *Appomattox, The Opera. Libretto Synopsis*, 28.

29. Qtd. in Braun, "The History Boys," 47.

# Contributors

DENYCE GRAVES, mezzo-soprano, made her debut at the Metropolitan Opera in 1995 and has appeared on the stages of leading opera houses and concert theaters throughout North America, South America, Europe, and Asia. Although her repertoire is extensive, her signature parts are the title roles in *Carmen* and *Samson et Dalila*. It was at the Metropolitan Opera after a performance of *Carmen* during the 1997–1998 opera season that Grammy Award–winning composer Richard Danielpour approached her with the plan of writing an opera about Margaret Garner and casting her in the title role. Graves's meetings later with the directors of the Michigan (Detroit) and Philadelphia opera companies led to the co-commissioning of Danielpour's opera by those two companies and a third, Cincinnati Opera, located in the Ohio city where Margaret Garner in 1856 killed her two-and-a-half-year-old daughter to protect her from the horrors of slavery.

MICHAEL HALLIWELL, an associate professor at the University of Sydney, teaches vocal studies and is a respected academic whose work on the operatic adaptation of literature has been widely published. He studied literature and music at the University of Witwatersrand in Johannesburg. In his current position he has served as Head of Vocal Studies and Opera, Pro-Dean and Head of School, and Associate Dean (Research) at the Sydney Conservatorium of Music. His book *Opera and the Novel: The Case of Henry James* was published by Rodopi in 2005. *Myths of National Identity in Contemporary Australian Opera* will be published by Ashgate in 2017. Halliwell also continues a successful career as an opera singer and as a recording artist. He was awarded scholarships to study with Otakar Kraus at the London Opera Centre and with Tito Gobbi in Florence. As principal baritone with the Netherlands Opera and the Hamburg State Opera, he has performed over fifty major roles in London, Munich, Berlin, Frankfurt, Paris, and Moscow. He has premiered five song cycles by Lawrence Kramer in Edinburgh, Vienna, Santa Fe, London, and New York over the past nine years.

LA VINIA DELOIS JENNINGS, Distinguished Professor in the Humanities and Professor of Twentieth-Century American Literature and Culture at the University of Tennessee, Knoxville, specializes in women's literature, African-American literature, the twentieth-century novel, diaspora religions, and whiteness studies. She is the author of *Toni Morrison and the Idea of Africa* (2008), which won the 2008 Toni Morrison Society Prize for Best Single-Authored Book on the literary work of the Nobel laureate and Pulitzer Prize–winning author. A reprint of the hardcover edition appeared in 2009, followed by the first paperback edition in 2010. Her study on Morrison also received the College Language Association's 2009 Outstanding Scholarship Award. In addition to attending performances of Margaret Garner in the premiere cities, Professor Jennings also attended the 2007 Lincoln Center performance of the opera directed by Tazewell Thompson that featured mezzo-soprano Tracie Luck in the title role. In June 2015, she was the keynote speaker at the two-day symposium at Columbia University entitled "Restaging the Harlem Renaissance: New Views on the Performing Arts in Black Manhattan," devoted to the artistic reclamation of the opera composer and librettist H. Lawrence Freeman. She is presently editing Freeman's 376-page manuscript "The Negro in Music and Drama" and serving a second term on Knoxville Opera's Board of Directors.

AIMABLE TWAGILIMANA, a professor of English at SUNY Buffalo State, specializes in African-American literature, Africana studies, and world literature. He teaches graduate seminars on the works of Toni Morrison. A member of the Toni Morrison Society, he participated in its Fourth Biennial Conference in Cincinnati, Ohio, where he also attended the premiere of *Margaret Garner*.

DELORES M. WALTERS, who holds a doctorate in cultural anthropology from New York University, began researching the life of *Margaret Garner* while directing a family and local history-training program at the National Underground Railroad Freedom Center in Cincinnati and teaching at Northern Kentucky University. As a member of the *Margaret Garner* Steering Committee, she attended the opera's Detroit rehearsal performance and workshop and introduced the historical Margaret Garner to traditional and nontraditional operagoers in various cities. She is coeditor, with Mary E. Frederickson, of *Gendered Resistance: Women,*

*Slavery, and the Legacy of Margaret Garner* (2013). The collection of essays began as a symposium in 2005 on women's resistance to enslavement and violence in historical, contemporary, and global contexts.

STEVEN WEISENBURGER, Mossiker Chair in Humanities and Professor of English at Southern Methodist University, specializes in narrative fiction, American literature, history and slavery, and race studies. His book *Modern Medea: A Story of Slavery and Child-Murder from the Old South*, which reclaims the historical events surrounding the Margaret Garner infanticide case, was published in 1998. Weisenburger has given numerous lecturers on Margaret Garner. His January 2005 public lecture at Xavier University began the slate of educational programming for the Cincinnati premiere of *Margaret Garner: A New American Opera*. He was also the keynote speaker for the Authors' and Editors' Recognition Luncheon at the Toni Morrison Society's Fourth Biennial Conference, which took place during *Margaret Garner's* Cincinnati premiere.

CARL B. WESTMORELAND became deeply involved in the founding and development of the National Underground Railroad Freedom Center, which opened its doors in 2004 and has since become a major draw for Cincinnati visitors. He serves as senior advisor at the center and curator for its main exhibit, the Slave Pen. He was a member of the *Margaret Garner* Steering Committee and attended the opera's Detroit rehearsal performance and workshop. Westmoreland also participated in numerous panels and seminars designed to educate the public about the history of Margaret Garner and American slavery.

HELENA WOODARD, an associate professor at the University of Texas, Austin, specializes in eighteenth-century British literature, ethnic and third world literature, American literature, critical race theory, women's literature, and the works of Toni Morrison. Her book *African-British Writings in the Eighteenth Century: The Politics of Race and Reason* (1999) explores the discourses of race focusing on the slave narratives of Olaudah Equiano, Mary Prince, Ignatius Sancho, Ukawsaw Gronniosaw, and Ottobah Cugoano. Woodard attended the May 7, 2005, world premiere of *Margaret Garner* in Detroit; its July 14, 2005, premiere in Cincinnati; and a late-February performance of the opera in Philadelphia.

KRISTINE YOHE, an associate professor of English at Northern Kentucky University, specializes in African-American literature, the literary works of Toni Morrison, and Underground Railroad literature. She has served as newsletter editor, membership chair, and as a member of the Toni Morrison Society executive committee. She has also been a consultant for the Cincinnati Opera Educational Programming Committee and the National Underground Railroad Freedom Center. She was a member of the *Margaret Garner* Steering Committee and attended the opera's Detroit rehearsal performance and workshop. In 2005 she was the director for the Fourth Biennial Conference of the Toni Morrison Society that met in Cincinnati, Ohio, July 14–17. The conference concurred with the Cincinnati premiere of the opera.

# Index